Pascal Birnstill

# Privacy-Respecting Smart Video Surveillance Based on Usage Control Enforcement

Karlsruher Schriften zur Anthropomatik
Band 25
Herausgeber: Prof. Dr.-Ing. Jürgen Beyerer

Eine Übersicht aller bisher in dieser Schriftenreihe erschienenen Bände finden Sie am Ende des Buchs.

# Privacy-Respecting Smart Video Surveillance Based on Usage Control Enforcement

by
Pascal Birnstill

KIT Scientific Publishing

Dissertation, Karlsruher Institut für Technologie (KIT)
Fakultät für Informatik, 2016

**Impressum**

KIT Scientific Publishing

Karlsruher Institut für Technologie (KIT)
KIT Scientific Publishing
Straße am Forum 2
D-76131 Karlsruhe

KIT Scientific Publishing is a registered trademark of Karlsruhe Institute of Technology. Reprint using the book cover is not allowed.

www.ksp.kit.edu



Print on Demand 2016

ISSN 1863-6489
ISBN 978-3-7315-0538-9
DOI 10.5445/KSP/1000055556

# Privacy-Respecting Smart Video Surveillance Based on Usage Control Enforcement

zur Erlangung des akademischen Grades eines

Doktors der Ingenieurwissenschaften

von der KIT-Fakultät für Informatik
des Karlsruher Instituts für Technologie (KIT)

**genehmigte**

**Dissertation**

von

**Pascal Birnstill**

aus Offenburg

Tag der mündlichen Prüfung: 21.04.2016

Erster Gutachter: Prof. Dr.-Ing. habil. Jürgen Beyerer

Zweiter Gutachter: Prof. Dr. rer. nat. Alexander Pretschner

# Abstract

The number of video surveillance deployments in publicly accessible spaces is continuously increasing. At the same time, the call for technical assistance of human operators in terms of so-called smart video surveillance system has been growing ever louder and is addressed by research and development. With such systems, video analysis algorithms for activity recognition, tracking, and biometric identification of persons become reality. While aiming to improve the effectiveness and the efficiency of video surveillance, these developments coincidentally increase the diversity and intensity of intrusions into observed individuals privacy and the potential for misuse. Legal scholars agree that applicable data protection laws cannot sufficiently cover the technological evolution of smart video surveillance and demand further regulations. In this sense they expect that a lawful operation of smart video surveillance will require effective mechanisms for protecting privacy and preventing misuse.

This research introduces a conceptual framework for lawful and privacy-respecting smart video surveillance, which enforces privacy-related constraints based on the current threat situation and the type of incident that has been detected. It thus constitutes the first approach towards situation-dependent smart video surveillance as opposed to adjusting the privacy level of disclosed data exclusively to the authorization levels of observers. This framework also increases the selectivity of smart video surveillance in terms of restricting data processing to individuals associated to an incident under investigation and in terms of data disclosure by means of enforcing privacy privileges for authenticated individuals or groups. Constraints are enforced by means of usage control technology, which is instantiated for video surveillance systems for the first time. Based on the proposed generic smart video surveillance architecture extended with usage control enforcement capabilities, smart video surveillance systems can be tailored for various purposes in publicly accessible spaces in a proportionate and privacy-respecting manner.

Two further parts of this work are concerned with extensions of the conceptual framework with privacy filters for video data and with information flow tracking across system boundaries.

With their potential to hide identities of captured individuals, privacy filters for video data are essential for realizing situation-dependent smart video surveillance. This research contributes the first user study to consider the utility of obfuscated video data in terms of recognizing activities that are specific for common purposes of (smart) video surveillance, e.g., fighting, stealing, or abandoning objects. The results indicate that certain privacy filters allow situation assessment by a human operator and protect the identities of observed individuals at the same time.

The integration of inter-system information flow tracking of explicit flows is motivated by works, which found that the communication between control rooms and emergency personnel on-site is crucial for the effectiveness of video surveillance measures. This need can also be observed in terms of the increasing number of mobile applications for video surveillance, which recently appear on the market. This work provides a generalization from inter-layer to inter-system information flow tracking and a generic specification syntax for describing information flow semantics depending on monitored events. Instantiating inter-system information flow tracking with usage control enables the protection of video data disseminated from a video surveillance system to mobile clients against illegitimate redistribution.

# Zusammenfassung

Die Anzahl der Videoüberwachungsmaßnahmen in öffentlichen Räumen nimmt weiterhin zu. Gleichzeitig wird der Ruf nach technischer Unterstützung der Operatoren durch sogenannte intelligente Videoüberwachungssysteme immer lauter und von der Forschung und Entwicklung aufgenommen. Mittels Algorithmen der Videoanalyse stellen solche Systeme Funktionalität zur Erkennung von Aktivitäten und zur Verfolgung und biometrischen Identifizierung von Personen zur Verfügung. Diese Entwicklungen sollen einerseits die Effektivität der Videoüberwachung steigern, erhöhen andererseits aber auch die Vielfalt und die Intensität der Eingriffe in die Privatsphäre der Betroffenen und das Missbrauchspotential der Systeme. Rechtswissenschaftler stimmen darin überein, dass die heutigen Datenschutzgesetze der technischen Entwicklung im Bereich der intelligenten Videoüberwachung nicht mehr gerecht werden, und fordern zusätzliche Regulierung. Sie gehen allerdings davon aus, dass ein rechtskonformer Betrieb intelligenter Videoüberwachungssysteme effektive Mechanismen zum Schutz der Privatsphäre der Betroffenen und zur Verhinderung des Missbrauchs solcher Systeme voraussetzen wird.

Die vorliegende Arbeit schlägt ein konzeptionelles Rahmenwerk für die rechtskonforme und privatsphärenrespektierende Gestaltung intelligenter Videoüberwachung vor, das Datenschutzanforderungen angepasst an die aktuelle Bedrohungssituation und an die Art der detektierten Aktivität durchsetzt. Es stellt den ersten Ansatz einer situationsabhängigen intelligenten Videoüberwachung dar, bei der Zugriffs- und Nutzungsbeschränkungen nicht mehr nur von der Berechtigungsstufe des Benutzers abhängen. Das Rahmenwerk erhöht weiterhin die Selektivität der Überwachung, indem es sie auf Personen einschränkt, die zu einem zu untersuchenden Ereignis assoziiert sind, und indem es die Durchsetzung von Privacy-Privilegien für authentifizierte

Personen oder Gruppen ermöglicht. Restriktionen werden mittels verteilter Nutzungskontrolle durchgesetzt, welche erstmals für Videoüberwachungssysteme instanziiert wurde. Basierend auf einer generischen Architektur für intelligente Videoüberwachung, die mit Nutzungskontrollmonitoren ausgestattet wurde, können Systeme für unterschiedliche Einsatzzwecke im öffentlichen Raum auf das Verhältnismäßige zugeschnitten werden, so dass die Persönlichkeitsrechte der Betroffenen so weit wie möglich geschützt werden können.

Zwei weitere Beiträge dieser Arbeit erweitern das konzeptionelle Rahmenwerk um Anonymisierungstechniken für Videodaten und um systemübergreifende Informationsflussverfolgung expliziter Flüsse.

Aufgrund ihrer Eigenschaft, die Identitäten erfasster Personen zu verschleiern, sind Techniken zur Anonymisierung von Videodaten für die Realisierung situationsabhängiger Videoüberwachung unentbehrlich. Im Rahmen dieser Arbeit wurde die erste Nutzerstudie durchgeführt, welche die Nützlichkeit verschleierter Videodaten im Hinblick auf die Erkennung von Aktivitäten untersucht, die für Zwecke der Videoüberwachung charakteristisch sind, d.h., Gewalttaten, Diebstahl und das Zurücklassen von Objekten. Die Ergebnisse deuten darauf hin, dass bestimmte Anonymisierungstechniken die Beurteilung von Situationen durch Operatoren zulassen und gleichzeitig die Identitäten der erfassten Personen schützen können.

Die Integration der systemübergreifenden Informationsflussverfolgung ist motiviert durch Arbeiten, die gezeigt haben, dass die Kommunikation zwischen Leitstellen und Sicherheitskräften vor Ort (bspw. Polizeistreifen) für die Effektivität von Videoüberwachungsmaßnahmen entscheidend ist. Dies lässt sich auch nicht zuletzt anhand der steigenden Anzahl mobiler Videoüberwachungsapplikationen auf dem Markt beobachten. Die vorliegende Arbeit generalisiert einen existierenden Ansatz zur abstraktionsebenenübergreifenden Informationsflussverfolgung, so dass auch eine systemübergreifende Informationsflussverfolgung ermöglicht wird. Hierzu werden generische Informationsflussprimitive eingeführt, die eine einheitliche Beschreibung und Verarbeitung von Informationsflusssemantiken beobachteter Systemereignisse ermöglichen. Durch die Instanziierung systemübergreifender Informationsflussverfolgung im

Zusammenspiel mit verteilter Nutzungskontrolle können bereitgestellte Videodaten auch auf den mobilen Endgeräten von Einsatzkräften vor unrechtmäßiger Nutzung, bspw. Speicherung oder Weiterverbreitung, geschützt werden.

# Contents

# 1 Introduction

## 1.1 Motivation

While the benefit of video surveillance for public security is subject of highly controversial discussions in public,[1] media, [2, 3] policy, law, and in social sciences (cf. section 2.2), the number of video surveillance deployments and cameras in publicly accessible spaces is still increasing.[4] As an example, from 2007 to 2014, 150 million Euros were spent on extending the coverage of video surveillance in France. This investment increased the number of video surveillance cameras from 345961 to around 1.30 million.[5] Similar numbers have been reported for Austria (160000 in 2006, 1 million in 2013 [6]), and Great Britain, where already 1.85 million cameras were installed in 2011.[7] According to a report of the French Ministry of the Interior the purpose of these video surveillance deployments is the prevention and investigation of criminal offenses. In particular, they are considered useful for fighting and prosecuting assault and battery, violent robberies, theft and burglaries, as well as destruction and degradations.[8] Meanwhile the amount of video data produced by video surveil-

---

1 http://www.urbaneye.net

2 http://www.sz.de/bayern/videoueberwachung-wie-kameras-unser-verhalten-veraendern-1.1735946

3 http://www.zeit.de/digital/datenschutz/2013-04/videoueberwachung-panopticon

4 Note that the numbers of surveillance cameras deployed in private premises is likewise increasing. While applicable regulations of workplace privacy law are not as concise, fundamental rights of employees and employers have to be weighed carefully. Detailed arrangements are subject of employee co-determination.

5 Thierry Hartmann, French Ministry of the Interior. "Video Surveillance in France: Recent Developments and Challenges", keynote at 10th Future Security, Sept. 2015

6 orf.at/news/stories/2581260/

7 http://www.theguardian.com/uk/2011/mar/02/cctv-cameras-watching-surveillance

8 http://www.interieur.gouv.fr/Publications/Rapports-de-l-IGA/Securite/L-efficacite-de-la-videoprotection-Rapport-complementaire

lance deployments already exceeds the capacities of prosecution authorities. On this account, French prosecution authorities have been outsourcing the operation of video surveillance systems deployed in public spaces to private sector security companies in the last few years. Nevertheless, even proponents of an expansion of video surveillance already admit that the effectiveness and efficiency of police work can no longer be increased through manual video surveillance.[9] As a consequence, the call for technical assistance of operators by means of so-called smart video surveillance systems is growing ever louder. To be more specific, prosecution authorities and operators of video surveillance deployments do not only call for assistance in terms of automatically detecting certain activities, but also in terms of means to investigate offenders, victims, and witnesses more efficiently.[9]

Video surveillance systems in use have been evolving from single cameras connected to a screen over inter-connected Closed Circuit Television (CCTV) systems with numerous, often pan-tilt-zoom cameras (PTZ cameras) and large video walls to early smart video surveillance systems. The latter already provide operators with assistance functionality such as movable object detectors and basic object tracking capabilities [Ham+05; Shu+05]. The challenge of algorithmically pre-evaluating captured video data in order to purposefully draw human operators' attention to potentially critical incidents is addressed by research on video analysis. Algorithms for detecting activities such as violence and battery, collapsing people, and abandoning objects are becoming reality [RR06; FGR06; Rou+07; VA13; CWF13], albeit false positive detections of such algorithms cannot be eliminated completely (cf. section 4.2.3). With the substantial progress that has been made in biometrics and soft-biometrics, the increasing resolutions of cameras, and continuously decreasing costs of computational power, more features of persons can be extracted from video data in real-time or at least in hindsight, which enables automated retrieval of scenes involving an individual person with increasing accuracy. Current research indicates that future developments in smart video surveillance will

[9] Thierry Hartmann, French Ministry of the Interior. "Video Surveillance in France: Recent Developments and Challenges", keynote at 10th Future Security, Sept. 2015

involve situation recognition, i.e., more complex activities described as spatio-temporal constellations or inter-dependencies between persons, objects and their attributes [TD08; Gup+09; Mün+11; FB12b]. While aiming to improve the utility of video surveillance measures, it is obvious that these developments coincidentally extend the spectrum of possible privacy intrusions and the potential for misuse. Another trend is concerned with monitoring the dynamics of large crowds of people in order to ensure the safety of public events such as music festivals, fairs, large-scale demonstrations, and sports events [Joh+08; Mah+10; MFA15]. In such scenarios, emergency personnel of different organizations, such as police, paramedics, fire department, etc. must cooperate closely. Several studies also reveal that the effectiveness of video surveillance measures strongly depends on a sound coordination between operators in the control rooms and security personnel on-site [Goo03; Goo04; GH04; Kev06; BS07]. Meanwhile this issue is addressed by all leading suppliers of video surveillance technology, which provide mobile applications for accessing their systems via mobile devices such as smart phones and tablets.[10] These applications however neglect privacy- and security-related requirements such as to remain in control over the usages of sensitive data transmitted to mobile devices.

In contrast to the problem of surveillance technologies being utilized on the Internet, the scientific discourse on privacy issues concerning (smart) video surveillance is predominantly taking place within social sciences and law. A central argument is shared by both: When faced with surveillance cameras, the mere possibility of being observed tends to change the way we behave. Philosophers have been discussing this effect at least since Bentham introduced the architectonic concept of the *Panopticon* in the late $18^{th}$ century, which pursued the defined goal of constraining its inmates to constantly evaluate their own behavior with respect to rules given by an authority. While most notably prisons have been built as Panopticons, video surveillance transfers

[10] For example, the mobile applications of the video surveillance supplier *Axis Communications AB* have been downloaded more than 50.000 times from the Google Play Store for the Android operating system. There is also a considerable number of third-party suppliers offering mobile applications for accessing popular video surveillance solutions or controlling individual cameras.

their fundamental mechanism into public spaces, where they all the more interfere with the values of free societies. More specifically, it interferes with the fundamental right to free development of the individual,[11] which is codified in constitutional law of numerous states and also in the Universal Declaration of Human Rights (UDHR) of the United Nations adopted in 1948. Inhibition or discouragement of the legitimate exercise of a constitutional law by potential prosecution has also been referred to as *chilling-effect*[12] by the United States Supreme Court as well as by the European Court of Human Rights (ECtHR). With regard to video surveillance the chilling effect has been observed in legal literature by Granholm [Gra86] in 1986.

In general, individuals who are affected by video surveillance have not given a reason for such measures, which therefore constitute groundless and unjustified intrusions into their personal rights in contradiction to the presumption of innocence[13] of the state of law (originating from the German *Rechtsstaat*). In cases of public interest, the state of law allows intrusions into individual rights if and only if the legal principle of proportionality is retained [RDH11; BS12]. Together with the principles of purpose limitation and data economy from data protection law, this constitutes the legal framework within which (smart) video surveillance measures have to be developed, deployed, and operated.

Nevertheless, from the perspective of law, video surveillance shall only serve as ultima ratio for ensuring public security and fighting crime in a certain area. Given that applicable data protection laws have been enacted at a time when the evolutions of smart video surveillance have not been foreseeable, it is hardly expectable that jurisdiction and future regulations will permit the deployment of smart video surveillance systems without effective mechanisms for protecting privacy and preventing misuse. In this respect, the capabilities of smart video surveillance are not only considered as an even greater threat to privacy, but also as a chance for responsible design of such systems [BS12].

---

[11] Article 22 Universal Declaration of Human Rights of the United Nations (UDHR)

[12] `www.yourdictionary.com/chilling-effect`, Webster's New World Law Dictionary Copyright ©2010 by Wiley Publishing, Inc., Hoboken, New Jersey.

[13] Article 11 UDHR

Legal scholars around Roßnagel, Hornung, and Spiecker gen. Döhmann addressed this challenge in several publications [RDH11; HD11; BS12; Vag13; BK14]. A common idea is that as long as people under surveillance have not given a reason for investigating on them, a greater extent of privacy intrusions as constituted by conventional video surveillance systems is not justified, i.e., the baseline privacy impact of the system must be kept as low as possible. Therefore, while the systems' pre-evaluation capabilities, i.e., activity recognition algorithms, necessarily have to be executed continuously in order to detect potentially critical incidents, their object detection capabilities can also serve as prerequisites for privacy protection mechanisms, since they enable the application of privacy filters (i.e., anonymization functions) for protecting observed people's identities when disclosing video data to an operator. The application of such privacy filters can also prevent unnecessary privacy breaches due to false positive detections of video analysis algorithms. This suggests that primarily operators are considered as threats to monitored individuals' privacy. A threat analysis of smart video surveillance indeed revealed that *malicious operators* constitute the group of attackers, which poses threats that are difficult to recognize yet particularly critical in terms of privacy intrusions and misuse (cf. section 4.2.1). The focus of this research is thus put on mechanisms against malicious operators.

As an orientation for lawful technical design and organizational embedding of smart video surveillance, Roßnagel et al. [RDH11] propose a three-step model motivated by danger levels that are known in law. A video surveillance measures is typically deployed to counter an *abstract danger*, i.e., at a dangerous or endangered place. Operators or video analysis algorithms evaluate video data with respect to suspicious activities that indicate *suspected threats.* These include characteristic activities pointing to potential violent confrontations, theft, or vandalism. A *concrete danger* requires that without an outside intervention a legal asset will be harmed, e.g., life and limp of individuals, property, etc. These danger levels justify different levels of privacy intrusions, which have to take place with increasing selectivity (cf. figure 1.1).

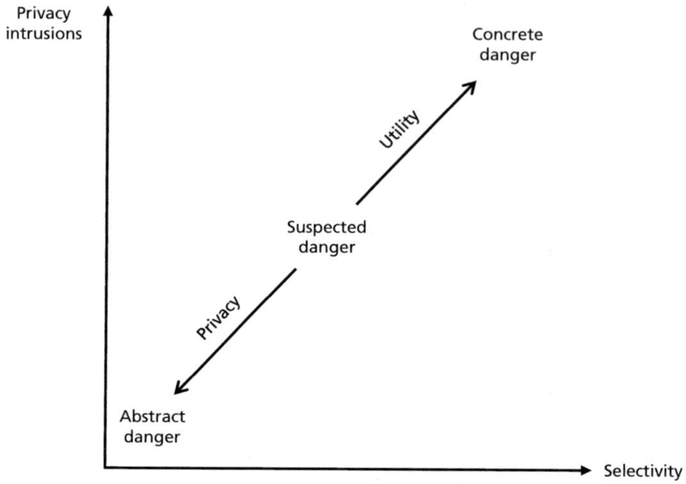


**Figure 1.1:** Danger levels of Roßnagel's three-step model

In this context *selectivity* is conceived as only affecting a minimal set of persons related to (potential) incidents when allowing deeper privacy intrusions as well as only unlocking a minimal set of (privacy-intrusive) system functions for a given type of incident, i.e., depending on the legally protected right concerned and the substantiation of danger. *Privacy intrusions* have a quantitative as well as a qualitative aspect. The types of information video analysis extracts from video data relates to the extent to which personal circumstances of an observed individual are collected and processed (e.g., time, place, clothing, company). A larger set of such non-unique features attributed to an individual may also allow inferences of persons' identities. On the other hand, biometric features directly enable the identification of individuals. Thus, the extent of analysis must be proportionate to a given danger level, but also the usage of algorithms collecting strongly identifying personal data. Generally speaking, low selectivity has to be balanced with a low privacy impact, deeper privacy intrusions have to be compensated with high selectivity and accountability (cf. figure 1.2). According to this model, at least as long as no potentially critical incident has been detected by an algorithm or an operator, the privacy impact of smart video surveillance is reduced in comparison to conventional video surveillance by means of enforcing access und usage restriction as well as the application of privacy filters. Suspected threats justify targeted monitoring of the individuals that are involved. At this stage, however, privacy filters can still be applied as far as they do not render activity recognition and hence situation assessment impossible. Before smart video surveillance systems unfold additional functionality (e.g., person retrieval, biometrics, etc.) for investigation purposes and preservation of evidence, the assessment of a human operator is required and needs to be logged in order to make misuse of the system traceable.

Altogether, an analysis of these works suggests a system design, which separates the systems' capabilities in situation-dependent operating modes with proportionate levels of functionality and privacy protection as illustrated in figure 1.2. Designing a smart video surveillance architecture capable of enforcing according operating workflows, i.e., the necessary restrictions and mechanisms, leads to the objective of this thesis.

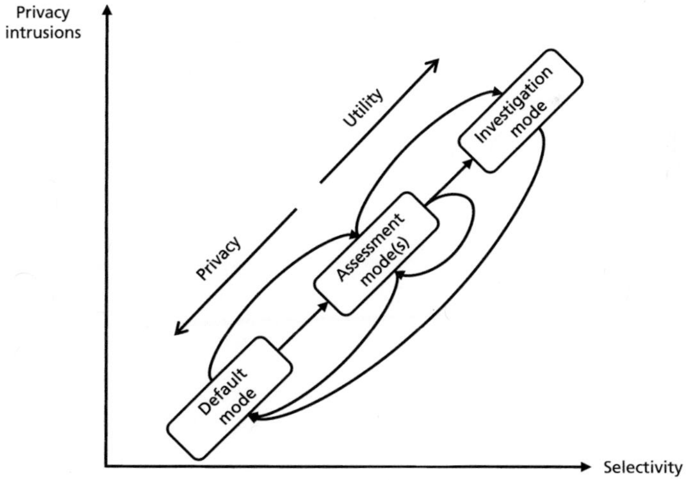


**Figure 1.2:** Situation-dependent operating modes according to danger levels

## 1.2 Objective

The objective of this thesis is an architecture and a prototype for privacy-respecting and lawful smart video surveillance, which involves the enforcement of privacy-related requirements, such as:

- usage restrictions on surveillance functionality,
- application of privacy filters (anonymization functions),
- spatial restrictions when visualizing and processing live data,
- temporal and spatial restrictions when visualizing or processing recorded data,
- object- and incident-based restrictions during investigation,
- obligations in terms of logging and notifications,
- privacy privileges for individual persons or groups.

These requirements are derived from interpretations of applicable law that can be found in legal literature [RDH11; HD11; BK14]. The particular classes of restrictions are essential for realizing a smart video surveillance system with low baseline privacy impact and enforcement of human situation assessment before possibly allowing more severe privacy intrusions during investigations, which have to take place in a selective and accountable manner.

The prototype system must further provide acceptable utility, at least in comparison to a conventional video surveillance system:

1. *Situation assessment:* Privacy filters must not be applied on the cost of the utility of video data. Operators must still be able to recognize activities with high probability, but not identities.
2. *Incident handling:* Despite of privacy-preserving mechanisms being in place and operational, operators must still be able to preserve evidence with comparable efficiency.

## 1.3 Research Questions

According to the objective, lawful and privacy-respecting smart video surveillance is characterized by a low baseline privacy impact as well as stepwise and selective privacy intrusions in proportion to the degree of substantiation of potentially critical incidents. The analysis of requirements and related work (cf. chapter 4) done in this dissertation has shown that the following research questions have to be addressed in order to meet this objective:

- How can situation-dependent workflows for operating smart video surveillance systems according to the aforementioned legal considerations be enforced based on usage control [PHB06]?
- How to ensure that sensitive detections, e.g., biometric attributes, are processed in a selective manner?
- How can identities of captured persons be protected when video data is disclosed to an operator?
- How can (video) data disseminated to mobile video surveillance applications be protected against illegitimate redistribution?
- Given that these privacy-preserving mechanisms are in place: Is it possible to preserve the utility of the smart video surveillance system?
  - Situation assessment: Is there a trade-off relationship between privacy protection and utility when applying privacy filters before releasing video data to an operator?
  - Investigation: Do the restrictions prevent operators from resolving incidents and preserving evidence?

The answers to these questions will substantiate the hypothesis that

> It is possible to realize smart video surveillance in accordance with legal requirements by means of protecting the identities of observed individuals against malicious operators through usage control enforcement and privacy filtering, while at the same time preserving utility in terms of allowing situation assessment and collection of evidence with acceptable efficiency.

Note that if smart video surveillance is only considered admissible if effective privacy-preserving mechanisms are in place, then we must also accept that the efficiency of the technology is reduced to some extent (cf. section 2.3).

The analysis of requirements and related work has shown that certain aspects are necessary conditions with respect to the objective. These are the following ones, on which the focus of this work is put.

**TS-1** A smart video surveillance architecture extended with usage control enforcement technology is able to enforce the privacy-related restrictions (cf. section 1.2) required to realize situation-dependent smart video surveillance workflows.

**TS-2** When video data is to be disclosed to an operator, privacy filters are able to protect observed individuals' identities while preserving the utility for situation assessment, i.e., the individuals' activities remain recognizable.

**TS-3** During investigation of incidents, the selectivity of collecting and processing sensitive data such as biometric face templates can be increased by means of monitoring algorithmic detections and according information fusion events within the system.

**TS-4** Video data can be protected against illegitimate redistribution when being forwarded to mobile devices of emergency personnel by means of inter-system information flow tracking and usage control enforcement.

**TS-5** Even though restrictions and privacy filters are in place, the utility of the system for resolving incidents and preserving evidence is preserved in terms of only inducing acceptable operating overhead and delay.

## 1.4 Solution Strategy

The aforementioned objective is addressed in the following steps:

1. Considerations from legal literature are refined into technical requirements for privacy-respecting smart video surveillance in compliance with law. These requirements are specified with respect to a generic smart video surveillance architecture derived from technical literature.

2. The generic smart video surveillance architecture is extended with a usage control infrastructure and components so as to enforce the identified requirements. The focus is on (i) decreasing the baseline privacy impact by enforcing privacy filters before releasing video data to an operator and (ii) increasing the selectivity of inevitable privacy intrusions when investigating confirmed incidents by enforcing temporal, spatial, functional, and object-based access and usage restrictions.

3. In order to remain in control of video data that is transmitted to mobile devices of emergency personnel and in particularly to inhibit illegitimate redistribution of such data, an approach towards inter-layer information flow tracking of explicit flows [Lov15] is generalized to inter-system information flow tracking and instantiated along with usage control for the Android operating system [FP12].

4. Privacy filters for video data are evaluated with respect to their ability to protect the identities of captured persons and also with respect to the utility of obfuscated video data in terms of still allowing human operators to recognize specific activities.

5. The utility of the final prototype system is evaluated by means of an application study. Participants are asked to operate the system, which is set up for detecting and investigating incidents concerning abandoned objects. Utility is compared to a conventional video surveillance system as well as a smart video surveillance system without privacy-preserving

mechanisms and measured in terms of the time the operator is occupied for assessing and documenting a given incident. Constraints being relaxed in a stepwise manner as well as privacy filters being applied should only induce a small overhead in terms of additional processing time to be spent by the operator.

## 1.5 Contributions

The following research contributions have been made to answer the research questions introduced in section 1.3:

**A Conceptual Framework for Lawful and Privacy-respecting Smart Video Surveillance.** Legal requirements and considerations found in literature have been translated into and complemented with technical requirements. This leads to a concept denoted as *situation-dependent smart video surveillance workflows* (cf. section 4.4), which is the first approach towards enforcing privacy-related constraints based on the current threat situation and the type of incident to be handled instead of adjusting the privacy level of disclosed data exclusively to the authorization levels of observers (cf. chapter 5). Constraints are enforced by means of usage control technology, which is instantiated for video surveillance systems for the first time [BP13; Fis+14]. Based on the proposed generic smart video surveillance architecture extended with usage control, video surveillance systems can be tailored for various purposes in public and publicly accessible spaces in a proportionate and privacy-respecting manner. This approach has been implemented and evaluated for Fraunhofer IOSB's smart video surveillance prototype *Network Enabled Surveillance and Tracking (NEST)* (cf. chapters 5 and 8).

**Enforcement of Selective Processing of Sensitive Personal Features.** Two mechanisms are introduced to increase the selectivity of smart video surveillance by (i) making use of the system's awareness of situations or incidents and (ii) making use of its ability to recognize persons occurring in the fields of view of different cameras. Incidents detected by smart video surveillance are associated to one or several individuals. Intrusive analysis functions such as biometric face detection are unlocked for collecting evidence concerning a particular incident. Based on tainting detections from video analysis and monitoring information fusion it is ensured that tainted detections of unrelated persons are not processed, but deleted as early as possible (cf. section 5.4). Selectivity is also improved by means of a novel approach to granting privacy privileges to individuals or groups in a non-transferable manner [Bir13; Bir+15]. An optical and a cryptographical authentication of a protected individual are fused into the abstracted object representation of this person within a smart video surveillance system. By this means, privacy privileges such as the application of privacy filters can be stuck to person objects and enforced upon authentication with the system (cf section 5.3).

**A Generalization of an Approach to Inter-Layer Information Flow Tracking to Inter-System Settings.** This research contributes a generalization from inter-layer information flow tracking of explicit information flows as introduced by Lovat [Lov15] to inter-system information flow tracking (cf. chapter 6). It also introduces a set of generic primitives for unifying the specifications of information flow semantics of events intercepted by run-time monitors as well as an asynchronous protocol for processing information flow-relevant events in distributed settings. With the demonstrated instantiation of usage control and inter-system information flow tracking, video data disseminated from a video surveillance system to mobile clients of emergency personnel can be protected against illegitimate redistribution [KBB16].

**An Evaluation of Anonymization Functions for Video Data with Focus on Privacy Protection and Utility.** Based on a formalized methodology the first large-scale online user study (103 respondents) asked participants to identify persons and to recognize activities in video clips on which common privacy filters were applied (cf. chapter 7). Using the *privacy evaluation video data set (PEViD)* [KE13] this study is also the first one to consider utility with respect to activities that are specific for common purposes of (smart) video surveillance [BRB15], i.e., fighting, stealing, and abandoning objects. With respect to these activities taking place in the used video clips, the results of the study indicate that recognizing activities based on obfuscated video data is indeed possible for operators. Certain privacy filters were at the same time able to hide observed individuals' identities with high probability, which contradicts with the common hypothesis that privacy and utility of video data are necessarily trade-off. An investigation of the influence of explicit and implicit evidences for identifying people also revealed that body shapes and clothes are the most important factors for identification. The stronger privacy filters such as *reduction to silhouette* and *pixelization* are also capable to protect against racial discrimination by operators.

## 1.6 Outline

This thesis is structured as follows. Chapter 2 introduces the prerequisites of the topic, such as smart video surveillance, the legal framework and the surrounding discourse in social sciences, as well as the usage control framework. In chapter 3, a generic smart video surveillance architecture is derived from literature and serves as a basis of all subsequent considerations. Chapter 4 derives requirements from legal literature as well as from a threat analysis based on the generic architecture and translates them into a technical concept denoted as *situation-dependent smart video surveillance workflows*. Chapter 5 describes how the generic smart video surveillance architecture must be extended with usage control enforcement mechanisms in order to enforce the operation of the system according to such workflows. In chapter 6 inter-system information flow tracking and usage control for the Android operating system are instantiated for protecting video data, which is transmitted to mobile devices of security or emergency personnel. Chapter 7 addresses the question of how to evaluate privacy filters for video data in terms of privacy protection and utility of obfuscated video data by introducing an evaluation model and presenting the results of an according user study. In chapter 8, the utility of a smart video surveillance system operated with a situation-dependent workflow for detecting, assessing, and investigating incidents concerning abandoned objects is evaluated in an application study. Chapter 9 provides conclusions and outlook.

# 2 Prerequisites

Beginning with definitions of *conventional video surveillance* and *smart video surveillance* that are used throughout this thesis, this chapter gives an overview regarding the socio-ethical discourse (cf. section 2.2) as well as the legal frameworks of the Federal Republic of Germany and the European Union (cf. section 2.3) regarding (smart) video surveillance. Furthermore, section 2.4 introduces the conceptual framework of Usage Control (UC), on which essential contributions of this research are based.

## 2.1 Definitions

### 2.1.1 Conventional Video Surveillance

Conventional video surveillance, which is often denoted as CCTV, is characterized by large walls of monitors, one screen for each camera of a video surveillance deployment. This one-to-one relation of cameras and monitors is necessary, since the cameras' video streams are observed and evaluated by human operators. Nowadays, digital cameras are gradually superseding the analogous ones that have been deployed in the earlier times of video surveillance. Cameras often provide so-called pan-tilt-zoom capabilities (PTZ cameras), allowing operators to adjust the perspective and the magnification to facilitate the assessment of a scene.

Deployments of conventional video surveillance may or may not be equipped with recording technology. Whether or not video data is being recorded and accessible for operators or prosecuting authorities is a question of balancing interests according to the principle of proportionality (cf. section 2.3). With regard to preservation of evidence, particularly prosecution authorities often argue in favor of recording of video data. In terms of intrusiveness into fundamental rights, video surveillance without recording or at least with a very constrained storage period is considered to be a less severe means.

### 2.1.2 Smart Video Surveillance

Throughout this thesis the term *smart video surveillance* denotes systems, which

1. employ computer vision algorithms for pre-evaluating video data in order to point operators' attention to detected activities or situations that may be critical,
2. provide operators with an abstracted representation of the observed area, consisting of static meta data as well as dynamically collected meta data concerning the objects in the observed area,
3. are to some extent able to perform evaluations on abstracted data, e.g., from detecting people entering a certain area to evaluating streams or densities of people (*heat maps*).

More details can be found in chapter 3, which outlines a generic architecture for smart video surveillance systems.

## 2.2 Ethical and Social Discourse

The following paragraphs give a brief and necessarily incomplete overview of the discourse on video surveillance in ethics and social sciences. It becomes apparent that technical measures for preserving privacy can only address specific parts of the problems that are attributed to the expansion and technical advancements of video surveillance.

**Panoptism.** Humanities scholars have been discussing the mechanisms of surveillance and its effects on society at least since Bentham introduced the *Panopticon* in the late $18^{th}$ century. The Panopticon is an architectonic design conceived for prisons in the first place, but also for other institutions with assumed surveillance needs such as schools, factories, or hospitals. A circular building with an observation tower in the center of an open space is surrounded by an outer wall containing cells for the inmates. Bentham explained the objective of the Panopticon as constraining its inmates to constantly evaluate their own behavior with respect to rules given by an authority so as to optimize the efficiency of surveillance. According to Foucault, inmates become the principle of their own subjection [Fou77]. This principle that inmates must expect to be observed by an invisible observer at any time ensures the internalization of given norms of conduct and thus gives the Panopticon the "ability to penetrate men's behavior". Many authors such as Koskela [Kos00; Kos02], Lyon [Lyo01], and Krasmann [Kra05] have since considered video surveillance in the light of Foucault's theories of governmentality (originating from the French term *gouvernmentalité*). Referring to the psychoanalytical concept of subjectification Kammerer characterizes the Panopticon as a super-ego turned stone [Kam08]. Foucault also notes that the Enlightenment did not only discover the idea of individual freedoms, but also invented the mechanisms of discipline [Fou77], which in a paradoxical fashion enabled the development of state power as well as democratic civil rights [Kam08]. Lyon and Kammerer accordingly characterize video surveillance as a modern expression of these ambivalent disciplinary mechanisms, which "both enables and constraints, involves care and control" [Lyo01].

In 1984 Foucault already posed the question how the increasing technical possibilities for accumulating knowledge about the individual can at all be decoupled from a greater imbalance of power structures [Fou84]. According to Microsoft's identity architect Cameron [Cam05], one must also ask the question whether technical approaches to oppose surveillance, such as privacy-enhancing technologies (PETs), will not only further increase society's dependency on technology in a non-desirable fashion.

**Social Exclusion.** A variety of publications see video surveillance as an instrument of exclusion of unwanted groups of persons employed for the commercialization of urban spaces [McC98; Lyo01; Wak02; Van07; HB07].

Wehrheim [Weh02], Klauser [Kla06], and Rolfes [Rol07] explain how video surveillance contributes to a reorganization of public spaces: Initially the presence of video surveillance depreciates public spaces as hazardous environments, which also cause a feeling of insecurity among citizens [Van07]. It takes effect inwardly in terms of a disciplinary measure as well as outwardly in terms of physical access control. By this means it displaces petty crime [Weh02; Töp07] and drives away unwanted people such as beggars and homeless people [Kla07; HB07]. Norris thus characterizes video surveillance as a "powerful tool in managing and enforcing exclusion" [NMW02]. Eventually public space under video surveillance suggests public order and safety, is appreciated, and marketed as shopping streets. Töpfer characterizes this effect of video surveillance as a fortification of cities and predicts further losses of urban space [Töp07]. Referring to Domosh [Dom98], Koskela also remarks that one has to be critical about the extent to which public spaces were ever public, since many public spaces were already controlled by private interests in the $19^{th}$ century [Kos00].

Homeless people interviewed by Huey [Hue10] stated directly that they consciously seek out public and private places where cameras are sited because the presence of the cameras makes them feel safer. A slight majority of the respondents perceives the presence of video surveillance cameras as an intrusion into their lives. With regard to the dense video surveillance network in London, McCahill also notes that suspicious facts could be passed on from space to space so as to lock known thieves out of any shopping mall [MN02].

Several works also stress the point that video surveillance in practice is not a democratic mechanism in a sense that everyone captured by cameras is treated equally [NA99; Fis01; Van07]. For instance, Norris and Armstrong [NA99] observed that being male, young, and black significantly increases the probability to come into focus of operators. Referring to such forms of discrimination, Lyon claims that "surveillance today is a means of sorting and classifying populations and not just of invading personal space or violating the privacy of individuals" [Lyo01].

It has also been observed that video surveillance opens up new possibilities of harassment [H+92; Ain98]. For voyeuristic reasons women are more likely to be targeted by deliberate misuse of video surveillance systems [NA99], which Koskela characterizes as an "extension of the male gaze" [Kos00].

**Feeling of Safety.** An often mentioned objective of video surveillance is to increase the feeling of safety of people within observed areas. This aspect has also been investigated in several studies, which reveal mixed results. According to Ditton [Dit00], when compared over time, there is no improvement of the feelings of safety after the installation of video surveillance (whereby the presence of cameras did also not discourage people from visiting places under surveillance). Gill and Spriggs [GS05] observed that people who were aware of the cameras actually worried more often about becoming a victim of crime than those who were unaware of them. Knowing that cameras were installed in an area did not necessarily lead to a reinforced feeling of safety. Similar results have been published by Elsbergen [Van07], and Rothmann [Rot10], while Dixon et al. [DLM03] as well as Zurawski [Zur07] found that a majority of the respondents feels safer in areas under surveillance.

**Public Acceptance.** Public attitudes towards video surveillance have been investigated in numerous studies, which in general observed a high acceptance [Dit00; Reu01; FHW08; Spr+05; GBA07]. Gill et al. also found that although the public are generally positive, it is less so after having experience with cameras [GBA07]: "Prior to installation people believed video surveillance would be an effective crime fighting tool, but after the event they were more realistic." While Forster remarked that only a minority of the respondents noticed surveillance cameras at all [FHW08], the interviews conducted by Dixon et al. [DLM03] showed that many of the interviewed people felt that video surveillance was a necessary evil and a sad reflection on society. Degli Esposti found that perceived effectiveness is the most important factor for public acceptance of surveillance technology [Esp14]. As Nogala [Nog02] and Kammerer [Kam08] remark, video surveillance is neither as powerful and effective nor as threatening as suggested by media reporting. Accordingly, video surveillance seems to be widely overestimated and misconceived, which may explain why public acceptance and perceived effectiveness do not match empirical effectiveness.

**Effectiveness.** Studies on the effectiveness of video surveillance, i.e., on its impact on crime reduction indeed show mixed result. They found small but measurable effects in some areas, but no effects in other areas. A large-scale meta study conducted by Welsh and Farrington [WF02] observed an overall reduction in crime by only two per cent. Gill and Spriggs [GS05] also found that out of 13 systems evaluated six showed a relatively substantial reduction in crime in the target area compared with the control area, but only two showed a statistically significant reduction relative to the control area. Video surveillance seemed to be more effective in reducing crimes in train stations and car parks, but not in city centers or residential areas [GBA07]. The meta studies further showed that video surveillance has no effect on violent or impulsive crimes (from five studies), but has a significant desirable effect on vehicle crimes. The effectiveness of video surveillance is also questioned due to not eliminating the actual causes of crime [SS07; Kam08]. It is thus considered to only have a displacing effect on crime [Van07; Kam08].

**Effectiveness Through Coordination.** Several studies observed that the effectiveness of video surveillance measures strongly depends on the cooperation and coordination between control rooms and police on site [Goo03; Goo04; GH04; Kev06; BS07]. Control rooms are typically owned and managed by the local authority, and staffed by either local authority employees or private security personnel. Gill et al. [Gil05] found through interviews with police officers and analysis of incident and occurrence logs that a good communication from and to control rooms is vital for detecting and handling incidents. The logs revealed that timely intervention is indeed possible if the control room staff is able to efficiently direct the police to critical incidents. The contents and purposes of incident logbooks of control rooms have also been described by Gill et al. [Gil05]. On the one hand logs serve as evidence, are used to pass on intelligence between operators on different shifts, and enable the police, or other external agencies to track an incident after the event. Then again they are used for data protection purposes and accountability. Operators have to use the logbooks to be able to explain and to justify why they had focused on a target individual, such that it can be checked what the operators have been monitoring and for how long. Interestingly, the analysis of incident logs also revealed that control room staff only spent 2.6% of total monitoring time on investigating incidents. Norris similarly found that typically less than one incident is investigated per shift [Nor03].

**Summary** Altogether, video surveillance is viewed sceptically, not least because of its unverified effectiveness in terms of crime reduction. Garland [Dav01] and Leopold [Leo05] interpret the regular calls of politicians for an expansion of video surveillance as a merely symbolic action strategy, i.e., "a mode that is concerned not so much with controlling crime as with expressing the anger and outrage that crime provokes". With a view to the future, linking data obtained from modern surveillance systems to data from other information sources such as the Internet and other telecommunications networks is considered as the greatest threat to privacy and civil rights [Nor03; Cam05; Kam05]. Hempel also remarks that video surveillance already started to cause undesired effects on moral courage, emergency calls, and reporting of offenses [HB07], since people seemingly assume that everything is observed by the omnipresent cameras.

## 2.3 Legal Framework

The legal discourse around video surveillance shows parallels with the debate on data retention in Germany and also within the European Union. This is particularly the case for video surveillance systems, which are not only used for live monitoring of certain spaces, but also store data in archives for a certain period of time. In general, individuals affected have not given a concrete reason to be subject of such surveillance technologies. In order to respect the presumption of innocence,[1] the state of law thus prohibits intrusive measures that put citizens under general suspicion. By this means, the state of law implicitly accepts that certain criminal offenses could not be resolved or only with greater effort. Accordingly, if smart video surveillance is only considered admissible if effective privacy-preserving mechanisms are in place, then it must also be accepted that these mechanisms reduce the effectiveness of the technology to a certain extent. In cases of public interest, the state of law allows intrusions into individual rights under certain circumstances as summarized in the following overview on the legal frameworks applicable for (smart) video surveillance in Germany respectively in the European Union. In particular, regulations with respect to lawful technology design are explained, which govern the collection, processing, and usage of personal data.

### 2.3.1 Legal Framework in Germany

On the level of the **Basic Law of the Federal Republic of Germany**, video surveillance and particularly smart video surveillance concerns several manifestations of the *general right of personality*. Manifestations concerned are the right of one's own image, the right to privacy, and most importantly the right to *informational self-determination*, which the Federal Constitutional Court developed in its census verdict (Volkszählungsurteil) in 1983.[2] The right to informational self-determination empowers individuals to decide when and to what extent their personal circumstances are published, i.e., when their personal data is used. Hornung and Desoi [HD11] argue that stays at a particular time at a certain place, condition and kind of clothing, behavior, or the presence of companions constitute personal circumstances. Therefore video surveillance necessarily interferes with the right to informational self-determination. Moreover, as capabilities such as tracking across multiple cameras based on recognizable visual features as well as activity recognition involve the possibility of creating long-term movement and behavioral profiles, smart video

[1] Article 11 UDHR
[2] cf. Federal Constitutional Court of Germany (Bundesverfassungsgericht) (BVerfGE) 65, 1

surveillance enables considerably deeper intrusions into the right to informational self-determination compared to conventional video surveillance. The knowledge of being exposed to such powerful technologies may also reinforce the panoptical effect/chilling effect (cf. section 2.2) of video surveillance and thus prospectively constitute a new quality of interference with the *general freedom of action* [3] and the *freedom of the person*,[4] from which people can only elude by avoiding areas that are monitored by smart video surveillance.

Interferences with constitutional rights can only be justified if they comply with the *principle of proportionality*. Accordingly, a video surveillance measure must pursue a legitimate aim and it must be *suitable*, *necessary*, and *reasonable* with respect to that aim. A measure is suitable if and only if there is evidence or at least confidence that it substantially contributes to the achievement of the aim. It is necessary if and only if no less serious measures with the same effectiveness are available. Eventually, it is reasonable if and only if the disadvantages in terms of interferences with constitutional rights of individuals concerned (e.g., interferences with the right to informational self-determination) do not outweigh the security interests to be pursued (by a given video surveillance measure). According to Roßnagel et al. [RDH11] this assessment of reasonableness implies that groundless surveillance measures must not interfere with fundamental rights. Depending on the legally protected interest which is concerned as well as on the intensity of the impending danger, also intrusive measures may be justified. An indicator for intrusions into the right to informational self-determination is the collection and processing of person-related or personal data.

In 2008, the Federal Constitutional Court formulated the *right to the guarantee of confidentiality and integrity of information technology* [5]as a further manifestation of the general right of personality. Hereby an effective protection of information technology systems, particularly of those processing personal

[3] Article 2(1) of the Basic Law
[4] Article 2(2) and Article 104 of the Basic Law
[5] cf. BVerfGE 120, 274, 302

or person-related data, against illegitimate access and manipulation is granted as a constitutional right.

Further possible interferences of smart video surveillance systems with constitutional rights may concern the *general principle of equality*[6] and the *freedom of assembly*.[7] If such systems are able to automatically detect the emergence of groups, they render intrusions into the latter constitutional right even more severe [HD11].

If subjective experiences influence definitions of suspicious behavior, which requires interventions, this entails the risk of selection effects and discrimination and thus constitutes an infringement of the general principle of equality. This is also the case if criminalistic experience justifies an intensified observation of certain groups, since objectively unrelated and innocent persons are affected, who are not imposing a threat [HD11]. If prejudices influence the modeling of suspicious behavior or if anomalies are detected based on machine learning, smart video surveillance may systematically discriminate certain social or cultural groups. On the other hand, if learning processes are observed and selection effects according to outer appearances like skin color, age, or gender are technically prohibited, smart video surveillance may also contribute to safeguarding constitutional rights [HD11].

In sub-constitutional law the **Federal Data Protection Act**, i.e., the German **Bundesdatenschutzgesetz (BDSG)**, prescribes the requirements to protect the right to informational self-determination. Its applicability requires that collected, processed, and used data exhibits personal connections. Hornung and Desoi [HD11] as well as Bier and Spiecker gen. Döhmann [BS12] argue that (smart) video surveillance may not necessarily establish personal connections due to restrictions on overview images and the possibility to apply anonymization functions before disclosing video data. However, personal connections cannot be generally excluded in the practice of video surveillance.

According to *§ 3a BDSG* the principles of *data avoidance* and *data economy* must be observed when designing systems, which collect, process, and use

[6] Article 3 of the Basic Law
[7] Article 8 of the Basic Law

personal data. These principles are reviewed in the course of the assessment of necessity of a surveillance measure and demands that technical and organizational procedures are implemented so as to process no or at least as few as possible personal data. For this, procedures must be reviewed, and any reduction of personal data usage that turns out to be possible, e.g., by means of avoidance, anonymization, or pseudonymization, becomes a legal obligation [Roß11].

*§ 6b BDSG* regulates the requirements concerning the *monitoring of publicly accessible spaces with optic-electronic devices (video surveillance).* According to *§ 6b para. 1 BDSG* video surveillance is allowable only in so far as it is necessary to fulfill public tasks, to exercise the right to determine who shall be allowed or denied access, or to pursue rightful interests for precisely defined purposes and under the condition that the rightful interests of the controller and the legitimate interests of the data subject are weighed up. Moreover, *§ 6b para. 3 BDSG* prescribes the same balancing of interests for the processing and usage of data collected by video surveillance. Although smart video surveillance is not explicitly mentioned (its evolution has not been foreseeable in 2001), legal experts agree that technologies, which automatically detect and recognize persons, track them across multiple cameras via recognizable (soft-biometric) features, analyze their behavior, and possibly collect uniquely identifying biometric features are subsumed under § 6b para. 3 BDSG [RDH11; HD11; BS12]. As a consequence, for the employment of smart video surveillance both weighings of interests between the controller and the data subjects are mandatory, i.e., according to § 6b para. 1 and § 6b para. 3 BDSG.

Smart video surveillance enables its controller to automatically extract sensitive personal data, which is indeed already contained in images, but which up to recently could not be extracted at all or at least not efficiently, i.e., only with considerable personnel expenditures. It is thus considered to constitute a substantially deeper interference with the legitimate interests of the data subjects compared to conventional video surveillance [RDH11; HD11]. This must be taken into account in both weighings of interests, which accordingly may shift towards the legitimate interests of the data subjects. If these prevail, the employment of smart video surveillance is not lawful (whereas conventional video surveillance may be lawful given the same facts of the case). Hornung and Desoi thus argue that smart video surveillance is only admissible in exceptional cases or may at least require a specific justification regarding its necessity, such as an extraordinary threat situation or particularly endangered objects [HD11].

*§ 6b para. 5 BDSG* demands that data must be deleted without delay, if it is *no longer needed for the pursued purpose or if the data subject's legitimate interests stand in the way of any further storage.* Furthermore, the *purpose limitation principle* requires that the purpose of collected personal data may only be changed in exceptional cases such as legal prosecution or averting a concrete danger, and must be preserved throughout any processing steps and during storage. The BDSG does not provide storage periods for personal data (collected by video surveillance systems). However, according to jurisdiction storage periods of up to ten days may be admissible depending on the concrete purpose of a given video surveillance measure.[8]

*§ 6a BDSG* is concerned with *automated individual decisions. § 6a para. 1 BDSG* prescribes that decisions, which have legal consequences for or substantially impair the interests of the data subject, must not be based exclusively on the automated processing of personal data, which serves to evaluate individual personal characteristics. In particular, a decision not made by a natural person based on the evaluation of content shall constitute a decision based exclusively on automated processing. According to Hornung and Desoi this regulation does not apply for conventional video surveillance or biometric systems. It is indeed applicable for smart video surveillance, since activities recognized by computer vision algorithms constitute an automated evaluation of individual personal characteristics [HD11]. Hence legal or actual adverse consequences, such as intense identity checks and luggage inspections, must not be based on such automated analysis methods. Conversely, decisions entailing adverse consequences must be taken by a natural person with genuine discretionary powers. Automated indications to suspicious activities are admissible provided

[8] cf. Higher Administrative Court (Oberverwaltungsgericht) (OVG) Lüneburg (11 LC 114/13)

that decisions regarding legal prosecution or measures for averting a danger are taken by operators in the control rooms of smart video surveillance systems or by security officers on site [HD11; BS12; BK14].

### 2.3.2 Legal Framework in the European Union

In April 2016 the European Parliament adopted the **General Data Protection Regulation of the European Union (GDPR)**. It unifies data protection within the European Union in a single law and will take effect as of Mai 2018. In contrast to the prior **Directive 95/46/EC**, regulations are directly applicable in the member states. Thus the GDPR also overrides the German BDSG.

According to Bretthauer et al. [BKB15] the GDPR formulates an objective point of view in its definition of personal data: *Art. 4 no. 2 GDPR* requires that a natural person is identifiable. In addition, recital 26 demands that in order to determine whether a person is identifiable all reasonable means have to be taken into account, which could be used either by the controller or by any other person to identify the individual. Accordingly, unmodified images of persons (captured by video surveillance cameras) can practically be considered as personal data.

Just as the Directive 95/46/EC the GDPR still does not contain an explicit regulation concerning video surveillance. *Art. 5 GDPR* postulates the *principles relating to personal data processing* and thus demands an explicit and legitimate purpose. Processing of personal data is only allowed if at least one of the criteria in *Art. 6 GDPR* is fulfilled, whereby (smart) video surveillance may be founded on Art. 6 no. 1 lit. d-f GDPR, i.e., processing is necessary in order to protect the vital interests of the data subject or of another natural person, for the performance of a task carried out in the public interest or in the exercise of official authority vested in the controller, orfor the purposes of the legitimate interests pursued by the controller or by a third party, except where such interests are overridden by the interests or fundamental rights and freedoms of the data subject which require protection of personal data, in particular where the data subject is a child.

Furthermore, the use of video surveillance must be proportionate, i.e., video surveillance may only be deployed for purposes that actually justify recourse to such systems. Just as in German law the principle of proportionality [9] demands that such systems may only be deployed if other prevention, protection and/or security measures requiring no image acquisition clearly prove insufficient and/or inapplicable with respect to the legitimate interests of the controller.

Similar to German law the principle of proportionality entails an obligation to data minimization. Data minimization is demanded in Art. 5 lit. c GDPR, i.e., processed personal or person-related data must be adequate, relevant and limited to what is necessary in relation to the purposes for which they are processed. Moreover, Art. 5 lit. e GDPR requires that storage periods of personal data are minimized, i.e., personal data shall be kept in a form which permits identification of data subjects for no longer than is necessary for the purposes for which the personal data are processed. Art. 5 lit. f GDPR adds the security-related requirements of integrity and confidentiality by prescribing that personal data is processed in a manner that ensures appropriate security of the personal data, including protection against unauthorized or unlawful processing and against accidental loss, destruction or damage, using appropriate technical or organizational measures.

Transparency, as another fundamental principle of data protection, is explicitly demanded by Art. 5 lit. a GDPR and requires that the processing of personal data is comprehensible for the data subjects. *Art. 14 GDPR* regulates the extent of information regarding the processing of personal data, which must be provided to data subjects. This includes information about the existence of profiling as well as meaningful information about the logic involved in any automated processing.

*Art. 22 GDPR* regulates automated individual decision-making. Art. 22 no. 1 GDPR demands the data subject shall have the right not to be subject to a decision based solely on automated processing, including profiling, which produces legal effects concerning him or her or similarly significantly affects him or her.

[9] Articles 8(2) and 52(1) of the Charter of the Fundamental Rights of the European Union

Profiling is defined in *Art. 4 no. 4 GDPR* as automated processing of personal data consisting of the use of personal data to evaluate certain personal aspects relating to a natural person, in particular to analyze or predict aspects concerning that natural person's performance at work, economic situation, health, personal preferences, interests, reliability, behavior, location or movements.

*Art. 35 no. 3 lit. c GDPR* prescribes a so-called *data protection impact assessment* for a systematic monitoring of a publicly accessible area on a large scale through video surveillance. It stipulates that whenever processing operations bare specific risks to the rights and freedoms of data subjects by virtue of their nature, their scope or their purposes, the controller or the processor acting on the controller's behalf shall carry out an assessment of the impact of the envisaged processing operations regarding the protection of personal data. The assessment must contain at least a general description of the envisaged processing operations, an assessment of the risks to the rights and freedoms of data subjects, the measures envisaged to address the risks, safeguards, security measures and mechanisms to ensure the protection of personal data and to demonstrate compliance with this regulation, taking into account the rights and legitimate interests of data subjects and other persons concerned.

## 2.4 Distributed Usage Control

*Usage control (UC)* generalizes access control to the time after initial access to data [PHB06]. Requirements include rights and duties, e.g., *data may not be forwarded, a privacy filter must be applied on data before disclosure, data must be logged and deleted after thirty days*, etc. UC requirements are typically specified in policies using formally verifiable languages such as the *Obligation Specification Language for usage control policies (OSL)* [Hil+07].

In distributed settings, e.g., forwarding a data item with an attached policy to another system, UC requirements can be enforced on the receiver's machine, too, requiring UC enforcement mechanisms at the receiving end [KP13].

Because data usually comes in different representations—an image can be a pix-map, a file, or aggregated into the set of objects shown on the image—

UC mechanisms have been augmented by information flow tracking technology [PLB11]. One can then specify policies not only for specific fixed representations of data, but also on *all* representations of that data. These representations are tracked by information flow detection technology. Policies then do not need to rely on events but can forbid undesired information flows in terms of specific representations to be created, also in a distributed setting [KP13].

The following paragraphs describe the components of the conceptual framework of usage control, the policy scheme in XML, and the assumptions on which the security guarantees of usage control enforcement are based.

## 2.5 The Conceptual Framework of Usage Control

Usage control requirements, i.e., policies, are typically specified in terms of events, which are intercepted by so-called *Policy Enforcement Points (PEPs)* (cf. figure 2.1). PEPs forward events to a *Policy Decision Point (PDP)*, which evaluates them against policies and replies with an *authorization action* so as to *allow*, *modify*, *inhibit*, or *delay* events. In addition, the PDP may trigger mandatory or optional obligations specified in policies as so-called *execute actions*. Execute actions are provided by *Policy Execution Points (PXPs)* include for instance sending a notification, writing a message to a log file, invoicing billing, and also deploying policies on other machines. In the latter case, the *Policy Management Point (PMP)*, which is responsible for deploying, retrieving, and shipping of policies, acts as a PXP. Usually a *Policy Retrieval Point (PRP)* is attached to a PMP. It provides a persistent policy storage from which policies can be retrieved via policy identifiers or data identifiers. Generally, the deployment of policies is triggered by a *Policy Administration Point (PAP)*, which may also implement a human-machine-interface for the usage control framework.

In order to perform information flow tracking across different applications, different layers of abstraction [Lov15] of a system or across different systems, a multitude of PEPs, each observing an individual set of information flow-relevant events, have to be integrated into the information flow tracking system. The so-called *Policy Information Point (PIP)* maintains and interprets the information flow semantics of events and accordingly keeps track of new representations of data items being created and of information flows between representations. By this means, when evaluating an event concerning a container (such as a file, a process, or a window), the PDP can ask the PIP whether this container is a representation of a protected data item, for which a policy must be enforced.

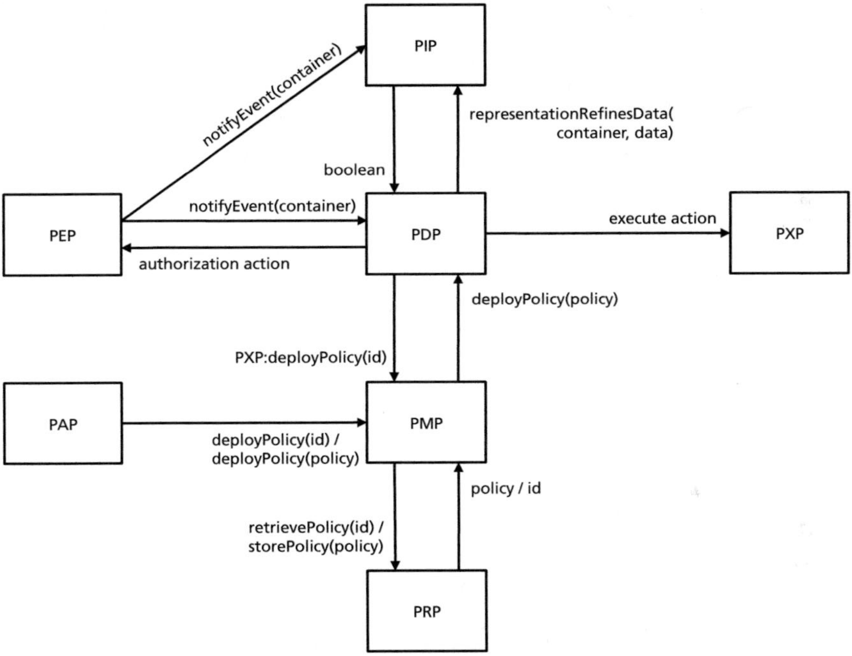


**Figure 2.1:** Components of the conceptual framework of usage control

### 2.5.1 XML-Representation of Usage Control Policies

Machine-readable policies are specified according to an XML scheme in the form of *event-condition-action rules (ECA rules)*. Listing 2.1 illustrates the basic structure of policies, which is sufficient for an understanding of the policies shown in this thesis (cf. appendix C.1 for the full XML scheme of the usage control policy syntax).

```
<policy>
  <preventiveMechanism>
    <timestep amount="10" unit="SECONDS" />
    <trigger action="someEvent" isTry="true">
      <paramMatch name="containerId" value="c1"/>
      <paramMatch name="dataId" value="d1" type="dataUsage"/>
    </trigger>
    <condition>
      <someCondition/> <!-- OSL formula, xpath formula, etc.-->
    </condition>
    <authorizationAction>
      <inhibit/> <!-- / <allow/> <modify/> / <delay/> -->
    </authorizationAction>
    <executeAction name="notifyReceiver">
      <parameter name="receiver" value="someReceiver"/>
      <parameter name="message" value="Policy violated"/>
    </executeAction>
    <!-- ... -->
  </preventiveMechanism>
</policy>
```

**Listing 2.1:** Simplified usage control policy structure

Usage control requirements can be enforced in a *preventive* or *detective* way as indicated by means of an enclosing *preventiveMechanism* or *detectiveMechanism* tag. Detective mechanisms are not capable of inhibiting, modifying, or delaying events, and are typically employed if data consumers are generally trustworthy, if illegitimate data usage is supposed to be unintentional rather than intentional, and if the value of the protected data is moderate. Requirements specified as detective mechanisms often concern compensating actions, e.g., to invoice billing or to send notifications. The *timestep* attribute defines the granularity of regular evaluations of a given policy by the PDP, which is particularly important when temporal or cardinality constraints are to be enforced. In addition, the PDP evaluates preventive mechanisms whenever it is notified of an event, which matches the specification in the *trigger action* section of the policy. An event matches a trigger action if and only if all parameter values of the event match the according parameter values specified in the trigger action. Parameters are tagged with the *dataUsage* type to indicate that a given policy is to be enforced for all representations of a given data item identified by the value of this parameter. Thus, an according event must be evaluated by the PIP, which will reply with the value `true` in case the given event concerns a representation of the data item specified using the dataUsage type.

Depending on the evaluation of the *condition*, e.g., a formula specified in OSL, an `xpath` statement,[10] or a regular expression, the remainder of the policy is either enforced or not. In terms of the enforcement of preventive mechanisms the *authorizationAction* specifies whether the event is to be inhibited, allowed, modified, or delayed. In addition, *executeActions* are triggered. In case of authorization actions other than inhibit, execute actions can also be specified as mandatory preconditions of the authorization actions by putting them into the authorization action section. By this means, for instance, the permission of an event is granted only if the execute action is performed successfully.

### 2.5.2 Assumptions of Usage Control

Guarantees concerning the security and the effectiveness of usage control mechanisms are based on several security-related assumptions regarding their implementation as well as the execution environment. It is assumed that the usage control infrastructure as well as application monitors are up and running, have not been tampered with, that they are correctly implemented and free of bugs, and that they do not exhibit side channels. Likewise, the integrity of policies must be ensured. A necessary, but not sufficient condition for these assumptions to be valid is the presence of state of the art mechanisms for user authentication, permission assignment, and access control, as well as the absence of operating system vulnerabilities. Moreover, secure communication channels must be used in order to ensure that protected data is exchanged confidentially and that users are not able to spoof the communication between components of the usage control infrastructure. If communication between

[10] `http://www.w3.org/TR/xpath20/`

components of the usage control infrastructure fails, events are inhibited by default. Some proposals on how to fulfill the aforementioned assumptions can be found in appendix A.

# 3 A Generic Architecture for Smart Video Surveillance

This chapter outlines a generic architecture of smart video surveillance systems, which has been published in [BP13] and [Fis+14]. It will serve as a basis for analyzing privacy- and security-related requirements as well as for developing according enforcement mechanisms. This generic architecture as outlined in figure 3.1 abstracts from earlier works on smart video surveillance architectures introduced by Fidaleo et al. [FNT04], Hampapur et al. [Ham+05], Bauer et al. [Bau+08], and Monari et al. [MVK08]. The leading paradigm of these works, a duality of video analysis and semantic analysis of extracted data, still prevails. Video analysis algorithms can be considered as signal processing algorithms aiming to transform a stream of images into a stream of objects and objects' attributes. Moreover, the detection of various kinds of activities already became reality (cf. section 3.1). Semantic analysis of extracted data, however, is still at an early stadium of research. Basic tasks such as object-based tracking across multiple cameras, counting persons within a specified area, detecting intrusions into a given area, or deviations from a pre-calculated route can be assigned to smart video surveillance systems. However, modeling and recognizing complex situations remains a major challenge (cf. section 3.2), also in terms of further interdisciplinary efforts, which are required to translate the domain knowledge of security and safety experts into machine-readable semantics. It is thus safe to assume that smart video surveillance systems of the foreseeable future will gradually experience advancements in terms of situation recognition, but will by no means substitute human operators. These systems' objective still remains assistance, while operators remain in charge of evaluating and handling reported incidents. Thus, also the smart video surveillance systems of the future will have to disclose video data for situation assessment as well as for investigation purposes.

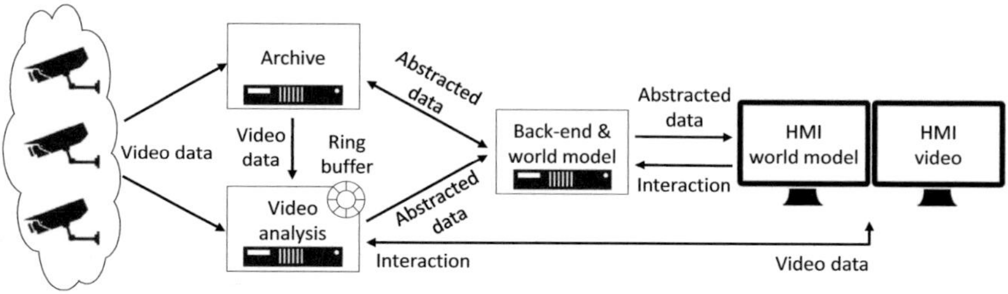


**Figure 3.1:** Data-flow perspective on the generic architecture for smart video surveillance systems

## 3.1 Video Analysis

In smart video surveillance systems the streams of images captured by the cameras are processed by video analysis algorithms in order to recognize basic activities, such as fighting or a person falling to the floor, but also to detect objects (i.e., persons and things) and specific attributes of them [RR06; FGR06; Rou+07; VA13; CWF13]. Based on these detections the system creates an abstracted representation of the monitored area, which allows to analyze scenes on a semantic level as will be explained in section 3.2. As illustrated in figure 3.1, image exploitation algorithms are not assumed to be fully integrated into video surveillance cameras. Due to the computational requirements of such algorithms as well as the camera hardware's limitations in terms of computing power, it is not foreseeable that image exploitation will be entirely encapsulated in video surveillance cameras in the near future.

Typically, dedicated video analysis components are deployed for each camera and maintain received images in ring buffers, from which they are read by the video analysis algorithms. Depending on their actual size, these ring buffers can also be used to replay potentially critical situations to have to be assessed by the operator, especially so in video surveillance deployments without an archive component.

The particular image exploitation algorithms to be integrated into a concrete smart video surveillance system depend on the specific purpose of the video surveillance measure. However, image exploitation algorithms can be differentiated into two classes according to their objective within the video surveillance process. The first class detects potentially critical incidents and must be executed continuously in the background, e.g., to detect violence, people falling down, or abandoned objects. In the following, this class is referred to as *detective algorithms.*

The second class is used for investigations purposes as well as for preserving evidence and involves algorithms for extracting biometric features or backtracking of individuals. Compared to detective algorithms, executions of these are mostly considered as deeper intrusions into observed individuals' privacy, even though they are only activated on-demand. This class is hence denoted as *reactive algorithms.*

Note that multi-camera object tracking algorithms constitute a borderline case, since they could be filed into both classes. If the purpose of a surveillance measure requires, for instance, to detect people or cars leaving an expected route, then object tracking is employed as a detective algorithm.[1] It is employed as a reactive algorithm if it is used in terms of backtracking, e.g., in order to retrieve the owner of an abandoned object. Note further that executing tracking algorithms does not mean that a complete history of detections of each person is stored persistently.[2] A person's current position and certain visual features (such as a color histogram or soft-biometric features) may be sufficient.

[1] Note that this also constitutes a type of incident requiring semantic analysis to be performed on an abstracted representation of the monitored area (cf. section 3.2).

[2] A Kalman filter, for instance, works recursively and requires only the last "best guess", rather than the entire history to predict a new position.

## 3.2 World Model of the Observed Area

Assigning more complex surveillance tasks to a smart video surveillance system requires an awareness for certain situations of interest. Situations of interest can be modeled as spatio-temporal constellations or inter-dependencies between persons, objects and their attributes in the observed environment [TD08; Gup+09; Mün+11; FB12a]. In order to recognize such situations of interest, an abstracted representation of the observed environment containing the persons, objects and attributes relevant to the situations of interest needs to be established and maintained. Such abstracted representations of monitored areas are referred to as (object-oriented) *world models*. Notable approaches towards building up world models have been proposed by Hampapur et al. [Ham+05] and Bauer et al. [Bau+09]. Fischer represents situations of interest as nodes in a dynamic Bayesian network, in which the evidences are based on the state of the world model [FB12b].

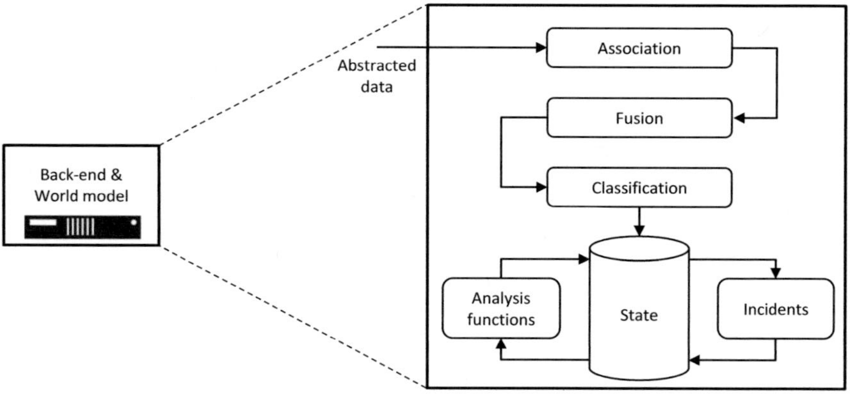


**Figure 3.2:** Data-flow perspective on an object-oriented world model

A world model is established and maintained by aggregating and consolidating sensor detections, i.e., detections of image exploitation algorithms, which are capable of extracting the relevant objects and according attributes from image streams (cf. figure 3.2). For this, detections of image exploitation algorithms and possibly other sensors are typically processed as follows. In an *association* step the world model determines whether an incoming detection refers to a known object. Subsequently a *fusion* step either aggregates the new information with an existing object or creates a new one. By this means, an attribute of the respective object may be changed or added. As the types of objects are modeled in terms of characteristic attributes, a *classification* step eventually (re-)determines the given object's type given its updated vector of attributes. A person may, for instance, be re-classified to a more specific group of persons, such as police officers, as soon as the system detects that the given person is wearing a uniform.

As explained above, the purpose of the world model is recognizing, representing, and managing situations of interest, which are also denoted as incidents. Incidents are themselves world model objects holding references to associated persons and things.[3] They also include more elementary situations of interest to be handled, such as a person has fallen to the floor, an object has been left behind, or a fire has been detected in some section of the building.

## 3.3 Archive for Video Data and Abstracted Data

Just as conventional systems, smart video surveillance systems often include an archive component for recording video data and abstracted data. Whether or not an archive is used depends on the purpose of the deployment, since persistent recording is considered to raise the privacy impact of a video surveillance measure. This applies in particular if personal identifiable information such as raw video data or biometric data is stored, which will usually be the case since archives are typically used for preserving evidence. In principle it would be sufficient to record video data, since abstracted data could be reproduced by means of re-processing recorded video data. In practice, however, abstracted data is recorded as well in order to accelerate operations, which can hardly be

[3] Note that associations of persons to incidents may be inaccurate due to the complexity of the scene or to due to not being triggered by persons directly (e.g., detection of abandoned objects). Thus, in some cases persons are associated to incidents via spatio-temporal corridors in which they have been detected.

performed in near real-time, such as searching for occurrences of a specific person in a spatio-temporal corridor. Thus, smart video surveillance systems may also perform analysis functions off-line, i.e., on recorded data. The archive is therefore not only accessed by operators, but also by components of the smart video surveillance system.

## 3.4 Human Machine Interface

The duality of video data and abstracted data of the world model is also reflected in the design of human machine interfaces (HMIs). The considered system architecture accordingly provides separate screens for visualizing video data as well as abstracted data (cf. figure 3.3).

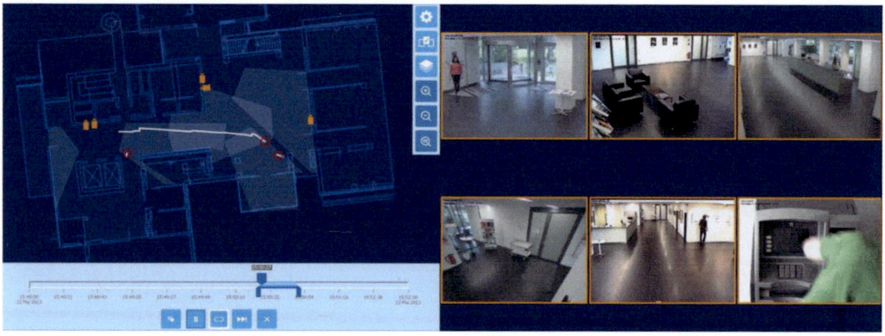

**Figure 3.3:** Exemplary HMI of Fraunhofer IOSB's smart video surveillance prototype system *NEST* [MVK08; Bau+08; MRV10]

The screen for viewing video streams includes controls for PTZ cameras. Abstracted data is visualized in an overview map of the observed area, which is also used to indicate potentially critical incidents. This is particularly helpful whenever positions of moving objects and their trajectories are relevant for situation assessment and also for visualizing streams and densities of persons in certain areas. The overview map may also offer information about cameras, such as their locations and fields of view, and can be used to select related cameras in the proximity of an incident under investigation. Eventually the

HMI provides controls for analysis functions and for accessing off-line data in case the system is equipped with an archive.

# 4 Privacy- and Security-related Requirements

This chapter introduces legal requirements concerning the operation of smart video surveillance. Legal scholars derived these requirements from applicable law (cf. section 2.3), particularly from German data protection law, which contains explicit regulations with regard to video surveillance. They are mainly privacy-related requirements that aim to protect individuals against disproportionate interferences with their personality rights and have to be complemented and refined from a technical perspective (cf. section 4.2). The technical analysis particularly emphasizes on the dimensions in which the selectivity of the monitoring process can be increased to enable a differentiated use of smart video surveillance technology. These requirements and insights are eventually incorporated into the concept of *situation-dependent smart video surveillance workflows* (cf. section 4.4).

## 4.1 Legal Requirements

In their analysis of German data protection law in respect of smart video surveillance Hornung and Desoi [HD11] provide brief indications regarding the requirements of lawful design of smart video surveillance technology. According to them smart video surveillance measures can only be proportionate if it is ensured that in the course of the surveillance process privacy intrusions take place in a stepwise manner depending on the degree of substantiation of a (potentially) critical situation. They propose a three-step model according to the extent of personal references of collected and processed data. Roßnagel et al. elaborate on this concept and provide concrete suggestions regarding a differentiated operation of smart video surveillance systems, which they address to technological research and development [RDH11]. As introduced in section 1.1, the three-step model is inspired by danger levels known in law (cf. figure 4.1). The particular steps or levels of operation in this model are characterized as follows.

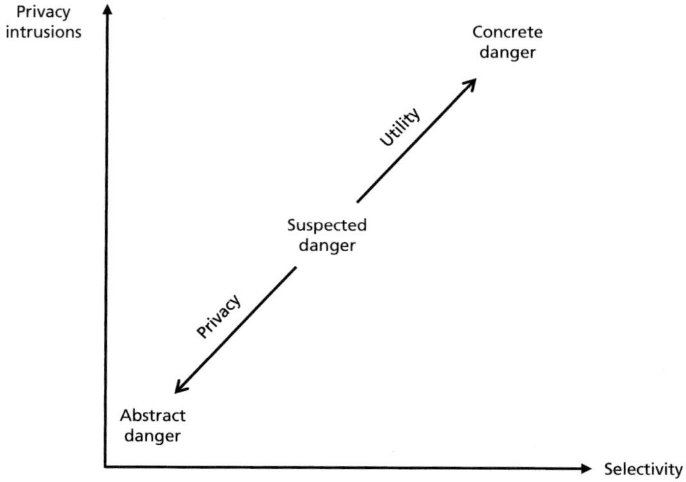


**Figure 4.1:** Danger levels of Roßnagel's three-step model

At the first/default level, video surveillance is employed against an *abstract danger*, i.e., at a dangerous or endangered place. As observed individuals have not given a reason for being monitored, intrusions into observed people's privacy, e.g., the collection and processing of their personal data, must be kept to a minimum. Video analysis pre-evaluates video streams in the background in order to draw the operator's attention to potentially critical incidents. Personal data must not be disclosed, i.e., the current situation is to be presented using abstracted representations, overview images from a distance without the possibility to zoom into the scene, or by applying privacy filters (anonymization functions) on disclosed data in order to avoid identifiability. Automated notifications to suspicious scenes are admissible as far as situation assessment and decisions regarding interventions or legal consequences remain in the responsibility of operators or security personnel on site [HD11; RDH11].

The second level is intended to provide appropriate means for the assessment of a *suspected danger* [RDH11] once an observed activity indicates a potentially critical situation. It is triggered by an operator's interaction or a notification based on automated exploitation of data. Severe privacy intrusions are not justified at this point, i.e., identities of monitored persons are not relevant as long as the operator has not rated the situation as actually critical. Collecting and processing personal data must be avoided, i.e., privacy filters must still be applied on disclosed video data. However, disclosing tracking information without personal connection is considered admissible just like selectively collecting and storing additional incident-specific data (specific surveillance of suspects). According data may also be used to prepare a potential intervention of security or emergency personnel [HD11].

The collection of personal data is justified once a situation has been assessed as a *concrete danger* to public safety, to the physical integrity of an individual, or as a criminal offense. A concrete danger requires an observation such as a person crossing a barrier, throwing a stone, or stealing a handbag. Accordingly, the third level provides means for identifying suspects, e.g., by means of access to unmodified video data as well as the extraction of biometric features [RDH11].

Altogether, intrusions into the right to informational self-determination must be minimized at the default level and balanced according to the operator's assessment of the threat situation as well as the legally protected interest at risk. If this can be ensured by means of technical mechanisms, privacy intrusions take place in a proportionate, justified, and selective manner. As by this means personal data is only disclosed in rare cases (third level), the principle of data economy is realized and the potential for misuse of the system is reduced.

An automated transition from one level to another does in itself not constitute an automated individual decision to be avoided, since it does not entail adverse legal or actual consequences such as interventions of security personnel or prosecution [RDH11; BK14]. Decisions concerning the initiation of such measures are taken exclusively by operators.

Once a situation turns out to be uncritical the purpose of collected personal data becomes obsolete. As a consequence the purpose limitation principle (cf. section 2.3) demands its deletion. This also requires that the association between personal data and the purpose of its collection is maintained [BS12].

A further requirement arises from the principle of equality. Social and cultural groups must neither be discriminated by operators nor by the technology itself, i.e., the probability of being monitored at the second or third level must not depend on one's ethnicity, religion, gender, or age (cf. section 2.2). Thus privacy filters to be applied before disclosing video data must not only hide the identity of captured individuals, but ideally also further visual features which indicate to specific social and cultural groups. Just as for privacy filters this anti-discrimination requirement must be considered when modeling suspicious behavior and when developing algorithms which are capable to automatically classify abnormal behavior. However, the latter issues are not covered in this research, since it does not address the level of internals of particular video analysis algorithms.

From a technical perspective the aforementioned legal requirements can be met in terms of enforcing access and usage constraints to increase selectivity (principle of proportionality), enforcing the application of privacy filters before disclosing video data (principle of data economy and data avoidance, principle of equality), as well as enforcing storage periods and deletion (principle of purpose limitation). The particular dimensions of selectivity concerning smart video surveillance are discussed later in the course of this chapter. The enforcement of according mechanisms is subject of section 5.1.1. Privacy filters for video data are covered in section 5.1.2 and chapter 7, whereas mechanisms concerning storage and deletion are introduced in section 5.1.4.

## 4.2 Technical Requirements

In a sub-project of the Competence Center for Applied IT Security Technology at Karlsruhe Institute of Technology (KASTEL), threats to smart video surveillance systems have been analyzed.[1] The methodology of this analysis was inspired

[1] Joint work with Erik Krempel

by Winkler and Rinner [WR14] and starts from different attackers and goals (cf. figure 4.2). Attackers are characterized according to their capabilities and possibilities and pose specific threats to the system. As a result of this threat analysis, *malicious operators* of smart video surveillance systems constitute the group of attackers, which poses such threats that are difficult to recognize yet particularly critical in terms of privacy intrusions and misuse. The focus of this research is thus put on mechanisms to prevent attacks that could be performed by malicious operators as highlighted in figure 4.2.

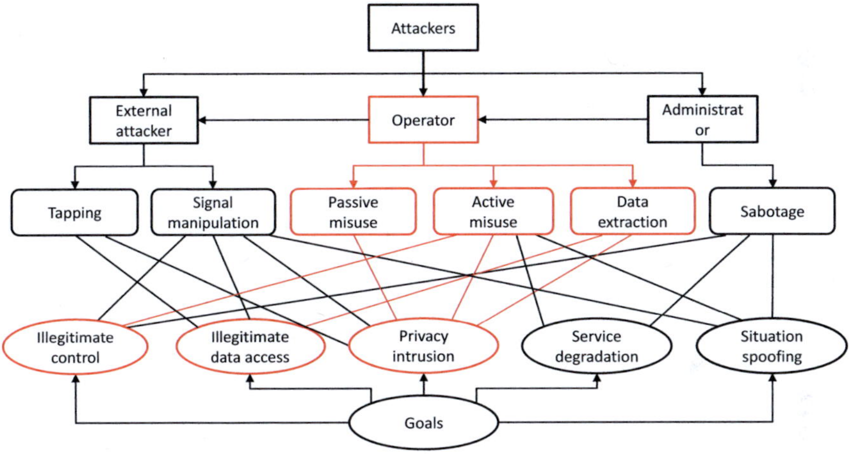


**Figure 4.2:** Attackers, threats, and goals regarding smart video surveillance

### 4.2.1 Attackers, Attack Goals, and Threats

The following paragraphs briefly describe the considered attackers, their goals, as well as according threats to a smart video surveillance system.

**Attackers.** In principle, each attack that can be accomplished by operators could also be conducted by *administrators* and by the organization, which operates a given smart video surveillance system. However, due to their extensive privileges, technical measures on the level of systems and software as proposed in this thesis are not sufficient to address the threats that are posed by them. In order to exacerbate according attacks additional physical and organizational measures have to be in place, such as physical access control for the computing center of the smart video surveillance system and the assertion of the four-eye-principle whenever the system is to be maintained or altered. Certain attacks can also be performed by *external attackers.* According threats can be mitigated by means of physical measures as well as measures on the level of the network infrastructure, such as employing encrypted communication channels, network access control,[2] and network separation. Further details concerning infrastructure security with regard to the operation of smart video surveillance systems can be found in appendix A.2.

**Multi-party Attacks.** In case attackers team up, particularly in teams consisting of an external attacker and an operator, new attacks on smart video surveillance systems are imaginable. Assume a smart video surveillance deployment, which only unlocks its object tracking capabilities in areas where potentially critical activities have been detected. A team of a malicious operator and an accomplice on the observed site can misuse the system with only a small risk of getting discovered. The accomplice can trigger fake detections in order to cause the system to unlock intrusive analysis functions, which the operator then employs for malicious purposes. As the detection can be traced back to a specific image exploitation algorithm and evidently has not been triggered manually by the operator, such kinds of misuse can hardly be discovered. However, such multi-party attacks, while theoretically possible, are difficult to rate from a risk assessment perspective. While attackers have to spend considerable effort on being close to the person on whom they want to spy, the benefit of such attacks is rather unclear.

**Attack Goals.** Attackers' goals can be differentiated according to the following categories, which are not strictly distinct from each other.

[2] e.g., IEEE 802.1X (Extensible Authentication Protocol (EAP) over IEEE 802) as specified in RFC 3748 (`https://tools.ietf.org/html/rfc3748`)

*Illegitimate control.* An attacker aims to gain (partial) control over the system in order to employ certain system functionality for his own purposes, e.g., control PTZ cameras or analysis functions in order to cover/uncover certain areas.

*Illegitimate data access.* An attacker illegitimately evaluates data in order to spy out areas or profile people while being undetectable. Whenever an operator or administrator misuses data collected by a video surveillance system beyond its defined purpose this is considered an illegitimate data access.

*Privacy intrusion.* The attacker attempts to commit unjustified privacy intrusions for an own malicious benefit, which may range from voyeurism right up to blackmailing people with gathered information. (Each video surveillance system interferes with observed people's privacy. However, as discussed in section 2.3, the degree of privacy intrusion must be proportionate given the legal purpose of its operator organization.)

*Service degradation.* The attacker's goal is to disturb the system's operation either to be unobserved or as an act of vandalism. In the context of smart video surveillance an attacker may not necessarily aim to disturb the entire system, but may break into the system in order to covertly manipulate or deactivate particular analysis components, e.g., to disable a detector for abandoned objects in order to covertly place explosives for committing a terrorist attack.

*Situation spoofing.* Situation spoofing includes attacks that aim to hide certain activities, e.g., by means of injecting fake video streams and/or suppressing detections of video analysis algorithms, or to distract the operator by means of spoofing detections that lead to false alerts. Situation spoofing could also be part of a multi-party attack as described before.

**Threats.** Threats appear as real attacks depending on attackers' goals and capabilities. (As pointed out by Beyerer and Geisler [BG15], they also depend on the attackers' resources, i.e., on attackers' cost-benefit functions).

*Tapping.* The attacker taps the cameras or the communication infrastructure without actively inserting signals. Tapping attacks are usually attempted in order to access video streams and to eavesdrop the communication between components. Such passive attacks are conducted for instance to spy on people or to learn when certain areas are unsupervised.

*Signal manipulation.* Signal manipulation constitutes an active tapping attack, which is performed to inject fake signals into the communication infrastructure., i.e., manipulated video streams or control messages in order to manipulate the system's operation or behavior.

*Passive misuse.* Passive misuse takes place whenever the system is used beyond its defined purpose to achieve malicious goals, but without violating procedural instructions and also without degrading the system's utility with respect to its actual purpose. Voyeurism constitutes the most prominent case of passive misuse of (smart) video surveillance [Kos02].

*Active misuse.* Active misuse constitutes a threat concerning which smart video surveillance poses a considerably higher risk as compared to conventional systems: It involves the misuse of the system and its analysis functions in order to illegitimately collect personal information due to private and/or criminal interests or to cover crimes.

*Data extraction.* Data extraction includes attacks such as stealing recorded data, deletion or alteration of data before it can be used as evidence, or analysis of data for creating profiles of certain people within an area under video surveillance. Data extraction also differs from active misuse since data is processed off-line, after it was recorded, and outside the system. It does not change the system's behavior. Example purposes of data extraction involve blackmailing people with gathered data as well as covering crimes.

*Sabotage.* Sabotage is constituted by manipulations of the system's behavior for the benefits of a malicious administrator. It encloses the deactivation of cameras, the deactivation of algorithms and analysis function, but also undisclosed extensions with algorithms to be executed for the attacker's malicious purpose, e.g., for covertly creating movement profiles.

As explained above, this research concentrates on the threats of *passive misuse, active misuse,* and *data extraction.* Passive misuse performed by a malicious operator cannot be prevented completely. However, the potential for passive misuse can be minimized if the system discloses personal identifiable information and in particular unmodified video data only in concrete threat situations. Passive misuse during concrete threat situations also does not seem very likely, because once people are harmed or property is damaged or destroyed, this will typically involve further investigations. Active misuse and data extraction performed by malicious operators requires "guarding the guards". It must be minimized in terms of enforcing strict constraints on function usage and data access by default, which are only relaxed in a situation-dependent and selective manner. Furthermore, in order to make misuse of privacy-intrusive functionality traceable, according user interactions are logged.

### 4.2.2 Unintentional Policy Violations and Assistance

Attempted violations against constraints do not necessarily occur on purpose. Assume that an operator is handling an incident for which it is allowed to access recorded data of up to 60 seconds prior to the detection. The operator may not be able to memorize all policies in detail and try to access data from 70 seconds prior to the detection. In addition to logging of such attempted policy violations, the system should explain to the operator why the action was inhibited. Policy violations can also be avoided by means of proactive assistance, e.g., by highlighting the timeframe, which is accessible according to the applicable policy.

### 4.2.3 False Detections

Since acts of violence, collapsing people, etc. must not be missed, activity recognition algorithms employed in smart video surveillance systems are parametrized conservatively. False negative errors are minimized on the cost of a certain false positive rate. Accordingly, even if automated individual decisions were not prohibited by law (cf. section 2.3 and section 4.1), the assessment of an operator is indispensable. At this stage, however, further intrusions into the personality rights of individuals, which are associated to a potentially critical incident, are still not justified. As explained in section 4.1 intrusions into observed persons' privacy shall only take place in the presence of concrete danger. Thus, people must not be identifiable on the basis of data, which is disclosed to the operator for the purpose of situation assessment. To achieve this, anonymization functions (privacy filters) must be applied on video data prior to visualization.

### 4.2.4 Secure Integration of Mobile Devices

Related work discussed in section 2.2 revealed that the effectiveness of video surveillance measures strongly depends on a sound coordination between operators in the systems' control rooms and security personnel on-site. In order to facilitate this coordination, meanwhile all leading suppliers of video surveillance technology provide mobile applications for accessing their systems via mobile devices such as smart phones and tablets.[3] The development towards video analysis and smart video surveillance for public events (crowd monitoring scenarios, cf. chapter 1) also implies that (video) data is exchanged with mobile emergency personnel of different organizations, such as police, paramedics, fire department, and the event organizer's own staff.

Furthermore, in certain application areas video surveillance is already operated without a central control room [KBB16]. Bretthauer and Krempel [BK14] analyzed the requirements of smart video surveillance for the purpose of detecting medical emergencies in hospitals and nursing facilities.[4] They found that incidents such as patients collapsing on the corridors must be assessed by qualified medical personnel. As these nurses or doctors are concerned with medical duties in the first place, they cannot permanently occupy a control room. Accordingly, they must be notified about potentially critical incidents via mobile devices, on which they must also be able to access video data.

In any case data disseminated to mobile devices must be protected against illegitimate redistribution since it may either show people in emergency situa-

[3] For example, the mobile applications of the video surveillance supplier *Axis Communications AB* have been downloaded more than 50.000 times from the Google Play Store for the Android operating system. There is also a considerable number of third-party suppliers offering mobile applications for accessing popular video surveillance solutions or controlling individual cameras.

[4] Note that such systems are predominantly used at night times when wards are occupied with minimum personnel.

tions or provide information on the current situation, which must not come into the possession of unauthorized persons. This requirement is addressed in chapter 6.

## 4.3 Mechanisms: Reductions and Restrictions

According to the previous section, three types of mechanisms are required to fulfill the legal requirements and to prevent misuse by a malicious operator:

- *Reduction mechanisms:* Anonymization functions (privacy filters)
- *Restriction mechanisms:* Enforcement of constraints regarding function usage and data access
- *Accountability and assistance mechanisms:* Enforcement of logging, notifications, and assistance functions

Anonymization functions are applied to balance groundless and unselective observation by means of *reducing* the personal connection of video data, i.e., they address the qualitative aspect of privacy intrusions. Privacy filters for video data are discussed in chapter 7.[5] *Restriction mechanisms* address the quantitative aspect of data collection. They increase and ensure the selectivity of function usage and data access so as to minimize the potential for misuse even when privacy intrusions are justified due to a concrete danger. However, selectivity also demands that only a minimal set of persons related to (potential) incidents is affected by deeper privacy intrusions. The particular dimensions in which the selectivity of smart video surveillance can be dispensed are discussed in the following. *Accountability and assistance mechanisms* are employed to make potential misuse traceable and to avoid unintentional misuse. All three types of mechanisms can be implemented based on the conceptual framework of usage control (cf. section 2.5). The concrete mechanisms to be enforced also depend on the current situation. Inspired by Roßnagel et al. [RDH11], section 4.4

[5] Note that privacy filters working on abstracted data are out scope of this thesis, but have been investigated i.a. by Vagts [VBB11; Vag13].

introduces the concept of *situation-dependent smart video surveillance workflows*, which encapsulates mechanisms into *operating modes* of the system. Operating modes prepare the system for suspected and concrete dangers, also depending on the type of incident to be handled.

### 4.3.1 The Dimensions of Selectivity

Smart video surveillance systems are characterized by an awareness of incidents, i.e., specific potentially critical activities or situations they are able to detect. The type of an incident is the first leverage point at which the selectivity of the surveillance process can be increased. It refers to the legally protected interest at risk. Another is the concrete instance of an incident type. Incidents have a temporal and spatial reference according to which constraints can be defined and evaluated. Eventually, incidents are triggered by or associated to one or more persons, i.e., person objects in the world model (cf. section 3.2). Thus a differentiation between persons that are associated to a given event and those who are not is the most fine-grained level of selectivity that can be reached.

**Incident Types.** Different incident types, i.e., predefined activities or situations that are detected by the system, may correspond to different legally protected interests being at risk, which in turn may justify different levels of privacy intrusions. Such levels of allowed privacy intrusions have to be expressed in terms of constraints for each incident type. *Spatial constraints* for access to video data and abstracted data can be specified in terms of a perimeter. Within this perimeter, additional data becomes accessible, beyond the perimeter access permissions do not change. Granting access to additional data may also involve the enforcement of appropriate privacy filters for video data and abstracted data depending on the particular incident type.In case the system is equipped with storage archives or at least small ring buffers for video and/or abstracted data, *temporal constraints* with respect to the accessible timeframe can be defined separately for each type of incident. *Optional analysis functions* of the system are disabled by default, but become unlocked and operational depending on the type of a current incident to be handled. Such additional analysis functions include further image exploitation algorithms, such as biometric face recognition, the execution of which is also restricted to cameras within a predefined perimeter of the incident. Further analysis functions to become unlocked may also work on abstracted data, such as exploring where a person associated to a current incident actually came from. Such optional analysis functions may be performed on live data, but also off-line, i.e., on recorded data. However, they are again restricted in terms of the aforementioned spatial and temporal access constraints.

**Incidents.** Instances of incident types, i.e., concrete incidents, take place at a certain location at a certain point in time. Based on this spatial and temporal reference of an incident, the spatial and temporal constraints according to the incident type are evaluated, i.e., the permissible perimeter and timeframe to be accessed during further investigations are calculated. Typically one or more persons (and possibly other world model objects) are associated to an incident. [6]According to these relations the selectivity of deeper intrusions into individuals' privacy can be increased. If, for instance, a biometric face recognition algorithm is unlocked and employed for preserving evidence concerning a current incident, then the processing of biometric face templates can be restricted to the persons associated to this specific incident. Biometric face templates of other persons that are collected coincidentally can be deleted at the earliest possible data processing step.

While conventional video surveillance systems only provide all-or-nothing approaches with regard to data storage, smart video surveillance also enables an incident-based approach to recording (video) data to an archive. By default, data is collected, written into ring buffers, processed, and cyclically overwritten, whereby the capacities of ring buffers only last for a few minutes of recording.

[6] Note that associations of persons to incidents may be inaccurate due to the complexity of the scene or to due to not being triggered by persons directly (e.g., detection of abandoned objects). Thus, in some cases persons are associated to incidents via spatio-temporal corridors in which they have been detected.

In case of an incident, independent of whether it is detected by video analysis or reported by an operator, data is forwarded from the ring buffers to the archive. As this approach increases the selectivity of data storage, it is considered a less severe intrusion into observed individuals' privacy in comparison to continuous recording [BKB15].

**Privacy Privileges for Persons and Groups.** In addition to restricting severe privacy intrusions to the circle of persons associated to an incident confirmed by an operator, the selectivity on the level of objects can also be increased in terms of granting privacy privileges to specific individuals or groups. Assume that a smart video surveillance system is deployed in an airport for the purpose of ensuring aviation safety. On the one hand, an airport constitutes a publicly accessible space for air passengers, visitors, etc. But then there are also employees of the airport operator and of airlines, who have to spend the major part of their working day within the monitored area. From the perspective of the airport operator the video surveillance system provides indispensable support for the security staff. However, the airport operator trusts in his own employees and hence wants to relieve them from the pressure of permanent surveillance by means of granting certain privacy privileges to them. Assume further that the system visualizes trajectories of captured persons on an overview map of the observed area. Now, if the system is able to keep track of the association of a given person and the person's status as a staff member, the privacy privilege of being hidden on the overview map can be enforced.

Even though tracking and object recognition is often considered to be privacy-intrusive, it also enables the application of privacy protecting mechanisms such as the enforcement of the aforementioned privacy privileges for specific individuals or groups, e.g., excluding persons from visualization or from certain analysis functions. This seemingly paradoxical situation that tracking technologies may contribute to privacy protecting mechanisms has been observed by Birnstill and Pretschner [BP13] and further investigated by Greiner et al. [Gre+13] as well as Birnstill et al. [Bir+15].

## 4.4 Approach: Situation-Dependent Smart Video Surveillance Workflows

The legal and technical requirements as well as the considerations regarding the dimensions of selectivity as discussed in the previous sections suggest an approach, which is denoted as *situation-dependent smart video surveillance workflows* and which separates the systems' capabilities into situation-dependent operating modes. This approach refines and extends ideas from Roßnagel [RDH11] and has been published in [BP13].

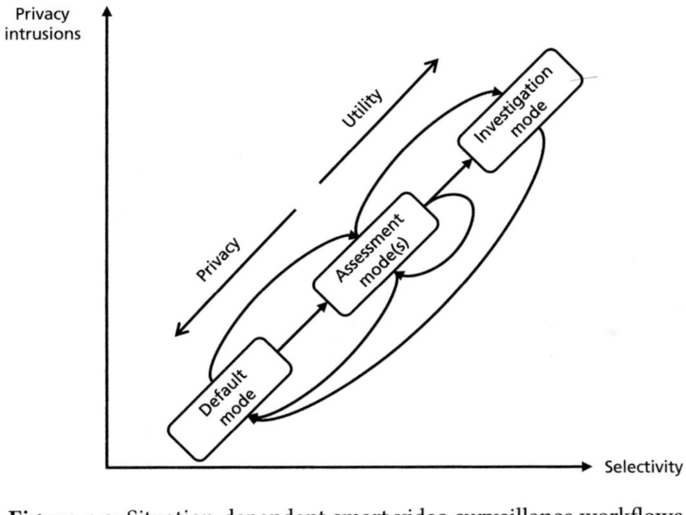


**Figure 4.3:** Situation-dependent smart video surveillance workflows

Operating modes encapsulate function usage constraints, data access constraints, as well as privacy filters and accountability requirements to be enforced according to the substantiation of a threat situation and depending on the type of incident that has been detected by the smart video surveillance system (and thus implicitly depending on the legally protected interest at risk). By this means low selectivity can be balanced with a low privacy impact while deeper privacy intrusions are compensated with a high selectivity and accountability.

Situation-dependent smart video surveillance workflows are characterized by at least three operating modes with increasing selectivity and proportionally decreasing privacy levels (cf. figure 4.3):

1. *Default mode:* Sensing for potentially critical incidents (abstract danger)
2. *Assessment mode(s):* Supporting situation assessment by the operator (suspected danger)
3. *Investigation mode:* Providing means for further investigations upon confirmation of the incident (concrete danger)

**Default Mode.** The system is operated in the *default mode* as long as no potentially critical incident has been detected. The default mode is therefore not incident-specific. Sensing for potentially critical incidents has to be performed continuously and necessarily takes place in an unselective manner. Even though the video surveillance measure by itself should be a consequence of prior incidents, from the perspective of an individual concerned it constitutes a groundless and unjustified observation. Accordingly the default mode is optimized to protect observed individuals' privacy, i.e., disclosed data is reduced to a minimum and must not exhibit personal connections. Disclosing video data should either be avoided, or, if not possible, privacy filters must be applied in order to protect the identities of individuals in the monitored area.

**Assessment Modes.** Assessment modes are incident-specific and activated once the system detects a potentially critical incident, which is initially considered as a suspected danger that may need to be taken care of by an operator. Accordingly, they create views of the scene, possibly enriched with abstracted data, so as to enable an operator to distinguish actual threats from false alarms, while still not disclosing data, which might reveal captured individual's identities. This is typically realized by applying privacy filters on disclosed data. Multiple cascaded assessment modes are also imaginable in order to shift the trade-off between privacy protection and utility in a stepwise manner: Video data may initially get obfuscated using a strong privacy filter, which the operator can adjust or switch to a weaker privacy filter in case a reliable situation assessment is not possible. Assessment modes may also unlock functions such as keeping track of the persons associated to the incident, or tracking back where these persons came from. The system is executed in an assessment mode until the operator either recognizes and confirms a concrete danger or discards the incident as a false detection or as uncritical. In the latter case the system returns into its default mode.

**Investigation Modes.** An *investigation mode* is entered once the operator confirmed an incident as a concrete danger. At this point, the physical integrity of people is at risk, property is damaged, or a criminal act is observed. As a consequence, further investigations involving the collection and processing of personal data for the purpose of identifying offenders is justified as well as the initiation of countermeasures. In other words, the utility of the system is increased to a level, which is appropriate for handling a given type of incident. At the same time the selectivity of the surveillance process is further increased, i.e., operations are restricted onto persons that are associated to the incident. If, for instance, a biometric face recognition algorithm is unlocked in order to obtain data, which allows the identification of an offender by prosecution authorities, it must only collect biometric face templates of persons that are associated to the incident under investigation. Usages of such intrusive functions are logged so as to be able to reveal misuse in hindsight.

Assessment modes as well as investigation modes are typically executed on appropriate subsets of the system's cameras, i.e., the remaining cameras will still be operated in the default mode. The technical enforcement of operating modes is subject of the subsequent chapter.

## 4.5 Preserving the Utility of the Smart Video Surveillance System

Privacy-preserving mechanisms, i.e., the enforcement of situation-dependent smart video surveillance workflows, must not be applied on the cost of the system's utility, i.e., they must not render a given smart video surveillance system ineffective with respect to its rightful purpose. The be more specific, this research considers the following aspects of the utility of a smart video surveillance system:

1. *Situation Assessment:* Privacy filters must not be applied on the cost of the utility of video data. Operators must still be able to recognize activities with high probability, but not identities.

2. *Incident Handling:* Despite of privacy-preserving mechanisms being enforced, operators must still be able to resolve incidents and to preserve evidence with acceptable operating overhead and delay.

These aspects of utility are evaluated in chapter 7, which investigates the utility of video data, which has been obfuscated using different privacy filters, and in chapter 8, which looks into the utility of an exemplary situation-dependent smart video surveillance workflow during incident handling.

# 5 Usage Control for Smart Video Surveillance

In order to enforce the requirements of situation-dependent smart video surveillance workflows as introduced before (cf. section 4.4) the generic architecture of chapter 3 is extended with usage control technology. In particular, this chapter addresses the research questions **TS-1** and **TS-3** (cf. section 1.3):

- Enforcing the constraints of operating modes for implementing situation-dependent smart video surveillance workflows based on usage control mechanisms (cf. section 2.4).
- Increasing the selectivity of data processing during investigation modes by means of tainting detections from video analysis and monitoring according information fusion events.

Section 5.1 explains how the state concerning situation-dependent smart video surveillance workflows is kept, which components of the generic architecture must be monitored by PEPs, and which PXPs have to be integrated in order to enforce the required rights and obligations (cf. section 2.4). Each paragraph first explains the purpose of a particular component extended with usage control capabilities in a generic fashion and subsequently discusses implementation-specific aspects. In section 5.2 an exemplary workflow is instantiated and according policies are explained. Section 5.3 explains how privacy privileges are enforced at the world model. Section 5.4 describes how selective processing of detections from video analysis algorithms is achieved, also based on usage control enforcement. Section 5.5 expands on the technical implementation of PEPs and PXPs for Fraunhofer IOSB's smart video surveillance platform *NEST* [MVK08; Bau+08; MRV10]. Section 5.7 concludes and discusses the assumptions under which the enforcement of the described mechanisms and policies can be guaranteed as well as the limitations of the approach.

## 5.1 Usage Control Enabled Architecture for Smart Video Surveillance

In the following, the generic architecture for smart video surveillance introduced in chapter 3 is extended with usage control components so as to enable the enforcement of situation-dependent smart video surveillance workflows.

### 5.1.1 Enforcing Operating Modes

As discussed in section 4.4, situation-dependent smart video surveillance workflows implement stepwise operating modes, along which the selectivity of privacy intrusions increases proportionally to the substantiation of potentially critical incidents.

The default mode of the system executes detective tasks, i.e., detecting certain activities or situations, which for most video surveillance deployments will be the same tasks across all cameras and observed areas. This is due to the fact that a video surveillance measure is deployed for a well-defined purpose, which does not change between different areas of the same deployment.[1] The default mode is basically realized by inhibiting actions by default, e.g., inhibit access to video streams, attributes of world model objects, recorded data, analysis functions, etc. Moreover, privacy privileges are enforced by means of inhibiting access to data or modifying data before access. World model objects or particular attributes of them can either be locked, or disclosed in an obfuscated form by applying privacy filters,[2] e.g., to coarsen an observed persons location attribute.

Assessment modes and also investigation modes are specific for the different types of potential incidents that are detected by the smart video surveillance system.[3] They selectively relax the access constraints and the application of

[1] Note that if required in the future, area-specific default modes can be implemented analogously to assessment and investigation modes as described in the following.

[2] Note that privacy filters working on abstracted data are out scope of this thesis, but have been investigated i.a. by Vagts [VBB11; Vag13].

[3] Note that smart video surveillance systems may also enable operators to report incidents by themselves. If this is done by pointing to the according video stream and choosing an incident type, situation-dependent smart video surveillance workflows can be enforced just as for automatically detected incidents.

privacy protection mechanisms, i.e., their relaxations are specified as deltas in relation to the previous constraints. An assessment mode for a certain type of incident is activated whenever the operator takes over the responsibility for handling a concrete incident. The operator typically does so by selecting an according alert that popped up in the HMI. Note that it is explicitly foreseen that several assessment modes can be defined for a certain type of incident. In case situation assessment is not possible due to a strong privacy filter being applied on video data in a $1^{st}$ level assessment mode, a $2^{nd}$ level assessment mode could either relax the parametrization of the current privacy filter or switch to a different one. An investigation mode is activated whenever an observed incident is confirmed by the operator. It will typically further relax access constraints of the previous assessment mode, particularly concerning objects that are associated to the incident under investigation, and provide access to incident-specific analysis functions for handling the incident and collecting evidences.

From both, assessment modes as well as investigation modes, the system must be reset into its default mode, whenever an assessment mode or investigation mode terminates, either because an incident is resolved or discarded in case it is recognized as a false detection.

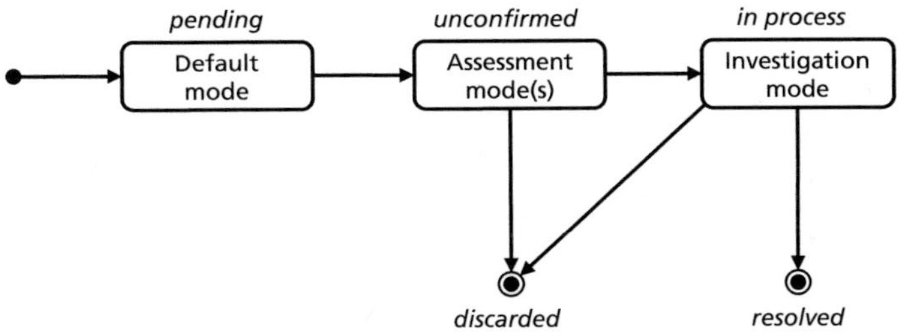


**Figure 5.1:** The lifecycle model of an incident handled in a situation-dependent smart video surveillance workflow

Accordingly, the current operating mode of the system is also reflected in the state of an ongoing incident. More specifically, the *status* attribute of an incident refers to a stage in the incident lifecycle model of situation-dependent smart video surveillance workflows, which is depicted in figure 5.1.

An incident's status is a precondition or a result of an operating mode and it also documents whether an incident has been resolved eventually or has been recognized as a false detection and was hence discarded. The status is *pending* until the operator takes up on handling the given incident. It remains *unconfirmed* until the incident has been assessed by the operator. Depending on the operator's assessment, the status either switches to *in_process* or to *discarded*, i.e., the incident is either confirmed by the operator or recognized as a false positive detection. During an investigation, an incident can still turn out to be uncritical. Thus, from *in_process* the status can either change to *discarded* or to *resolved*. The *discarded* status is particularly important if additional data has been collected during the investigation of an incident. In case the incident lifecycle terminates in the *discarded* status, either the instant deletion of such data can be enforced or it can be conferred to be deleted as soon as the regular storage period expires. Data collected during an investigation, which terminated in the *resolved* state, typically includes evidences required for documentation and prosecution purposes. It is thus explicitly excluded from deletion after expiration of the regular storage period. A world model object of type *incident* contains the following attributes:

- incident type,
- status,
- detection time reference,
- termination time reference,
- spatial reference,
- source camera,
- associated world model objects.

The time references point to the time when the incident has been detected and to the time when it has been discarded or resolved eventually. An incident's state also comprises its spatial coordinates and an identifier of the source camera. Both attributes are derived from detections of video analysis algorithms, based on which the incident has been recognized. Finally, the state contains a list of identifiers of world model objects, i.e., persons or things, which have been associated to the incident. Primarily, objects are associated to incidents based on concrete activities that have been observed, but possibly also because they were captured very close to the incident. If, for instance, multiple persons are involved in a fighting scene, video analysis algorithms may not be able to accurately differentiate between passers-by, bystanders, and actual combatants. Nevertheless, even inaccurate associations of world model objects to incidents can contribute to an increased selectivity when processing data during investigations (cf. section 5.4).

Operating modes are conceptionally specified in *constraint profiles* addressed via tuples (*mode*, *incident type*) and contain the following types of constraints:

- temporal constraints,
- spatial constraints,
- constraints on world model data types,
- privacy filters to be applied on data that is disclosed to the operator,
- accessible analysis functions on video data and world model data,
- operator interactions to be logged.

The first three types of constraints specify which data is accessible in a given operating mode. These constraints are enforced globally, i.e., they apply for data to be accessed by the operator and also for data to be accessible for investigation mode analysis functions. A *temporal constraint* defines a timeframe of recorded video data or world model data, which the operator can access for situation assessment respectively investigation of an incident and which is interpreted relative to the incidents detection time reference. A *spatial constraint* is specified in terms of a perimeter or, in case the camera network is separated into a hierarchical structure, in terms of a hierarchy level.[4] It is interpreted relative to the spatial reference of the incident in either case. *Constraints on world model data types* define which objects types as well as which attributes of these objects are accessible within the given operating mode. Note that the aforementioned types of constraints cover both, live data and recorded data, depending on specified temporal constraints. This implies the assumption that live data and recorded data is accessible via equivalent interfaces.[5] Constraint profiles of assessment modes and investigation modes are interpreted as deltas in relation to the constraints of the previous mode, i.e., they selectively relax particular constraints, whereas constraints that are not relaxed do not have to be respecified.

*Privacy filters* are applied on data that is disclosed to the operator.[6] Since assessment modes are designated for viewing data related to a potentially critical incident and analysis functions are locked by default, *accessible analysis functions* are typically specified for investigation modes only. Similar to when the operator is granted access to recorded data, either video data or abstracted data to be reprocessed by such analysis functions is pulled from the archive into image exploitation respectively world model components. Data produced by investigation mode analysis functions becomes inaccessible as soon as the operating mode changes again (to the default mode) and will either be written back to the archive or deleted depending on whether the incident terminates in a *resolved* status respectively *discarded* status.

[4] Note that video data, i.e., live streams as well sequences of images from the archive, is usually not referenced via spatial coordinates. It is addressed via the identifier of its source camera, which actually has spatial coordinates, also for its field of view. Thus, a spatial constraint on video data access is translated into identifiers of accessible cameras.

[5] This may seem as a matter of course of well-conceived system design, however, in practice video surveillance systems and archive solutions are often obtained from different software suppliers.

[6] Note that the application of privacy filters could also be enforced when data is accessed by investigation mode analysis functions. However, since the attacker model of this thesis emphasizes on operators and operating organizations as the primary attackers or misusers, the focus is put on restricting the accessibility of intrusive functions and on protecting their output rather then on obfuscating their input.

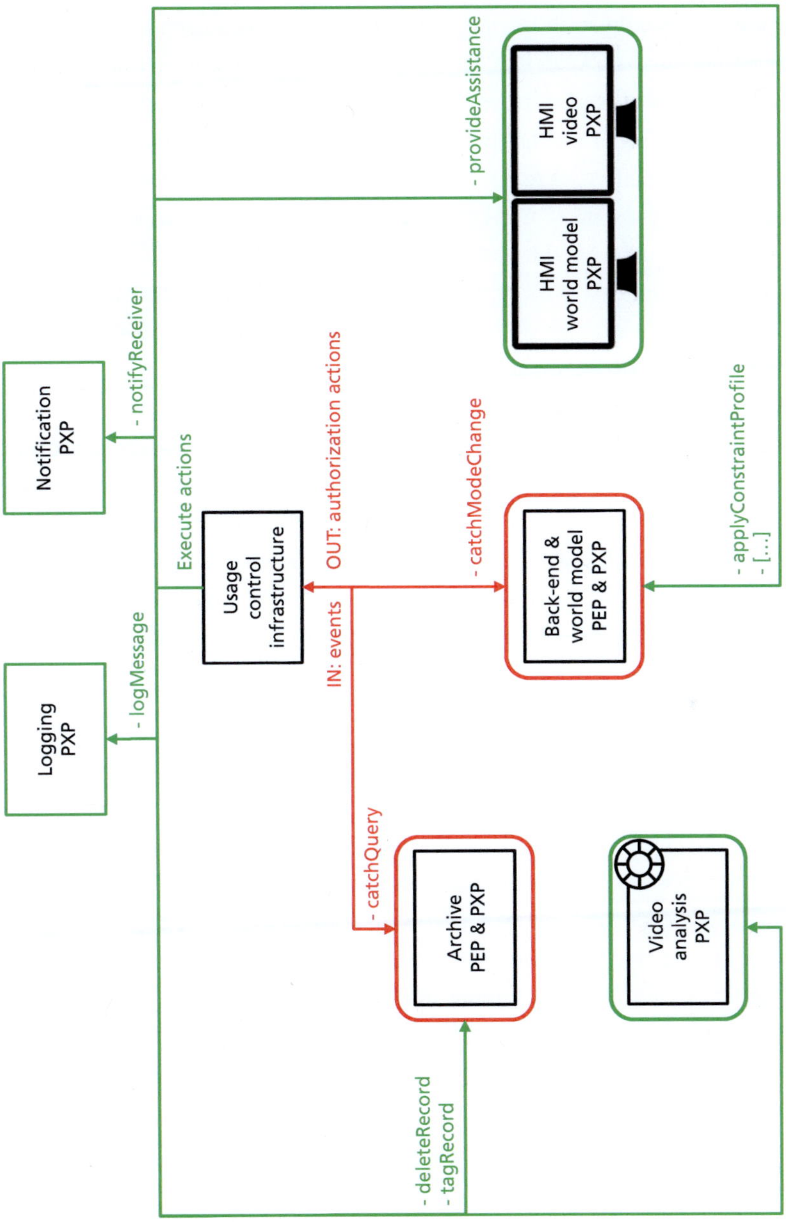


**Figure 5.2:** The generic smart video surveillance architecture instrumented with usage control capabilities

Finally, the constraint profile of an operating mode contains *operator interactions* to be written into the system's log. In an assessment mode, this typically involves the operator's assessment of an incident, i.e., whether the incident is confirmed, discarded, or ambiguous, where the latter indicates that the operator switched between different assessment modes, which the system provides for the given type of incident. For investigation modes, also the usage of unlocked analysis functions is logged in order to make misuse traceable in hindsight.

The particular constraints of a constraint profile have to be enforced on various components of the smart video surveillance system. There is a *root policy* for each constraint profile, which is triggered by mode changes observed by a PEP at the back-end (cf. figure 5.2). Root policies always evaluate to *allow*. Via calling execute actions of components acting as PXPs, they apply constraint profiles to the world model (*applyConstraintProfile*) and enforce the activation of privacy filters. Further policies control queries to the archive, enforce privacy privileges, and ensure selective processing of the detections of video analysis algorithms during investigations as is described in the following. Policies of an exemplary situation-dependent smart video surveillance workflow can be found in section 5.2.

### 5.1.2 Enforcement for Video Streams and Video Analysis

The cameras' video streams and also recorded video data are never accessed directly by the HMI. The HMI only visualizes video streams that are provided as output of video analysis components. In terms of usage control enforcement, video analysis components act as PXPs. By this means, the usage control infrastructure's PDP is able to control the video output of each image exploitation component depending on the evaluation of a policy, which is triggered by an event intercepted by some PEP – the back-end and world model PEP in this case. The video analysis PXP provides the following execute actions (cf. figure 5.2):

- *blockOutput*
- *unblockOutput*

- *enablePrivacyFilter*
- *disablePrivacyFilter*
- *disableAlgorithm*
- *taintAlgorithm*
- *enableBufferFwd*
- *disabledBufferFwd*

Depending on the constraint profile of the current operating mode, a video analysis component's output is either blocked, obfuscated by means of applying a specific privacy filter, or streamed without privacy filtering. This behavior is controlled using the PXP's execute actions *blockOutput*, *unblockOutput*, *enablePrivacyFilter*, and *disablePrivacyFilter*. Whenever recorded video data is accessed, either to be visualized to the operator or to be reprocessed with additional video analysis algorithms, video analysis components pull accessible video data (e.g., images) from the archive and process it exactly like live video data from a camera. Thus, the execute actions *enablePrivacyFilter* and *disablePrivacyFilter* are also used to enforce the application of privacy filters when visualizing recorded video data.

Optional video analysis algorithms are typically unlocked in investigation modes (e.g., biometric face recognition) and can be applied on live streams, but also on accessible video data, which is pulled from the archive. Such algorithms become available in the HMI once an according constraint profile is deployed at the world model/back-end. Whether they are actually required and hence enabled is up to the operator. However, once an incident is resolved or discarded, i.e., the system switches to its default mode, optional algorithms must be deactivated. For this, the video analysis PXP provides the *disableAlgorithm* execute action.

Furthermore, an incident-specific taint mark can be assigned to an optional video analysis algorithm by calling the *taintAlgorithm* execute action. As a consequence, each detection of the algorithm is tainted with this taint mark before it is transmitted to the world model. At the world model, the detections are associated to the according incident under investigation, which is a prerequisite for improving the selectivity of data processing, e.g., by deleting biometric face templates of persons that are not associated to the incident under investigation at the earliest possible data processing step. The details of this approach towards selective data processing are explained in section 5.4.

The execute actions *enableBufferFwd* and *disableBufferFwd* are used to trigger respectively terminate the forwarding of video data from ring buffers to the archive so as to realize an incident-based recording strategy (cf. section 4.3.1). Note that the exemplary situation-dependent smart video surveillance workflow introduced in section 5.2 does not implement an incident-based recording strategy, as it was intended to also illustrate how constraints concerning analysis functions on the archive are specified and enforced.

**Implementation.** Within the NEST prototype system, there is a dedicated video analysis component for each camera. By means of switching the image source, these components can be used for image exploitation on camera live streams, but also on video data from the archive. However, since in most scenarios live and off-line video analysis are operated concurrently, a system is usually equipped with two video analysis components per camera.

The video analysis components in NEST are designed as configurable chains of plug-ins, where each plug-in executes a specific image exploitation algorithm. The input of the first plug-in within the chain of a video analysis component is an image source, accessing a camera or the archive. The last plug-in is a video streaming server to which the HMI is connected. Intermediate plug-ins receive the current image from the previous plug-in, possibly together with data structures containing exploitation results of the previous plug-in. When activated, they continuously execute an image exploitation algorithm (or privacy filter), send detections to the world model, and pass images and other data structures on to the subsequent plug-in.

In order to provide the aforementioned execute actions, privacy filter plug-ins, video analysis plug-ins, and the video streaming server implement a PXP interface. Via this PXP interface, privacy filter plug-ins provide the execute actions *enablePrivacyFilter* and *disablePrivacyFilter* to the usage control infrastructure. Optional video analysis plug-ins provide the execute actions *disableAlgorithm* and *taintAlgorithm*, whereas the plugins that are executed continuously do not, i.e., the detective algorithms (cf. section 3.1) of the default mode of the smart video surveillance system. Eventually, the video streaming server plug-in implements the execute actions *blockOutput* and *unblockOutput* to either offer an output video stream of the camera attached to the given video analysis component or not.

### 5.1.3 Enforcement for the World Model

As discussed in chapter 3, the generic architecture for smart video surveillance outlined in this thesis models the back-end of the system and the world model as a single component (w. l. o. g.). This basically means that the considered component is responsible for creating and maintaining an object-oriented representation of the observed area, providing access to analysis functions on abstracted data and also on video data, as well as for the management of incidents, which are also represented as objects within the world model. Analysis functions to be executed on abstracted world model data include detecting intrusions into specified areas, counting people in specified areas, backtracking selected persons, comparing persons' positions with pre-estimated paths (anomaly detection), etc. Regarding usage control enforcement, this component acts as a PEP and also as a PXP (cf. figure 5.3). The following events are intercepted by this PEP:

- *catchModeChange*
- *catchFunctionUsage*
- *catchIncidentClosed*
- *catchFusion*
- *catchClassification*

*CatchModeChange* events are intercepted at the incident management module of the world model. As mentioned in section 5.1.1, these events indicate changes of the operating mode and trigger according *root policies.* In case additional analysis functions are unlocked in an assessment or investigation mode, their usage is observed by means of *catchFunctionUsage* events. *CatchIncidentClosed* events indicate that either a critical incident (status=*resolved*) or a false alert (status=*discarded*) is closed by the operator. In the latter case, data collected during incident handling is usually deleted, whereas data concerning a critical incident is tagged in order to prevent deletion, since it may include evidences that are relevant for prosecution. *catchModeChange*, *catchFunctionUsage*, and *catchIncidentClosed* events also reflect the operator's interaction with the system and hence trigger log messages or notifications in order to make misuse traceable (cf. section 5.1.6).

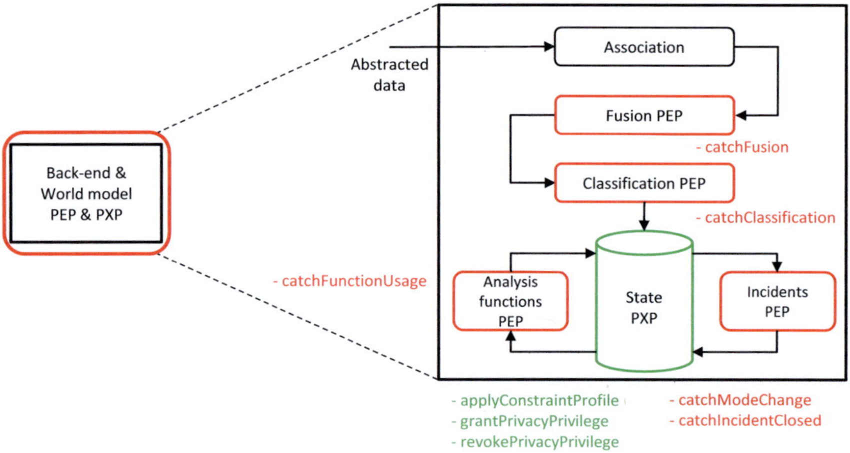


**Figure 5.3:** Zooming into the back-end and world model component instrumented with usage control capabilities

As introduced in section 3.2, *information fusion* is the data processing step, which updates the state of a world model object given new detections from video analysis that have been associated to this particular object. Since the association of a detection (e.g., an observed attribute of a person) to a world model object is a precondition of selective data processing, *catchFusion* events must be monitored. By this means, detections received from optional video analysis algorithms can be filtered at the earliest possible data processing step, so as to increase the selectivity of data processing as claimed in **TS-3** (cf. section 1.3). Section 5.4 explains the details of this approach.

In the *classification* step of data processing, persons that are *known* to the system are recognized, i.e., either an identity or a group affiliation is attributed to the corresponding world model object. Thus, *catchClassification* events must be observed in order to enforce privacy privileges that are granted to individual persons or groups (cf. section 5.3). The PXP interface of the back-end and world model provides the following execute actions:

- *applyConstraintProfile*
- *grantPrivacyPrivilege*
- *revokePrivacyPrivilege*

The *applyConstraintProfile* execute action is called when enforcing root policies of operating modes, i.e., whenever the operating mode of the system changes and an according constraint profile must be applied (cf. section 5.1.1). Temporal constraints,[7] spatial constraints, and constraints regarding world model data types are enforced when data is accessed by the HMI and by analysis functions that work on abstracted world model data. Specified privacy filters are applied on world model data, which is accessed by the HMI.[8] An operating mode's constraint profile also specifies accessible analysis functions, i.e., optional video analysis functions as well as analysis functions for abstracted world model data.

[7] Note that temporal constraints refer to data recorded in the archive. Data is pulled from the archive via the world model. Therefore, if it is ensured that the archive only accepts queries originating from the back-end/world model, temporal constraints could already be enforced here. However, this is consciously omitted, since monitoring queries at the archive provides an equivalent level of security, but allows a more flexible usage of the archive (cf. section 5.1.4).

[8] Note that privacy filters working on abstracted data are out scope of this thesis, but have been investigated i.a. by Vagts [VBB11; Vag13].

Such analysis functions become available in the HMI once they are unlocked within the back-end/world model according to the activated constraint profile.

Eventually, the execute action *grantPrivacyPrivilege* renders world model objects or specific attributes of them invisible or inaccessible for the HMI so as to grant privacy privileges for particular persons or groups (cf. section 5.3). Privacy privileges are revoked (*revokePrivacyPrivilege*) once a protected person becomes associated to a potentially critical incident.

**Implementation.** Within the NEST prototype system, the back-end is merely a communication backbone for modules, which process abstracted data. For instance, the world model itself, analysis functions on world model data, incident management, and archive access are implemented as adapters that are attached to the back-end. The PEP, which from a conceptional point of view intercepts back-end functionality such as status changes of incidents, is thus actually implemented as separated PEPs for specific adapters. The incident management adapter also provides a connector through which any other PEP can acquire parameters concerning the current operating mode of the system in order to enrich events before notifying them to the PDP.

### 5.1.4 Enforcement for the Archive

The archive component adds the time dimension to the operation of a smart video surveillance system. Additional analysis functions that are unlocked in investigation modes may also be executed off-line on recorded data. The archive persistently stores video data as well as abstracted data until a predefined storage period expires.[9] It is directly connected to the cameras' output streams, since only original video data is admissible as evidence in court in case an incident entails legal proceedings. The world model keeps a live state of a few seconds in its memory, which is then pushed to the archive. Video data as well as abstracted data is addressed via timestamps. Whenever the operator navigates

[9] Note that this approach is still applicable if video data and abstracted data are stored in separate archive components.

the HMI to a point in time in the past, recorded data is pulled transparently by video analysis components and by the world model. Thus, it can also be reprocessed using optional analysis functions during investigations.

However, the constraint profiles of operating modes also apply for recorded data. Therefore the archive acts as a PEP as it intercepts queries (*catchQuery* events) to be evaluated against the applicable constraint profile by the PDP.[10] To be more specific, queries have to be evaluated against temporal constraints, spatial constraints, and constraints on abstracted world model data types. As recorded data is only disclosed to the operator via video analysis components (cf. section 5.1.2) and via the world model (cf. section 5.1.3), the PXP interfaces of those components are used for applying privacy filters as specified in constraint profiles. The PXP interface of the archive provides two execute actions:

- *deleteRecord*
- *tagRecord*

In case an incident turns out to be a false alert during investigation, the *deleteRecord* execute action is called. It erases additional data, i.e., world model objects' attributes, which have been collected by optional analysis functions and are identified by means of their incident-specific taint marks. In contrast, the *tagRecord* execute action is used to exclude records from deletion when the regular storage period expires and is applied to preserve collected evidences once a critical incident has been resolved.

**Implementation.** The archive component of the NEST prototype system is built upon a NoSQL column data store. Video data, i.e., individual images, as well as abstracted world model data is kept in columns. Particular data items are organized by means of timestamps, spatial locations, source meta

[10] Note that if it is ensured that the archive only accepts queries originating from the back-end/world model, then it is sufficient to intercept and evaluate queries against the current constraint profile at the back-end/world model. However, this is consciously omitted, since monitoring queries at the archive provides an equivalent level of security, but allows a more flexible usage of the archive component.

data, i.e., the source camera and possibly the source algorithm, and data types. Data types include object types such as *person*, *suitcase*, *dog*, *police officer*, as well as objects' attributes such as visual and (soft-)biometric features (*glasses*, *hat*, *biometric face template*, etc.), inferred attributes (*age*, *gender*, etc.), and activities. However, recorded data is addressed via timestamps or timeframes primarily. The implementation of UC enforcement for the archive thus evaluates intercepted queries against temporal constraints of the current operating mode in the first place. Spatial constraints as well as constraints regarding data types are then enforced by means of filtering out according columns when answering queries, i.e., when transferring data to other components.

### 5.1.5 Enforcement for the Human-Machine-Interface: Providing Assistance to the Operator

The HMI visualizes accessible world model data (persons, objects, incidents, etc.) and video data, also from archives, and enables the operator to control the system, e.g., navigating PTZ cameras, activating optional analysis functions on video data as well as on abstracted data. W. l. o. g. it is assumed that the interaction between the HMI and other components of the system is realized using the model-view-controller pattern (MVC). Accordingly, the HMI only visualizes data and provides controls of analysis functions that are accessible at the moment. Thus, neither access to data nor to usage of analysis functions has to be monitored at the HMI.

The operator's interaction with the system also does not have to be monitored at the HMI, since it is already observed by the PEPs at the back-end/world model (cf. section 5.1.3) and at the archive (cf. section 5.1.4).

A smart video surveillance system is typically able to execute multiple situation-dependent workflows according to the incident types, which are detected and have to be handled by an operator. Thus, it cannot be assumed that operators memorize the constraint profile of each operating mode of each particular incident type. This leads to attempted policy violations, many of which happen unintentionally, and hence to frustration and unnecessary log messages to be reviewed. This issue is addressed by means of a PXP interface, which implements the execute action *provideAssistance*. This execute action is used to visualize access constraints whenever the operating mode changes (e.g., by highlighting the accessible timeframe of recorded data). It is also used to show messages in the HMI that explain attempted policy violations. By this means the usage control infrastructure supports the operator to avoid unintentional policy violation attempts and improves the usability of the smart video surveillance system.

**Implementation.** The PXP interface of the NEST prototype system's HMI is also used to reset controls to a permitted state. For instance, access to recorded data is provided via a slider control element on a timeline. This slider can also be navigated to points in time, which are not accessible given the temporal constraints of the current operating mode. Such attempted policy violations are detected when evaluating *catchQuery* events observed at the archive.[11] The PDP accordingly triggers that the timeline control is reset to a permitted state.

### 5.1.6 Observing the Observer: Logging and Notifications

Requirements concerning accountability (cf. section 4.2.1 and section 4.2.2) are realized via dedicated PXPs: a *Logging PXP* and a *Notification PXP* The logging PXP is called whenever a policy demands that a message is written to the system's log using the execute action *logMessage*. This is done in order to make misuse traceable in hindsight and typically involves changes of the operating mode, the operator's interactions with the system in assessment and investigation modes, or attempted policy violations committed by the operator. The notification PXP provides the execute action *notifyReceiver*. This execute action is used whenever a policy demands that a notification message is sent,

[11] Note that if it is ensured that the archive only accepts queries originating from the back-end/world model, then it is sufficient to intercept and evaluate queries against the current constraint profile at the back-end/world model. However, this is consciously omitted, since monitoring queries at the archive provides an equivalent level of security, but allows a more flexible usage of the archive component.

for instance to the responsible police station, the department head, or to the employee organization.

**Implementation.** Both PXPs, the logging PXP as well as the notification PXP, are implemented as stand-alone servers, which are only connected to the NEST prototye system via the usage control infrastructure.

## 5.2 Usage Control Policies of a Situation-dependent Smart Video Surveillance Workflow

The subsequent sections instantiate an exemplary situation-dependent smart video surveillance workflow by means of explaining the required policies in detail. Assume a smart video surveillance system, which is deployed at an airport. The considered workflow is concerned with handling incidents related to abandoned objects, which might be dropped due to carelessness and hence be completely harmless, but might also contain explosives for committing a terrorist attack. Accordingly, a video analysis algorithm for detecting abandoned objects is executed continuously during any operating mode of the system.

Note that this scenario as well as the constraints of each particular operating mode are intended to serve as an example of a situation-dependent smart video surveillance workflow and its specification in policies. Situation-dependent smart video surveillance workflows are aligned with legal requirements (cf. section 4.1) on a conceptional level, however, this specific workflow has not been analyzed in terms of its proportionality and lawfulness. Note further that multi-tenancy, i.e., multiple operators working with multiple front-ends in order to cover large areas and to handle concurrent incidents, is not explicitly covered here. Section 5.7.1 briefly outlines the modifications that are required for obtaining multi-tenancy capability in a smart video surveillance system which is equipped with UC.

### 5.2.1 Default Mode: Detecting Abandoned Objects

The constraint profile of the default mode is applied when the system is activated, and it is applied again whenever an incident is closed, either because it has been resolved or because it has been recognized as a false detection. Accordingly there are two root policies for the default mode, which are shown in the listings 5.1 and 5.2, and which are equivalent with regard to the constraints and privacy filters to be enforced. The XML policy scheme is explained in section 2.5.1 (cf. appendix C.1 for the complete XML scheme).

Both policies enforce that optional video analysis algorithms are disabled on all cameras, which are also reset to the default privacy filter, which reduces persons to silhouettes (cf. chapter 7). The constraint profile to be applied at the world model is likewise equivalent. Recorded data is not accessible,[12] while from the live state of the world model access is granted to the *location* attribute of all world model objects of type *person*, but to nothing else. They differ in terms of the execute actions to be performed at the archive and in terms of the messages that are written to the log. The policy triggered whenever an incident is closed as resolved (cf. listing 5.1) tags additional data collected during the investigation to be excluded from regular deletion, i.e., to preserve this data as evidence for prosecution. The second policy (cf. listing 5.2) matches on discarded incidents and ensures the deletion of all additional data that collected during the investigation. Another policy blocks any queries to the archive while the video surveillance system operates in its default mode (cf. listing 5.3).

A log entry is written for each illegitimate attempt to access the archive. At the HMI, controls are reset and a notification message is shown, which explains why the attempted access to the archive has been inhibited.

[12] Note that temporal constraints also have to be enforced at the world model, since its memory may still contain data, which must not be accessed according to the constraint profile.

```xml
<policy description="Reset to default mode after incident resolved" name="resetResolved">
  <preventiveMechanism name="resetAfterIncidentResolved">
    <description>Set up default mode after incident resolved</description>
    <trigger action="catchIncidentClosed" isTry="true">
      <paramMatch name="status" value="resolved"/>
    </trigger>
    <condition>
      <true/>
    </condition>
    <authorizationAction name="allow">
      <allow/>
    </authorizationAction>
    <executeAction name="videoAnalysis:disableAlgorithm">
      <parameter name="cameras" value="*"/>
      <parameter name="algorithm" value="*"/>
    </executeAction>
    <executeAction name="videoAnalysis:enablePrivacyFilter">
      <parameter name="cameras" value="*"/>
      <parameter name="filter" value="silhouetteFilter"/>
    </executeAction>
    <executeAction name="worldModel:applyConstraintProfile">
      <parameter name="timeframe" value="0"/>
      <parameter name="perimeter" value="*"/>
      <complexParameter name="objectDependentConstraints">
        <parameter name="objectType" value="person"/>
        <parameter name="attributeType" value="location"/>
        <parameter name="analysisFunctions" value=""/>
      </complexParameter>
    </executeAction>
    <executeAction name="archive:tagRecord">
      <parameter name="incidentIdentifier" value="string(//event/parameter[@name='incidentId']/@value)" type="xpath"/>
    </executeAction>
    <executeAction name="logMessage">
      <parameter name="incidentIdentifier" value="string(//event/parameter[@name='incidentId']/@value)" type="xpath"/>
      <parameter name="message" value="Incident closed as resolved"/>
    </executeAction>
  </preventiveMechanism>
</policy>
```

**Listing 5.1:** Policy to reset the system to its default mode after an incident has been resolved by the operator

```xml
<policy description="Reset to default mode after incident discarded" name="resetDiscarded">
  <preventiveMechanism name="resetAfterIncidentDiscarded">
    <description>Set up default mode after incident discarded</description>
    <trigger action="catchIncidentClosed" isTry="true">
      <paramMatch name="status" value="discarded"/>
    </trigger>
    <condition>
      <true/>
    </condition>
    <authorizationAction name="allow">
      <allow/>
    </authorizationAction>
    <executeAction name="videoAnalysis:disableAlgorithm">
      <parameter name="cameras" value="*"/>
      <parameter name="algorithm" value="*"/>
    </executeAction>
    <executeAction name="videoAnalysis:enablePrivacyFilter">
      <parameter name="cameras" value="*"/>
      <parameter name="filter" value="silhouetteFilter"/>
    </executeAction>
    <executeAction name="worldModel:applyConstraintProfile">
      <parameter name="timeframe" value="0"/>
      <parameter name="perimeter" value="*"/>
      <complexParameter name="objectDependentConstraints">
        <parameter name="objectType" value="person"/>
        <parameter name="attributeType" value="location"/>
        <parameter name="analysisFunctions" value=""/>
      </complexParameter>
    </executeAction>
    <executeAction name="archive:deleteRecord">
      <parameter name="incidentIdentifier" value="string(//event/parameter[@name='
            incidentId']/@value)" type="xpath"/>
    </executeAction>
    <executeAction name="logMessage">
      <parameter name="incidentIdentifier" value="string(//event/parameter[@name='
            incidentId']/@value)" type="xpath"/>
      <parameter name="message" value="Incident closed as discarded"/>
    </executeAction>
  </preventiveMechanism>
</policy>
```

**Listing 5.2:** Policy to reset the system to its default mode after an incident has been discarded by the operator

```
<policy description="Handle archive queries in default mode" name="queryArchiveDM">
  <preventiveMechanism name="inhibitArchiveQueriesDM">
    <description>Evaluate archive query against constraint profile</description>
    <trigger action="catchQuery" isTry="true">
      <paramMatch name="operatingMode" value="defaultMode"/>
      <paramMatch name="incidentType" value=""/>
    </trigger>
    <condition>
      <true/>
    </condition>
    <authorizationAction name="inhibit">
      <inhibit/>
    </authorizationAction>
    <executeAction name="logMessage">
      <parameter name="message" value="Attempted access to archive inhibited"/>
      <parameter name="lowerTimeframeBoundary" value="string(//event/parameter[@name='lowerTimeframeBoundary']/@value)" type="xpath"/>
      <parameter name="upperTimeframeBoundary" value="string(//event/parameter[@name='upperTimeframeBoundary']/@value)" type="xpath"/>
    </executeAction>
    <executeAction name="hmi:provideAssistance">
      <parameter name="notificationMessage" value="Access to the archive is not allowed in the default mode!"/>
    </executeAction>
  </preventiveMechanism>
</policy>
```

**Listing 5.3:** Policy to inhibit archive access in the default mode

### 5.2.2 Assessment Mode: Relaxing Constraints

The constraint profile of the assessment mode is applied whenever the operator take over the responsibility for an alert concerning an abandoned object. Listing 5.4 shows the according root policy.

Access constraints are relaxed in terms of granting access to the previous 60 seconds [13] of recorded data of cameras within the same area subset as the camera, which detected the abandoned object. Furthermore, the world model grants access to persons associated to the given incident via the corresponding incident object.[14] Within the relevant area subset, the cameras' privacy filters are switched to a Gaussian blurring filter (cf. chapter 7). A message concerning the mode change is written to the system log, and the HMI is triggered to highlight the accessible timeframe of recorded data, i.e., 60 seconds prior to the point in time when the abandoned object has been detected.

Two further policies are deployed for evaluating queries to the archive. The policy depicted in listing 5.5 specifies actions to be executed whenever a legitimate access takes place. Listing 5.6 shows the policy concerning attempted violations of the constraint profile. Queries to the archive are allowed if the requested timeframe does not reach back farther than 60 seconds and if a suitable response filter for the assessments mode's constraint profile is applied successfully or already in place. The constraint relaxations are the same as specified in the root policy, and the query is logged as a legitimate access.

Queries to the archive are inhibited if the requested timeframe reaches back farther than 60 seconds and are logged as illegitimate queries. At the HMI, controls are reset and a notification explains why the attempted access to the archive has been blocked.

---

[13] Note that temporal constraints also have to be enforced at the world model, since its memory may still contain data, which must not be accessed according to the constraint profile.

[14] Note that this association may not be perfectly accurate, i.e., it may constitute an over-approximation involving several person objects, since airports are typically crowded and the detector may have a small delay. This is because an abandoned object may not be recognized as a distinct object until its owner has clearly moved away from the object. In the meantime other persons could have passed similarly close to the abandoned object and would thus get associated to the incident as well.

```
<policy description="Set up assessment mode for abandonded object incidents" name="setupAMAbandonedObject">
  <preventiveMechanism name="enforceConstraintProfileAMAbandondedObject">
    <description>Apply AM constraint profile for abandonded object incident</description>
    <trigger action="catchModeChange" isTry="true">
      <paramMatch name="incidentType" value="abandonedObject"/>
      <paramMatch name="status" value="unconfirmed"/>
    </trigger>
    <condition>
      <true/>
    </condition>
    <authorizationAction name="allow">
      <allow/>
    </authorizationAction>
    <executeAction name="worldModel:applyConstraintProfile">
      <parameter name="timeframe" value="60"/>
      <parameter name="incidentLocation" value="string(//event/parameter[@name='incidentLocation']/@value)" type="xpath"/>
      <parameter name="perimeter" value="areaSubnet"/>
      <complexParameter name="objectDependentConstraints">
        <parameter name="objectType" value="incident"/>
        <parameter name="incidentIdentifier" value="string(//event/parameter[@name='incidentIdentifier']/@value)"/>
        <parameter name="attributeType" value="associatedObjects"/>
        <parameter name="analysisFunctions" value=""/>
      </complexParameter>
    </executeAction>
    <executeAction name="videoAnalysis:enablePrivacyFilter">
      <parameter name="cameras" value="areaSubnet"/>
      <parameter name="filter" value="blurringFilter"/>
    </executeAction>
    <executeAction name="logMessage">
      <parameter name="incidentIdentifier" value="string(//event/parameter[@name='incidentId']/@value)" type="xpath"/>
      <parameter name="message" value="Launched assessment mode for abandoned object incident"/>
    </executeAction>
    <executeAction name="hmi:provideAssistance">
      <parameter name="visualization" value="highlightAccessibleTimeframe"/>
    </executeAction>
  </preventiveMechanism>
</policy>
```

**Listing 5.4:** Policy to enforce the assessment mode constraint profile for incidents concerning abandoned objects

```xml
<policy description="Handle archive queries in assessment mode for abandoned object detection" name="queryArchiveAMAbandondendObjectAllow">
  <preventiveMechanism name="allowArchiveQueriesAMAbandonedObject">
    <description>Evaluate archive query against constraint profile</description>
    <trigger action="catchQuery" isTry="true">
      <paramMatch name="operatingMode" value="assessmentMode"/>
      <paramMatch name="incidentType" value="abandonedObject"/>
    </trigger>
    <condition>
      <xPathEval>
        //event/parameter[@name='lowerTimeframeBoundary']/@value &gt;= (//event/parameter[@name='incidentTime']/@value − 60)
      </xPathEval>
    </condition>
    <authorizationAction name="allowFilteredResponse">
      <allow>
        <executeAction name="applyResponseFilter">
          <parameter name="incidentLocation" value="string(//event/parameter[@name='incidentLocation']/@value)" type="xpath"/>
          <parameter name="perimeter" value="areaSubnet"/>
          <complexParameter name="objectDependentConstraints">
            <parameter name="objectType" value="incident"/>
            <parameter name="incidentIdentifier" value="string(//event/parameter[@name='incidentIdentifier']/@value)"/>
            <parameter name="attributeType" value="associatedObjects"/>
          </complexParameter>
        </executeAction>
      </allow>
    </authorizationAction>
    <executeAction name="logMessage">
      <parameter name="message" value="Legitimate access to archive allowed"/>
      <parameter name="incidentIdentifier" value="string(//event/parameter[@name='incidentIdentifier']/@value)" type="xpath"/>
      <parameter name="lowerTimeframeBoundary" value="string(//event/parameter[@name='lowerTimeframeBoundary']/@value)" type="xpath"/>
      <parameter name="upperTimeframeBoundary" value="string(//event/parameter[@name='upperTimeframeBoundary']/@value)" type="xpath"/>
    </executeAction>
  </preventiveMechanism>
</policy>
```

**Listing 5.5:** Policy to allow legitimate archive access in the assessment mode

```xml
<policy description="Handle archive queries in assessment mode for abandoned object detection" name="queryArchiveAMAbandondendObjectInhibit">
  <preventiveMechanism name="inhibitArchiveQueriesAMAbandonedObject">
    <description>Evaluate archive query against constraint profile</description>
    <trigger action="catchQuery" isTry="true">
      <paramMatch name="operatingMode" value="assessmentMode"/>
      <paramMatch name="incidentType" value="abandonedObject"/>
    </trigger>
    <condition>
      <xPathEval>
        //event/parameter[@name='lowerTimeframeBoundary']/@value &lt; (//event/parameter[@name='time']/@value - 60)
      </xPathEval>
    </condition>
    <authorizationAction name="inhibit">
      <inhibit/>
    </authorizationAction>
    <executeAction name="logMessage">
      <parameter name="message" value="Illegitimate access to archive inhibited"/>
      <parameter name="incidentIdentifier" value="string(//event/parameter[@name='incidentIdentifier']/@value)" type="xpath"/>
      <parameter name="lowerTimeframeBoundary" value="string(//event/parameter[@name='lowerTimeframeBoundary']/@value)" type="xpath"/>
      <parameter name="upperTimeframeBoundary" value="string(//event/parameter[@name='upperTimeframeBoundary']/@value)" type="xpath"/>
    </executeAction>
    <executeAction name="hmi:resetControls">
    </executeAction>
    <executeAction name="hmi:provideAssistance">
      <parameter name="notificationMessage" value="Only the previous 60 seconds of recorded data can be accessed for situation assessment!"/>
    </executeAction>
  </preventiveMechanism>
</policy>
```

**Listing 5.6:** Policy to inhibit illegitimate archive access in the assessment mode

### 5.2.3 Investigation Mode: Unlocking Analysis Functions

The root policy of the investigation mode (cf. listing 5.7) is triggered whenever the operator confirms an incident concerning an abandoned object. The investigation mode's constraint profile grants access to the previous 5 minutes [15] of recorded data from cameras of the entire terminal, in which the abandoned object has been detected. It additionally grants access to all attributes of persons that are associated to the given incident, and disables the privacy filtering on all cameras within this terminal of the airport.

As investigation modes are intended to provide the operator with analysis functions to handle the given type of incident, the according constraint profile unlocks functions for locating a selected person, recording current views to serve as evidences, as well as biometric face recognition. The *recordViewAsEvidence* function basically takes a screenshot of the HMI, which the operator considers suitable for documenting the incident. Such evidences are saved as attributes of the incident. They are kept in memory until the incident is closed and are then pushed to the archive. The analysis function for locating a selected person is used to determine the current location of a person, which is selected in offline data, e.g., when the operator has investigated the person who actually dropped the considered object in buffered data or in recorded data pulled from the archive. This function is based on tracking on abstracted world model data. Therefore, its application is directly restricted on person objects, which are associated to the incident in order to ensure selectivity (cf. research question **TS-3**, section 1.3). A selective application of analysis functions operating on video data, such as biometric face recognition,[16] requires the deployment of further mechanisms as will be explained in section 5.4, where the policy in listing 5.11 also shows how the usage of optional analysis functions in investigation modes is made traceable.

[15] Note that temporal constraints also have to be enforced at the world model, since its memory may still contain data, which must not be accessed according to the constraint profile.

[16] Remind the exemplary character of the depicted policies. Indeed, only prosecution authorities may be allowed to employ biometric methods for (later) identification of persons

```
<policy description="Set up investigation mode for abandonded object incidents" name="setupIMAbandonedObject">
  <preventiveMechanism name="enforceConstraintProfileIMAbandondedObject">
    <description>Apply IM constraint profile for abandonded object incident</description>
    <trigger action="catchModeChange" isTry="true">
      <paramMatch name="incidentType" value="abandonedObject"/>
      <paramMatch name="status" value="inProcess"/>
    </trigger>
    <condition><true/></condition>
    <authorizationAction name="allow"><allow/></authorizationAction>
    <executeAction name="worldModel:applyConstraintProfile">
      <parameter name="timeframe" value="300"/>
      <parameter name="incidentLocation" value="string(//event/parameter[@name='incidentLocation']/@value)" type="xpath"/>
      <parameter name="perimeter" value="terminal"/>
      <complexParameter name="objectDependentConstraints">
        <parameter name="objectType" value="incident"/>
        <parameter name="incidentIdentifier" value="string(//event/parameter[@name='incidentIdentifier']/@value)"/>
        <parameter name="attributeType" value="*"/>
        <parameter name="analysisFunctions" value="recordViewAsEvidence;locatePerson;faceRecognition"/>
      </complexParameter>
    </executeAction>
    <executeAction name="videoAnalysis:disablePrivacyFilter">
      <parameter name="cameras" value="terminal"/>
    </executeAction>
    <executeAction name="logMessage">
      <parameter name="incidentIdentifier" value="string(//event/parameter[@name='incidentId']/@value)" type="xpath"/>
      <parameter name="message" value="Launched investigation mode for abandoned object incident"/>
    </executeAction>
    <executeAction name="notifyReceiver">
      <parameter name="receiver" value="airportPoliceStation"/>
      <parameter name="message" value="Incident concerning an abandoned object under investigation"/>
      <parameter name="incidentLocation" value="string(//event/parameter[@name='incidentLocation']/@value)" type="xpath"/>
    </executeAction>
    <executeAction name="hmi:provideAssistance">
      <parameter name="visualization" value="highlightAccessibleTimeframe"/>
    </executeAction>
  </preventiveMechanism>
</policy>
```

**Listing 5.7:** Policy to enforce the investigation mode constraint profile for incident concerning abandoned objects

```
<policy description="Handle archive queries in investigation mode for abandoned object detection" name="queryArchiveIMAbandondendObjectAllow">
  <preventiveMechanism name="inhibitArchiveQueriesIMAbandonedObject">
    <description>Evaluate archive query against constraint profile</description>
    <trigger action="catchQuery" isTry="true">
      <paramMatch name="operatingMode" value="investigationMode"/>
      <paramMatch name="incidentType" value="abandonedObject"/>
    </trigger>
    <condition>
      <xPathEval>
        //event/parameter[@name='lowerTimeframeBoundary']/@value &gt;= (//event/parameter[@name='incidentTime']/@value - 300)
      </xPathEval>
    </condition>
    <authorizationAction name="allowFilteredResponse">
      <allow>
        <executeAction name="applyResponseFilter">
          <parameter name="incidentLocation" value="string(//event/parameter[@name='incidentLocation']/@value)" type="xpath"/>
          <parameter name="perimeter" value="terminal"/>
          <complexParameter name="objectDependentConstraints">
            <parameter name="objectType" value="incident"/>
            <parameter name="incidentIdentifier" value="string(//event/parameter[@name='incidentIdentifier']/@value)"/>
            <parameter name="attributeType" value="*"/>
          </complexParameter>
        </executeAction>
      </allow>
    </authorizationAction>
    <executeAction name="logMessage">
      <parameter name="message" value="Archive access allowed"/>
      <parameter name="incidentIdentifier" value="string(//event/parameter[@name='incidentIdentifier']/@value)" type="xpath"/>
      <parameter name="lowerTimeframeBoundary" value="string(//event/parameter[@name='lowerTimeframeBoundary']/@value)" type="xpath"/>
      <parameter name="upperTimeframeBoundary" value="string(//event/parameter[@name='upperTimeframeBoundary']/@value)" type="xpath"/>
    </executeAction>
  </preventiveMechanism>
</policy>
```

**Listing 5.8:** Policy to allow legitimate archive access in the investigation mode

```xml
<policy description="Handle archive queries in investigation mode for abandoned object detection" name="queryArchiveIMAbandondendObjectInhibit">
  <preventiveMechanism name="inhibitArchiveQueriesIMAbandonedObject">
    <description>Evaluate archive query against constraint profile</description>
    <trigger action="catchQuery" isTry="true">
      <paramMatch name="operatingMode" value="investigationMode"/>
      <paramMatch name="incidentType" value="abandonedObject"/>
    </trigger>
    <condition>
      <xPathEval>
        //event/parameter[@name='lowerTimeframeBoundary']/@value &lt; (//event/parameter[@name='time']/@value - 300)
      </xPathEval>
    </condition>
    <authorizationAction name="inhibit">
      <inhibit/>
    </authorizationAction>
    <executeAction name="logMessage">
      <parameter name="message" value="Attempted access to archive inhibited"/>
      <parameter name="incidentIdentifier" value="string(//event/parameter[@name='incidentIdentifier']/@value)" type="xpath"/>
      <parameter name="lowerTimeframeBoundary" value="string(//event/parameter[@name='lowerTimeframeBoundary']/@value)" type="xpath"/>
      <parameter name="upperTimeframeBoundary" value="string(//event/parameter[@name='upperTimeframeBoundary']/@value)" type="xpath"/>
    </executeAction>
    <executeAction name="hmi:resetControls">
    </executeAction>
    <executeAction name="hmi:provideAssistance">
      <parameter name="notificationMessage" value="Only the previous 10 minutes of recorded data can be accessed for investigation!"/>
    </executeAction>
  </preventiveMechanism>
</policy>
```

**Listing 5.9:** Policy to inhibit illegitimate archive access in the investigation mode

Furthermore, the mode change is logged, the airport police station is notified about the incident under investigation, and the HMI again visualizes the accessible timeframe of recorded data (5 minutes prior to the point in time when the abandoned object has been detected).

Again, two further policies are required for evaluating queries to the archive. Listing 5.8 depicts the policy concerning legitimate accesses, whereas the policy of listing 5.9 handles illegitimate queries violating the temporal access constraint. Queries to the archive are allowed if the requested timeframe does not reach back farther than 5 minutes and if a response filter according to the investigation mode's constraint profile is applied successfully or already in place. The constraint profile corresponds to the specification in the root policy, and the query is logged as a legitimate access.

Again, queries are blocked if the requested timeframe reaches back farther than allowed, i.e., more than 5 minutes, and are logged as illegitimate queries. HMI controls are reset and a notification explains why the attempted access to the archive has been inhibited.

## 5.3 Enforcement of Privacy Privileges for Individual Persons or Groups

Privacy privileges for individual persons or groups can be granted at the world model in terms of locking certain objects' records or locking specific attributes of those objects. Locked objects do not appear in the HMI and may also be excluded from analysis functions that are performed on abstracted world model data. If only certain attributes are locked, the person object is still accessible and visualized in the world model HMI, but without access to the locked attributes. Note that privacy filters such as coarsening a person's location information before visualization could be granted similarly. However, such privacy filters typically cannot be applied to individual objects [VBB11; Vag13]. Since further the purpose as well as the utility of obfuscated world model data is questionable, the effect attained by privacy filters may not differ substantially from locking objects or attributes.

Privacy privileges can be granted, for instance, to staff members of the airport operator or airlines in order to prevent location profiling, which otherwise could serve for illegitimate performance monitoring of these employees. To achieve this, persons with privacy privileges have to (i) authenticate with the smart video surveillance system and (ii) the authenticated identity, pseudo-identity, or group affiliation must be associated to the world model object representing the person to be protected.

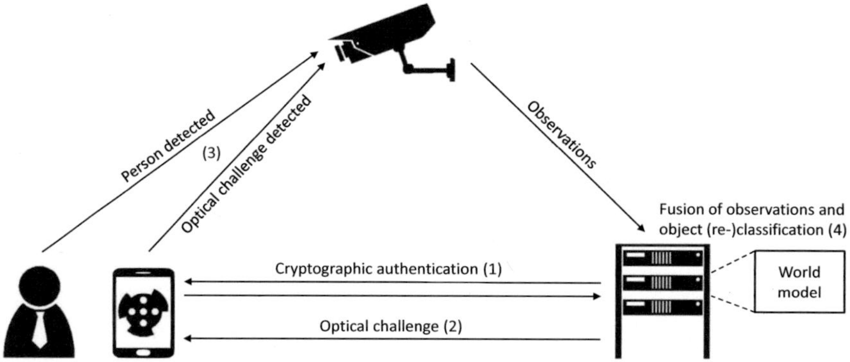


**Figure 5.4:** Cryptographic challenge-response procedure and optical authentication with a smart video surveillance system

As introduced by Vagts and Beyerer [VB11], optical challenge-response methods can be used to establish an association between the world model object representation of a person captured by a camera of a smart video surveillance system and a mobile communication device used by this person, i.e., a smart phone or tablet. This mobile communication device can also be used to perform a cryptographic authentication. By this means, privacy privileges according to an identity, or group affiliation can be associated to the world model object corresponding to the authenticated person. Thus, (i) and (ii) are achieved by means of combining an optical challenge-response method with a cryptographic authentication scheme as introduced by Birnstill and Pretschner [BP13] and refined by Greiner et al. [Gre+13] as well as Birnstill et al. [Bir+15]. This two-part authentication procedure is depicted in figure 5.4.

In the first step (1), the cryptographic authentication with the smart video surveillance system is performed over a wireless network. By this means it is ensured that the mobile device belongs to a person holding privacy privileges. This procedure creates a new world model object, which only contains the authenticated identity or group affiliation. In the second step (2), the system replies with a short-lived visual code, which is robustly recognized by cameras and refers to the new world model object. As soon as this visual code is presented to a camera (3), the according person object and the authenticated identity or group affiliation are fused at the world model (cf. section 3.2). The person object is hence reclassified as a privileged object (4). This is observed by the world model PEP in terms of an according *catchClassification* event (cf. figure 5.3). As a consequence, the *grantPrivacyPrivilege* execute action is called with the identifier of the object in order to lock the according world model object or some of its attributes. Privacy privileges can also be revoked in case a person gets associated to an incident using the *revokePrivacyPrivilege* execute action, which is typically called when entering the investigation mode for the given incident.

As long as the world model is able to keep track of a protected person object, the enforcement of privacy privileges can be guaranteed.[17] Note that tracking does not mean that a complete history of the detections of each person is stored persistently.[18] In contrast to other approaches towards implementing privacy privileges in smart video surveillance [Wic+04], the proposed two-step authentication scheme does not rely on locatable cryptographic tokens that can easily be passed on from one person to another. Thus, a protected person cannot transfer the privacy privileges granted due to identity or group

[17] Note that protected persons could be enabled to check whether their privacy privileges are still enforced using an application for mobile devices. In case the system has lost track, the authentication can be renewed.

[18] A Kalman filter, for instance, works recursively and requires only the last "best guess", rather than the entire history to predict a new position.

affiliation to someone else. Note further that instrumenting tracking to enable the enforcement of privacy privileges as demanded in section 4.3.1 constitutes an instance of the *tracking paradoxon* [BP13; Gre+13; Bir+15].

### 5.3.1 Example Policy for Enforcing Privacy Privileges

Listing 5.10 depicts a policy, which grants a privacy privilege to the group *staffMembers*. It is triggered by *catchClassification* events as described above. The policy is triggered whenever the classification of a world model object to the type *staffMember* is observed. The privacy privilege to be granted using the execute action *grantPrivacyPrivilege* of the world model locks the according world model object and thus renders it invisible for the world model HMI unless it is associated to an incident under investigation.

```xml
<policy description="Observe object classification to apply group−based privacy privileges"
      name="grantPrivacyPrivilegeToStaffMembers">
  <detectiveMechanism name="grantPrivacyPrivilege">
    <description>Grant privacy privilege according to classified object type</description>
    <timestep amount="1" unit="SECONDS"/>
    <condition>
      <always>
        <eventMatch action="catchClassification">
          <paramMatch name="objectType" value="staffMember"/>
        </eventMatch>
      </always>
    </condition>
    <executeAction name="worldModel:grantPrivacyPrivilege">
      <parameter name="privacyPrivilege" value="lockWorldModelRecord"/>
      <parameter name="objectId" value="string(//event/parameter[@name='objectId']/
          @value)" type="xpath"/>
    </executeAction>
  </detectiveMechanism>
</policy>
```

**Listing 5.10:** A policy to grant privacy privileges based on object classification

## 5.4 Increasing the Selectivity of Data Processing

Particularly investigation modes of smart video surveillance systems unlock additional analysis functions to be performed on video data or abstracted data. Such algorithms collect or extract additional types of data that explicitly serve for investigation and prosecution purposes. Thus, with regard to the goal of increasing the selectivity and achieving proportionality of intrusions into observed individuals' privacy, their application needs to be restricted to persons related to an incident under investigation. An example technology to be unlocked in an investigation mode is biometric face recognition.[19] Biometric face recognition algorithms are used for extracting biometric face templates of individuals from images. While often used as a an authentication method, in smart video surveillance biometric face recognition is used for identifying persons, either instantaneously (e.g., in case the system is operated by prosecuting authorities and connected to databases of police networks), or in the course of later investigations of an incident. In the following, the example of biometric face recognition is employed to explain how such algorithms can be applied in a selective manner.

As soon as biometric face recognition is activated, either on a particular camera or on a set of cameras covering a specific area, the algorithm searches for faces and, if possible, extracts biometric face templates of any person captured on the input images that are delivered by the camera(s). On this level of video analysis it is not possible to restrict data collection to those persons that are actually related to the incident under investigation. However, the selectivity can still be increased by filtering collected data at the earliest possible stage of data processing. By this means, irrelevant face templates of unrelated persons are deleted as soon as possible after their collection. As described in section 3.2 and section 4.3.1, the world model of the smart video surveil-

[19] Remind the exemplary character of the depicted policies. Indeed, only prosecution authorities may be allowed to employ biometric methods for (later) identification of persons

lance system associates incidents to persons and other objects.[20] It is also responsible for associating abstracted data collected by algorithms to world model objects and for consolidating the particular attribute values by means of information fusion. Thus, the selectivity of data processing can be increased by monitoring information fusion, recognizing sensitive data, and filtering out irrelevant attributes based on associations between persons and incidents under investigation. In particular, this enables the deletion of biometric face templates at an early stage of data processing in case the respective individual is not associated to an incident under investigation, which is allowed to process biometric face templates. Thus, if there is no justification for collecting an individual's biometric face template, it is deleted before being fused into the world model representation of the given person.

### 5.4.1 Approach: Tainting and Tracking Detections

Realizing the aforementioned idea to increase the selectivity of data processing requires that data collected by investigation mode algorithms (e.g., biometric face recognition) is recognized during the information fusion procedure of the world model (cf. section 3.2). This can be achieved by means of tainting detections of investigation mode algorithms.

The tainting-based approach consist of the following steps. Each incident is identifiable by means of a unique taint mark. Persons associated to the incident are tainted using this taint mark (e.g., a person performing a potentially violent activity). In case the incident is confirmed by an operator, investigation mode analysis functions are unlocked. Assume that a biometric face recognition algorithm is unlocked and activated in order to collect evidences allowing to identify the people involved in the fight under investigation. As soon as the face recognition algorithm is activated by the operator, the incident's taint

[20] Note that associations of persons to incidents may be inaccurate due to the complexity of the scene or to due to not being triggered by persons directly (e.g., detection of abandoned objects). Thus, in some cases persons are associated to incidents via spatio-temporal corridors in which they have been detected.

mark is passed to this algorithm. The algorithm then attaches this taint mark to each detection it disseminates until it is eventually deactivated.

Note that in case of multiple incidents being investigated concurrently by different operators, overlapping usages of investigation mode algorithms may occur due to overlapping permissions of the investigation modes according to incident types as well as overlapping areas. In such cases, detections are tainted with the taint marks of all authorized incidents and the corresponding attributes of world model objects are accessible from within the respective investigation modes. However, the problem of multi-tenancy of smart video surveillance systems as a whole is not addressed in detail in this work (cf. section 5.7.1).

### 5.4.2 Monitoring Information Fusion

When detections of video analysis algorithms are processed at the world model, information fusion of a detection (e.g., a biometric face template) into a person object is allowed if and only if the taint marks of the detection and the person object match, i.e., the individual from whom the biometric face template has been collected is associated to a currently investigated incident. Three cases of information fusion events have to be differentiated:

- Taint mark of detection ≡ taint mark of object ⇒ fusion allowed:
  The detection as well as the world model object belong to the same incident scope. Assuming that the association (cf. section 3.2) between the detection and the world model object is correct, then the detection is actually an attribute of this person, and the person is associated to the incident under investigation.

- Detection is tainted, object is not tainted ⇒ fusion inhibited:
  The world model object is not associated to any incident. The information fusion attempts to process a privacy-sensitive personal attribute of a person that is not associated to an incident under investigation, which is not allowed.

- Taint mark of detection $\not\equiv$ taint mark of object $\Rightarrow$ fusion inhibited: The detection and the world model object belong to different incidents, i.e., there is another incident under investigation concerning this object.

Tainted detections that do not get fused into a world model object have been collected from individuals that are not associated to incidents under investigation. They have been extracted coincidentally, since these people were captured in an area, in which an incident has been investigated by an operator. As such detections are deleted before being fused into the corresponding world model objects, the application of privacy-intrusive analysis functions such as biometric face recognition is restricted to persons that are associated to authorized incidents so as to increase the selectivity of the surveillance process.

### 5.4.3 Example Policies for Tainting and Monitoring Fusion

Ensuring selective processing of detections of optional video analysis algorithms of investigation modes requires two policies as will be explained using the biometric face recognition example.

The first policy is triggered by *catchFunctionUsage* events concerning the biometric face recognition algorithm (cf. listing 5.11). It enforces that the algorithm is initialized with an incident-specific taint mark. Each detection of the biometric face recognition algorithm is hence tainted using the given taint mark before being transmitted to the world model. The permission to activate the biometric face recognition algorithm also depends on the successful deployment of the second policy, which controls information fusion at the world model, and a log message to make the usage of this investigation mode analysis function traceable. The execute action *deployPolicy* is provided by the usage control infrastructure's PMP itself (cf. section 2.5).

```
<policy description="Taint biometric face recognition" name="taintFaceRecognition">
  <preventiveMechanism name="taintFaceRecognition">
    <description>Taint face recognition and deploy fusion policy</description>
    <trigger action="catchFunctionUsage" isTry="true">
      <paramMatch name="function" value="biometricFaceRecognition"/>
    </trigger>
    <condition>
      <true/>
    </condition>
    <authorizationAction name="allowFaceRecognition">
      <allow>
        <executeAction name="videoAnalysis:taintAlgorithm">
          <parameter name="algorithm" value="biometricFaceRecognition"/>
          <parameter name="taintMark"
            value="string(//event/parameter[@name='taintMark']/@value)" type="xpath"/>
          <parameter name="cameras"
            value="string(//event/parameter[@name='cameraList']/@value)" type="xpath"/>
        </executeAction>
        <executeAction name="deployPolicy">
          <parameter name="policyName" value="fusionPolicy"/>
          <parameter name="taintMark"
            value="string(//event/parameter[@name='taintMark']/@value)" type="xpath"/>
        </executeAction>
        <executeAction name="logMessage">
          <parameter name="message" value="Analysis function activated"/>
          <parameter name="function" value="biometricFaceRecognition"/>
          <parameter name="incidentIdentifier" value="string(//event/parameter[@name='
              incidentIdentifier']/@value)" type="xpath"/>
        </executeAction>
      </allow>
    </authorizationAction>
  </preventiveMechanism>
</policy>
```

**Listing 5.11:** A policy intercepting the activation of biometric face recognition in order to taint the video analysis algorithm and to deploy a policy for controlling the fusion of tainted detections

The policy depicted in listing 5.12 is triggered by *catchFusion* events. In case such events involve biometric face templates, taint marks of the detection and of the target world model object are compared. A *catchFusion* event is only allowed to be executed if the taint marks match. If the taint marks do not match, fusion is inhibited, since either the biometric face template and the target object do not belong to the same incident or the corresponding individual is not associated to any incident at all.

```
<policy description="Control fusion of biometric face templates" name="fusionPolicy">
  <preventiveMechanism name="controlFusion">
    <description>Inhibit fusion if taint marks do not match</description>
    <trigger action="catchFusion" isTry="true">
      <paramMatch name="detectionType" value="biometricFaceTemplate"/>
    </trigger>
    <condition>
      <xPathEval>
        //event/parameter[@name='detectionTaintMark']/@value != //event/parameter[
              @name='objectTaintMark']/@value
      </xPathEval>
    </condition>
    <authorizationAction name="inhibitFusion">
      <inhibit>
      </inhibit>
    </authorizationAction>
  </preventiveMechanism>
</policy>
```

**Listing 5.12:** A policy to inhibit fusion if the taint marks of the detection and the target world model object do not match

## 5.5 Implementation of PEPs and PXPs in the NEST Prototype System

All components of the prototype system NEST, which have been extended to act as PEPs, are written in the programming language Java. Calls to methods are monitored using aspect-oriented programming, i.e., by means of aspects written in AspectJ, which are also called *interceptors*. The particular interceptors communicate with the usage control infrastructure via a mediator component. This mediator holds a connector to the incident adapter at the back-end through which it acquires parameters concerning the current operating mode of the system in order to enrich events before notifying them to the PDP.

AspectJ provides two means of applying aspects to an application, which are *byte code weaving* and *compile time weaving*. Byte code weaving injects an aspect on the byte code level and is only applicable to interface methods. Compile time weaving requires access to the target application's source code and allows the interception of arbitrary methods. Moreover, aspects applied via compile time weaving can access public data structures and methods of the application. By this means it is easier to implement interceptors in such a way that the application is not left in an inconsistent state when method calls are inhibited due to decisions of the PDP. Because of this, compile time weaving has been used to integrate interceptors into the components of the NEST prototype system.

Components that act as PXPs, i.e., that are providing execute actions to the usage control infrastructure, are extended with communication servers, which implement the PXP interface. While Java-based PXPs are typically called via Remote Method Invocation (RMI), the usage control infrastructure also communicates via Transmission Control Protocol (TCP) and Java Messaging Service (JMS)/C++ Messaging Service (CMS), since there are also PXPs written in C++, such as the PXPs of the video analysis components.

## 5.6 Related Work

The analysis of related work reveals that some existing privacy mechanisms for video surveillance work at the level of video streams only and do not consider the level of object streams into which video streams are fused. Other mechanisms deactivate surveillance by default and only activate it when explicitly triggered, therefore making it impossible to track, for instance, suspicious luggage being dropped. A third class of existing privacy mechanisms is inherently bound to an observation purpose which, specifically so in publicly deployed video surveillance systems, is hard to render operational.

Fidaleo et al. propose a privacy-enhanced surveillance architecture in which a so-called privacy buffer detects and removes identifiable information, e.g., persons' faces, from input data [FNT04]. The operator is granted interactive control over certain system functions. This does not seem to be situation-dependent. When weighing the appropriateness of a video surveillance measure in terms of its intrusiveness, a system which is most of the time as little intrusive as possible is considered "better" than a system that persistently sticks to the same trade-off between privacy and utility. Aiming to reduce a smart video surveillance system's privacy impact by default, this research contributes mechanisms for restricting function usage and data usage as well as enforcing the application of privacy filters depending on incident types and threat situations. In [Sen+05] Senior et al. introduce a privacy-preserving video console for hiding sensitive details in video streams depending on authorization levels.

Thuraisingham et al. [Thu+06] propose an access control model for smart video surveillance systems characterized by their ability to maintain an abstracted representation of the monitored area (cf. section 3.2). It enables fine-grained control of access to abstracted data and video data depending on an extensive model of authorization levels also including maintenance personnel and administrators. These approaches suggests that the privacy level of exposed (video) data should be adjusted exclusively to the authorization level of the observer, as opposed to the authorization level induced by the current threat situation and the type of incident.

Vagts and Jacoby [VJ12] also introduce an access control model for smart video surveillance. In contrast to the aforementioned works, access to abstracted data is governed based on video surveillance tasks, which encapsulate all data collected for a specific purpose. However, a smart video surveillance system also needs to collect and analyze data, based on which tasks can be triggered, and it remains unclear how this data is protected (further works and aspects concerning task-based smart video surveillance are discussed below).

Saini et al. [Sai+12] quantify the loss of privacy due to video surveillance recordings by decomposing embedded information into *what*, *when*, and *where* evidence. Such evidence may (i) be sensitive in case the person's identity is unveiled and (ii) constitute context knowledge, which allows for drawing inferences about the identity. However, eliminating *when* and *where* evidence in addition to obfuscating personal features (cf. chapter 7) turns out to be hard in practice. Accordingly, situation-dependent smart video surveillance workflows as proposed in this research concentrate on minimizing the disclosure of personal identifiable information by means of enforcing situation-dependent access constraints and privacy filters.

Wickramasuriya et al. enforce privacy policies concerning the visualization of video surveillance data [Wic+04]. Surveillance is restricted to critical regions. Cameras are deactivated by default and activated by motion detectors if people enter such regions. Policies specify access rights to regions and privacy levels for individuals or groups. People are authenticated using radio-frequency identification (RFID) tags. When entering critical regions with an RFID tag granting access, one may also be granted a high privacy level, i.e., be erased from visualized data. This seems useful for monitoring people in constrained regions. However, even while staying in the observed area, people can easily transfer their identity to someone else by passing on their RFID tag. In contrast, the approach described in section 5.3 inhibits identity transfers by means of employing the system's tracking capabilities to persistently bind authenticated identities to captured objects.

Mossgraber et al. have introduced the notion of task-based smart video surveillance [MRV10], the benefits of which for privacy have been elaborated by Vagts and Bauer [VB10]. System functionality is separated into so-called surveillance tasks, which are triggered on behalf of an authorized operator, and which are not supposed to exchange data among each other. Thus, aiming at data minimization, video data must only be acquired, processed, and stored if required by an authorized task. This approach seems appropriate if the surveillance purpose does not require a significant extent of continuous video analysis. Furthermore, in order to apply a task-oriented approach, either the principal purpose of the surveillance measure must decompose into distinct sub-purposes, or multiple purposes must be intended from the beginning. In practice, surveillance measures in publicly accessible spaces are usually dedicated to a rather broadly conceived legal purpose (e.g., ensuring aviation safety in an airport) requiring a broad spectrum of detective functionality. A meaningful decomposition of this kind of purposes is not straightforward and does not directly seem to lead to increased privacy. Deploying a surveillance system for multiple distinct purposes is, for legal reasons (cf. section 2.3), almost only conceivable for deployments in non-public environments, e.g., in office buildings. In such scenarios, surveillance systems are typically utilized for monitoring critical areas, valuable objects, or on-demand tracking of specifically selected persons, such as unknown visitors. However, surveillance systems in non-public environments constitute a small fraction of privacy invasions induced by video surveillance technologies.

A separation of analysis functions into operating modes depending on incident types as well as the substantiation of threat situations (cf. section 4.4 and section 5.1.1) is thus favored over a separation into tasks. Note that according to their on-demand usage optional analysis functions to be unlocked in assessment modes or investigation modes of situation-dependent smart video surveillance workflows could also be considered as tasks. The concept of task-based video surveillance, however, neglects the requirements of a default mode, which continuously executes detective analysis functions, and of proportionate intrusions into observed people's privacy, as encapsulated in cascaded assessment modes and investigation modes.

## 5.7 Conclusions

As has been shown in this chapter, usage control monitoring capabilities enable the presented generic architecture to enforce the constraints that are required to implement situation-dependent workflows and hence to realize privacy-respecting smart video surveillance. Thus, the research question **TS-1** has been validated (cf. section 1.3). Such workflows, as motivated in chapter 4, separate the systems' capabilities into operating modes with different levels of functionality and different levels of privacy protection. Combined with the enforcement of privacy privileges and selective processing of detections from video analysis during information fusion, a system design has been introduced, which balances low selectivity with a low privacy impact, whereas deeper privacy intrusions are compensated with high selectivity and accountability so as to confirm research question **TS-3**.

This instantiation of usage control in the domain of smart video surveillance differs to a certain extent from the usual data-centric approach: Policies are not specified for particular data items, but for types of data and for analysis functions and privacy filters to be applied on data or not, depending on the current situation.

### 5.7.1 Assumptions and Limitations

The assumptions on which the security and reliability of usage control enforcement is based (cf. section 2.5.2) also apply for the usage control-enabled smart video surveillance system design introduced in this chapter. In particular, the assumption that components are not tampered with and do not leak any data via implementation errors must also be made for all components of the video surveillance system, which are instrumented with usage control enforcement capabilities. Appendix A provides further considerations on how a secure and reliable operation of usage control mechanisms can be ensured by the underlying infrastructure. Moreover, it is assumed that all components communicate via encrypted and authenticated communication channels. Operators are authenticated by the operating system of their front-end machine and are granted minimal permissions. Authentication of operators with the surveillance system is out of scope of this thesis. This implies that all operators are granted equivalent permissions by the surveillance system as specified in the constraint profiles of operating modes.

The presented system design does not explicitly cover the aspect of multi-tenancy capability. Particularly in vast environments such as airports, video surveillance systems may provide multiple front-ends to be operated by multiple operators concurrently. To achieve this, basically implementation-specific changes have to be made. Operating modes and according constraint profiles have to be enforced depending on the particular front-end instance, the operator of which took over the responsibility to handle a given incident. Video analysis components must be equipped with as many outputs as there are front-end instances attached to the system and also be enabled to execute different privacy filters for each output depending on the operating modes of the according front-ends. Executing two operating modes concurrently also means that recorded data is transferred from the archive to the world model whenever a legitimate query is posed by a front-end instance. This means that constraint profiles are enforced at the back-end/world model only, since filtering queries at the archive is not effective anymore.

Privacy breaches due to additional context knowledge that operators may have are not covered by this research. Assume that the considered system does not reveal identities of captured persons via video data disclosed to the operator in its default mode and its assessment modes due to privacy filters being applied such as those investigated in chapter 7. Identities of people in the monitored area may still leak via the site map view provided by the world model's HMI (cf. section 3.4), even if it only visualizes the positions of otherwise anonymous person objects as specified in the exemplary default mode of section 5.2.1. This is because operators may have additional context knowledge, which could allow to deduce a person object's identity. Assume a video surveillance deployment in a hospital. Its purpose is to support night nurses by detecting patients falling down or wandering about in corridors. Knowing the location of the nurses' room combined with the hospital's duty roster allows for creating movement profiles of individual nurses, which can be misused for performance monitoring, e.g., assessing a nurse's reaction time in case of paging patients. [Sai+12] constitutes a first step towards modeling such context knowledge.

Eventually, media breaks are beyond the scope of usage control mechanisms. If a malicious operator films the system's screens showing unmodified video data in investigation modes, the respective video clip is not protected.

# 6 Protecting Video Surveillance Data on Mobile Devices

The effectiveness of video surveillance measures strongly depends on a sound cooperation between the operators in the control rooms and the police as well as emergency personnel as explained in section 2.2 and section 4.2.4. This increasingly involves that (video) data is disseminated to mobile devices carried by the personnel on-site. Referring to the concept of situation-dependent smart video surveillance workflows (cf. section 4.4) this depicts a function to be unlocked in investigation modes of certain incidents.[1] Thus data to be exchanged may not be protected by means of privacy filters anymore. This chapter is concerned with the enforcement of usage control requirements such as *transmitted data must neither be stored nor redistributed by unauthorized recipients* (cf. research question **TS-4**). In order to achieve this, usage control is augmented with inter-system information flow tracking technology. As described in [KBB16], the mechanisms introduced in the following have also been integrated into a camera-based fall detection system for hospitals and nursing facilities. This "headless" system is operated without a control room, i.e., in case a potential emergency has been detected it notifies the medical staff via mobile devices and provides video data for situation assessment. This work contributes a generalization from inter-layer information flow tracking of explicit information flows as introduced by Lovat [Lov15] to inter-system information flow tracking. It further introduces a set of generic primitives for unifying the specifications of information flow semantics of events intercepted

[1] Note that this work assumes that data concerning an ongoing incident is specifically forwarded to law enforcement officers or security personnel on-site. Therefore operators can only forward data, which is accessible according to the constraint profile of the current operating mode. It is not assumed that the video surveillance system itself is operated by mobile users.

by run-time monitors as well as an asynchronous protocol for processing information flow-relevant events in distributed settings.

## 6.1 Information Flow Tracking

Because data usually takes different shapes and appears as files, in windows, in processes' memory, as Java objects, in network connections, in printer queues, etc., usage control mechanisms have been augmented with information flow tracking technology [HP09]. One can then specify policies not only for specific fixed representations of data, but also on *all* representations of that data. These representations are tracked by information flow detection technology. Policies then do not need to rely on events, but can forbid specific representations to be created, also in a distributed setting [KP13]. In other words, information flow tracking aims to answer the question into which representations within a (distributed) system a monitored data item has been propagated.

Semantics of explicit information flows are typically specified in terms of events that are observed by run-time monitoring components. In order to perform information flow tracking across different applications, different layers of abstraction of a system, or across different systems, a multitude of such monitors (i.e., PEPs, cf. section 2.4), each observing an individual set of information flow-relevant events, have to be integrated into the information flow tracking system. Events are then interpreted with respect to information flow semantics specifications by a super-ordinate information flow tracking component (per host system), the so-called *PIP*. The PIP keeps track of new representations of data being created and of information flows between representations (cf. figure 6.1). By this means, when evaluating an event concerning a container (such as a file or a window), the PDP can ask the PIP whether this container is a representation of a protected data item, for which a policy must be enforced.

The following problems are addressed in this work. Plugging new PEPs into an existing usage control and information flow tracking infrastructure requires a unified specification of the information flow semantics of observed events, which are interpreted by PIPs. In order to facilitate this, a set of *generic primitives* for describing information flow semantics is introduced, which can be used by engineers for specifying information flow semantics of the events intercepted by their monitors (cf. section 6.3). These generic primitives are derived from analyses of all available scenarios in which information flow tracking has been instantiated for UC [HP09; PLB11; WP12].

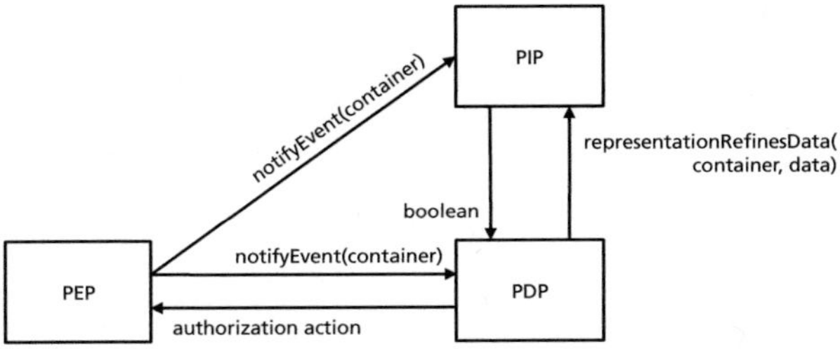


**Figure 6.1:** Generic usage control architecture with information flow tracking

This research also covers the modeling of inter-layer information flows, i.e., flows between applications and the operating system, as introduced by Lovat [Lov15] and generalizes this approach to inter-system information flows so as to enable monitoring of flows of protected data between systems equipped with usage control enforcement mechanisms. As this approach is prone to over-approximations, it requires an extension with monitoring technology of higher precision in future work (cf. section 6.1.1). Across system boundaries, information flows have to be handled asynchronously, triggered by different events on the particular machines. A distributed protocol is specified for processing inter-layer and inter-system flows based on semantics description primitives (cf. section 6.4.3). By this means, the interoperability of information flow tracking components is ensured so as to facilitate the enforcement of usage control policies on the granularity of representations, also in distributed settings.

This chapter is structured as follows. After discussing related work in section 6.1.1, section 6.2 explains the formal information flow model of Harvan and Pretschner [HP09]. Section 6.3 introduces generic primitives for specifying information flow semantics of events. In section 6.4 the model is extended so as to allow uniform processing extension of inter-layer and inter-system information flows. Section 6.5 instantiates this approach to inter-system information flow tracking for a smart video surveillance system. It protects video data from the surveillance system against illegitimate capturing and redistribution once it is disseminated to mobile devices of law enforcement or security teams on behalf of an operator.

### 6.1.1 Related Work

The subject of the work presented in the following is the specification and processing of information flow semantics depending on events that are intercepted by UC monitors, including inter-system and inter-layer information flows.

The distributed usage control model proposed by Pretschner et al. [PHB06] has been extended with information flow tracking [HP09; PLB11] to enable the enforcement of policies depending on the state of an information flow model, e.g., *no further representations of the referred data item must be created.* The aspect of distributed enforcement of usage control policies is considered in greater detail in [Bas+13; KP14], also focusing on efficient PDP-PIP communication.

This work builds on and extends [HP09; PLB11; Lov15]. It unifies information flow semantics specifications of monitoring components and adds a generalization from inter-layer to inter-system flows.

In [KP13] Kelbert and Pretschner introduced another approach towards state-based tracking of explicit flows across system boundaries based on system call interposition on the level of the Internet Protocol (IP) stack. By this means, inter-system flows are detected on the level of communication relationships between processes on remote systems (e.g., *write* system calls to TCP sockets). With this approach inter-system information flows do not have to be observed on the level of applications and therefore no specifications of according information flow semantics are needed. However, it requires a deep integration into the operating system. This is hard to implement for common operating systems for mobile devices, e.g., Android or iOS, and it requires a considerable amount of context switches between the kernel space and the user space to update each system's PIP.

Lovat et al. also proposed approaches to handle implicit flows [LOP14] and to address the issue of over-approximations of simple taint-based information flow tracking systems [LK14], which this work does not cover.

Information flows towards operating system resources and in-between processes are addressed by taint-based information flow tracking frameworks such as Panorama [Yin+07] and TaintDroid [Enc+14]. SeeC [Kim+09] also covers inter-system taint propagation. With Neon [Zha+10], Zhang et al. provide a virtual machine monitor for tainting and tracking flows on the level of bytes, which does not require the modification of applications and operating systems. Demsky's tool GARM [Dem11] tackles data provenance tracking and policy enforcement across applications and systems via application rewriting.

## 6.2 Information Flow Model

This approach to information flow modeling originates in earlier works of Harvan and Pretschner [HP09; PLB11]. An information flow model is a transition system that captures the flow of data throughout a system. Transitions of the state are triggered by events in the system that are observed by monitors, such as PEPs of a usage control infrastructure. A system's information flow tracking component, the PIP, interprets events given information flow semantics, which are provided by monitors when being deployed in an existing infrastructure. An usage control infrastructure extended with information flow tracking therefore typically consists of several PEPs monitoring various applications on different layers of abstraction and also on different machines. Each PEP contributes to the information flow model by intercepting a set of events. It propagates the information flow semantics of these events to the local PIP when being deployed. Accordingly, whenever the PDP evaluates a state-based usage control policy, i.e., a policy which applies for each representation of a certain data item (cf. section 2.5.1), it queries the PIP whether the data item concerned by a given event is a representation of the data item protected by the policy.

The state of the information flow model comprises three aspects. First of all, it reflects which data items are in which container, where a container may be a file within the file system, a window in the graphical user interface, an object in a Java virtual machine, a network connection, and so on. The state also captures *alias relations* between containers, which are used to express that a container is implicitly updated whenever some other container is being updated. This happens, for instance, when processes share memory. Finally, the state comprises different *names* that identify a container, e.g., a file container may not only be accessible by its file name, but also by a file handle.

### 6.2.1 Formal Model

As introduced by Pretschner and Harvan in [HP09; PLB11] the formal information flow model is a tuple $(D, C, F, \Sigma, E, R)$. $D$ is the set of data items for which usage control policies exist. $C$ is the set of containers in the system. $F$ is the set of names. $\Sigma = (C \to 2^D) \times (C \to 2^C) \times (F \to C)$ is the set of possible states, which consist of the *storage function* $s : C \to 2^D$, the *alias function* $l : C \to 2^C$, and the *naming function* $f : F \to C$. Chains of aliases are addressed using the reflexive transitive closure of the alias function denoted as $l^*$. The initial state of the system is denoted as $\sigma_I \in \Sigma$, where the state of the storage function $s$ is given by the initial representation of a data item a usage control policy refers to. *Events* $E$ are observed actions that trigger changes of the storage function $s$, the alias function $l$, or the naming function $f$. These changes are described in a (deterministic) transition relation $R \subseteq \Sigma \times E \times \Sigma$.

A notation introduced in [HP09] is used in the following to describe updates to the functions $s$, $l$, and $f$. Let $m : S \to T$ be any mapping and $x \in X \subseteq S$ a variable. Then $m[x \leftarrow expr]_{x \in X} = m'$ with $m' : S \to T$ is defined as

$$m'(y) = \begin{cases} expr & if\ y \in X \\ m(y) & otherwise. \end{cases}$$

## 6.3 Generic Semantics Specification for Information Flow Tracking

For any PEP, $R$ is specified in an *information flow semantics*, which the PEP deploys on the PIP when being added to a usage control infrastructure. For each event intercepted by a PEP, an information flow semantics specifies the state changes of the functions $s$, $l$, and $f$ using generic primitives that are introduced in the subsequent paragraphs.

When processing an event according to an information flow semantics (e.g., listing 6.3), the PIP picks the action description for the type of the given event, converts event parameters in order to match the signatures of the contained semantics primitives (i.e., it implicitly applies the naming function $f$ or the storage function $s$ on a given parameter: $F \xrightarrow{f} C \xrightarrow{s} D$), and finally modifies its state according to the given primitives.

### 6.3.1 Primitives for Updating the Storage Function

The storage function keeps track of representations, i.e., mappings between data items and containers. It is used for modeling the actual information flows.

$$\begin{aligned} &flow(container\ c, data\ \{d_i\}_{1 \leq i \leq n \in \mathbb{N}}) : \\ &\qquad s[c \leftarrow s(c) \cup \{d_i\}] \end{aligned} \tag{6.1}$$

The $flow$ primitive (cf. eq. (6.1)) indicates an information flow of a set of data items $\{d_i\}_{1 \leq i \leq n \in \mathbb{N}}$ into the container $c$. This primitive is used, for instance, when modeling that a process creates a new file, a child process, or that a file is copied. Data items will then also flow into containers of processes that currently have a read handle on this file.

$$\begin{aligned} &flow\_to\_rtc(container\ c, data\ \{d_i\}_{1 \leq i \leq n \in \mathbb{N}}) : \\ &\qquad \forall t \in l^*(c) : s[t \leftarrow s(t) \cup \{d_i\}] \end{aligned} \tag{6.2}$$

The $flow\_to\_rtc$ primitive (cf. eq. (6.2)) models a flow into containers of the reflexive transitive closure $l^*(c)$ of container $c$. It is used for processes reading from a file, writing to a file, or receiving data from the system clipboard.

$$\begin{aligned} clear(container\ c) &: \\ s[c \leftarrow \varnothing] & \end{aligned} \tag{6.3}$$

The *clear* (cf. eq. (6.3)) primitive is employed whenever a container is deleted, such as when deleting a file, closing a window, killing a process, etc.

### 6.3.2 Primitives for Updating the Alias Function

The alias function keeps track of relationships between containers that lead to implicit flows, i.e., whenever data items flow to container $c_{from}$, they also flow into container $c_{to}$ to which $c_{from}$ holds an alias.

$$\begin{aligned} create\_alias(container\ c_{from}, container\ c_{to}) &: \\ l[c_{from} \leftarrow l(c_{from}) \cup c_{to}] & \end{aligned} \tag{6.4}$$

The primitive *create_alias* shown in eq. (6.4) adds an unidirectional alias from container $c_{from}$ to container $c_{to}$ to the alias function of $c_{from}$. Unidirectional aliases are used, e.g., for memory-mapped file I/O if a process has read-only access to the file (cf. `mmap` system call on any POSIX-compliant UNIX and Linux operating system).

$$\begin{aligned} create\_bidir\_alias(container\ c_{from}, container\ c_{to}) &: \\ l[c_{from} \leftarrow l(c_{from}) \cup c_{to}], & \\ l[c_{to} \leftarrow l(c_{to}) \cup c_{from}] & \end{aligned} \tag{6.5}$$

Bidirectional aliases are added using the *create_bidir_alias* primitive (cf. eq. (6.5)). Examples to be modeled with bidirectional aliases include creating a new window, or a process having read and write access to a file.

$$\begin{aligned} rm\_alias\_locally(container\ c_{from}, container\ c_{to}) :& \\ l[c_{from} \leftarrow l(c_{from}) \setminus c_{to}]& \end{aligned} \tag{6.6}$$

The primitive *rm_alias_locally* removes an unidirectional alias from $c_{from}$ to $c_{to}$, e.g., aliases that have been added using the *create_alias* primitive of eq. (6.4).

$$\begin{aligned} rm\_alias\_globally(container\ c_{to}) :& \\ \forall c \in C : l[c \leftarrow l(c) \setminus c_{to}]& \end{aligned} \tag{6.7}$$

In some cases an unidirectional alias has to be removed from all containers in $C$, e.g., in case $c$ is a file, which is deleted. For this, the *rm_alias_globally* primitive is employed as shown in eq. (6.7).

$$\begin{aligned} rm\_bidir\_alias\_locally(container\ c_{from}, container\ c_{to}) :& \\ l[c_{from} \leftarrow l(c_{from}) \setminus c_{to}],& \\ l[c_{to} \leftarrow l(c_{to}) \setminus c_{from}]& \end{aligned} \tag{6.8}$$

Bidirectional aliases as added using the primitive *create_bidir_alias* (cf. eq. (6.5)) are removed using the primitive *rm_bidir_alias_locally* as shown in eq. (6.8).

$$\begin{aligned} clear\_aliases(container\ c) :& \\ l[c \leftarrow \varnothing]& \end{aligned} \tag{6.9}$$

*clear_aliases* removes all aliases with the given container as source from the state of the alias function (cf. eq. (6.9)), e.g., to clean up if a container is deleted.

### 6.3.3 Primitives for Updating the Naming Function

The naming function keeps track of different names referring to the same container. For instance, files can be addressed via file names and also via file handles or hard links; in the Windows operating system, a particular window can be identified via a window handle and also via a window name.

$$\begin{aligned} &add\_naming(naming\ n, container\ c): \\ &\qquad f[n \leftarrow c] \end{aligned} \tag{6.10}$$

A new name $n$ for a container $c$ is added to the state of the information flow model using the primitive *add_naming* (cf. eq. (6.10)) and removed via $rm\_naming$:

$$\begin{aligned} &rm\_naming(naming\ n): \\ &\qquad f[n \leftarrow nil] \end{aligned} \tag{6.11}$$

## 6.4 Inter-Layer and Inter-System Information Flows

So far, *inter-layer* and *inter-system* information flows are not covered by the semantics specification primitives. The term *inter-layer* refers to flows between different layers of abstraction such as between an application and the operating system. *Inter-system* flows take place in distributed scenarios, i.e., whenever data is exchanged between machines over a network connection. Monitoring such flows requires that an event indicating an *incoming* flow is matched to a preceding *outgoing* event on another system or layer of abstraction. In the following, an information flow model extension for inter-system flows is introduced. As this requires a synchronization of the PIPs of different systems, it can be conceived as a generalization of the approach to inter-layer information flow tracking introduced by Lovat [Lov15].

### 6.4.1 Extended Information Flow Model

As an example, consider the transfer of video data from a streaming server to a client, e.g., from a video surveillance system to a mobile device. Assume further that both, the server and the client, are equipped with PEPs that are capable of intercepting outgoing events respectively incoming events. All other components of the usage control infrastructure are deployed on both systems as well. Initially, the server side PEP observes an outgoing event indicating an information flow from a local container to a container representing the network connection between the server and the client. When receiving data of the video stream via this network connection, the PEP at the client side observes an according incoming event. Finally, when either the client disconnects from the video stream or the server closes the connection, a third event is observed at the server side, which terminates the information flow. Initially, these events are independent from the perspective of both PIPs. Detecting an inter-system information flow requires that both events are interpreted at both PIPs requiring according *remote* information flow semantics, which are provided by the according PEPs and exchanged between PIPs.

Within an information flow semantics a so-called *scope* specification indicates that an event is interdependent with an event at another system (or layer of abstraction). The particular events are matched to a certain scope by means of a *scope name* parameter, which is a label for an information flow mutually known by two systems (or layers of abstraction). Accordingly, the information flow model of section 6.2.1 is extended with a set of scopes $SCOPE$. The state $\Sigma$ is extended with the following two mappings: The *intermediate container function* $\iota : SCOPE \rightarrow C$ maps each scope to a dedicated intermediate container $c_\iota \in C$. The *scope state function* $\varsigma : SCOPE \rightarrow \{\text{ACTIVATED}, \text{DEACTIVATED}\}$ indicates currently open scopes. Intermediate containers of different systems are distinct containers. They are mapped on each other by means of scopes and hence virtually represent a connection between two systems. Each event belongs to at most one inter-layer or inter-system scope (also denoted as XLAYER and XSYSTEM respectively). In the initial state $\sigma_I$ of the system, there is one dedicated intermediate container $c_\iota$ for each scope $\iota$ and $\varsigma(sc)$ is DEACTIVATED for all $sc \in SCOPE$. A scope has the following three attributes, which define how the model state is modified when processing an according event:

$$X_{SCOPE} : \Sigma \times E \rightarrow SCOPE \times BEHAVIOR \times DELIMITER \times INTER$$

$$DELIMITER = \{\text{OPEN}, \text{CLOSE}, \text{NONE}\}$$

$$BEHAVIOR = \{\text{IN}, \text{OUT}, \text{INTRA}\}$$

$$INTER = \{\text{XLAYER}, \text{XSYSTEM}\}$$

The *DELIMITER* of a scope describes whether a given event indicates a new inter-system or inter-layer flow. The delimiter OPEN changes the state of the scope within which the event is processed to ACTIVATED. CLOSE changes the state of a given scope to ACTIVATED, whereas the delimiter NONE is used for flows within a specific layer of abstraction of a system. The *BEHAVIOR* describes whether the given event indicates an outgoing information flow to (OUT), or an incoming information flow (IN) from another system or layer of abstraction. The *BEHAVIOR* of a scope affects the processing of semantics primitives when handling inter-system or inter-layer information flows as will be described in section 6.4.3 (INTRA is the default behavior, i.e., a flow within a layer of abstraction, which does not affect the interpretation of primitives). Finally, *INTER* differentiates between inter-system (XSYSTEM) and inter-layer (XLAYER) information flows.

### 6.4.2 Selecting the Appropriate Scope Semantics for an Event

For each type of event a PEP's information flow semantics contains an *action description*, which specifies its interpretation in terms of information flow using semantics primitives (cf. section 6.3). In other words, an event is an observable indicator for an action performed by a user or process. Action descriptions give information flow semantics to events, e.g., an event indicating that the user takes a screenshot constitutes the creation of a new representations of the data items that are currently visualized on the system's screen(s). An action description also includes an ordered list of all scope specifications that potentially apply for the given type of event. The XML scheme for information flow semantics can be found in appendix D.

The notification about the event only contains the scope (as a name-value pair, where the value is the scope itself). When processing an event, the PIP needs to check, in the given order of the action description, which scope specification is applicable. For each eventual scope specification, the PIP evaluates the following three conditions:

1. Does the scope name in the scope specification match the name of a parameter of the given event?
2. If $DELIMITER = \text{OPEN}$ in the scope specification: Is this scope deactivated?
3. If $DELIMITER = \text{NONE}$ or $DELIMITER = \text{CLOSE}$ in the scope specification: Is this scope activated?

If only one of the conditions is not fulfilled, the respective scope specification is skipped. The PIP processes the ordered list until the appropriate scope specification $X_{SCOPE}$ has been found.

### 6.4.3 Scope Processing

The transition relation $R$ is modified when processing a scope specification. Algorithm 1 describes how $R$ is modified in order to obtain $R_{mod}$, i.e., the transition relation for inter-system or inter-layer information flows.

**ALGORITHM 1:** $R_{inter}(\sigma,e)$

$(scope, behav, delim, inter) \longleftarrow X_{SCOPE}(\sigma, e)$;
**if** $scope \neq \emptyset$ **then**
  $ic \longleftarrow \iota(scope)$;
  $R_{mod} \longleftarrow R$;
  **if** $delim = \textsc{open}$ **then**
    $\sigma \longleftarrow \varsigma[scope \leftarrow \textsc{activated}]$;
  **if** $behav = \textsc{out}$ **then**
    $R_{mod} \longleftarrow R_{mod}\Big[s[c \leftarrow s(c) \cup \{d_i\}]$
      $\overset{\text{subst.}}{\Longleftarrow} s[ic \leftarrow s(ic) \cup \{d_i\}]\Big]$;
    $R_{mod} \longleftarrow R_{mod}\Big[\forall t \in l(c) : s[t \leftarrow s(t) \cup \{d_i\}]$
      $\overset{\text{subst.}}{\Longleftarrow} \forall t \in l(ic) : s[t \leftarrow s(t) \cup \{d_i\}]\Big]$;
    $R_{mod} \longleftarrow R_{mod}\Big[\forall t \in l^*(c) : s[t \leftarrow s(t) \cup \{d_i\}]$
      $\overset{\text{subst.}}{\Longleftarrow} \forall t \in l^*(ic) : s[t \leftarrow s(t) \cup \{d_i\}]\Big]$;
  **if** $behav = \textsc{in}$ **then**
    $R_{mod} \longleftarrow R_{mod}\Big[s[c \leftarrow s(c) \cup \{d_i\}]$
      $\overset{\text{subst.}}{\Longleftarrow} s[c \leftarrow s(c) \cup s(ic)]\Big]$;
    $R_{mod} \longleftarrow R_{mod}\Big[\forall t \in l(c) : s[t \leftarrow s(t) \cup \{d_i\}]$
      $\overset{\text{subst.}}{\Longleftarrow} \forall t \in l(c) : s[t \leftarrow s(t) \cup s(ic)]\Big]$;
    $R_{mod} \longleftarrow R_{mod}\Big[\forall t \in l^*(c) : s[t \leftarrow s(t) \cup \{d_i\}]$
      $\overset{\text{subst.}}{\Longleftarrow} \forall t \in l^*(c) : s[t \leftarrow s(t) \cup s(ic)]\Big]$;
  $\sigma \longleftarrow R_{mod}(\sigma,e)$
  **if** $delim = \textsc{close}$ **then**
    $\sigma \longleftarrow \varsigma[scope \leftarrow \textsc{deactivated}]$;
    $\sigma \longleftarrow s[ic \leftarrow \varnothing]$;
**else**
  $\sigma \longleftarrow R(\sigma,e)$;
**return** $\sigma$

In the used notation $R[left \xleftarrow{\text{subst.}} right]$ denotes that the term on the left referring to $R$ is substituted with the term on the right in $R_{mod}$. If the delimiter of the scope equals OPEN, the scope is activated (cf. line 5); if the delimiter of the scope equals CLOSE, the scope is deactivated after handling the event (cf. line 22). In between (cf. line 7 ff.), depending on the scope's behavior, either the left argument (target) (cf. line 14 ff.) or the right argument (source) of the storage function primitives $flow$ or $flow\_to\_rtc$ is substituted with the scope's dedicated intermediate container. Finally, the modified transition relation $R_{mod}$ is applied on the state $\sigma$ (cf. line 21).

In case the processed information flow is an inter-system flow ($inter$ = XSYSTEM), the PIP needs to enable its counterpart on the remote system to process the given event. As described in section 6.5.1 this is achieved by forwarding a remote information flow semantics to the remote PIP.

## 6.5 Instantiation: Protecting Streamed Video Data at the Client Side

The subsequent paragraphs describe an instantiation of usage control and inter-system information flow tracking for protecting video data streamed from a video surveillance system to mobile clients against duplication and redistribution after receipt. In order to enforce this usage control requirement, (i) an according policy must be deployed at the usage control infrastructure of the client, (ii) the information flow of the video stream must be tracked from the server to the client system, and (iii) video data must be monitored at the client side in order to inhibit further representations to be created. The following protocol steps have to be performed in order to achieve (i) and (ii):

1. Intercept an event signaling *outgoing* video data at the server side PEP
2. Evaluate the event against an according policy at the server side PDP
3. Deploy a policy for the video data at the client side PDP
4. Process the event at the server side PIP

5. Create a new representation of the video data at the client side PIP
6. Process the outgoing event also at the client side PIP using an information flow semantics provided by the server side PIP
7. Intercept an event signaling *incoming* video data at the client side PEP
8. Evaluate the event at the client side PDP
9. Process the event at the client side PIP
10. Intercept an event signaling the termination of the video data transfer at the server side PEP (*close* event)
11. Process the event at the server side PIP
12. Process the close event also at the client side PIP using an information flow semantics provided by the server side PIP

The details of the protocol steps are explained by means of figure 6.2 before (iii) is addressed in section 6.5.2. As introduced in section 2.4 the PMP is responsible for policy deployment and inter-system policy shipment. All other components of a system's usage control infrastructure are registered at the local PMP, which provides according communication connectors via a lookup function.

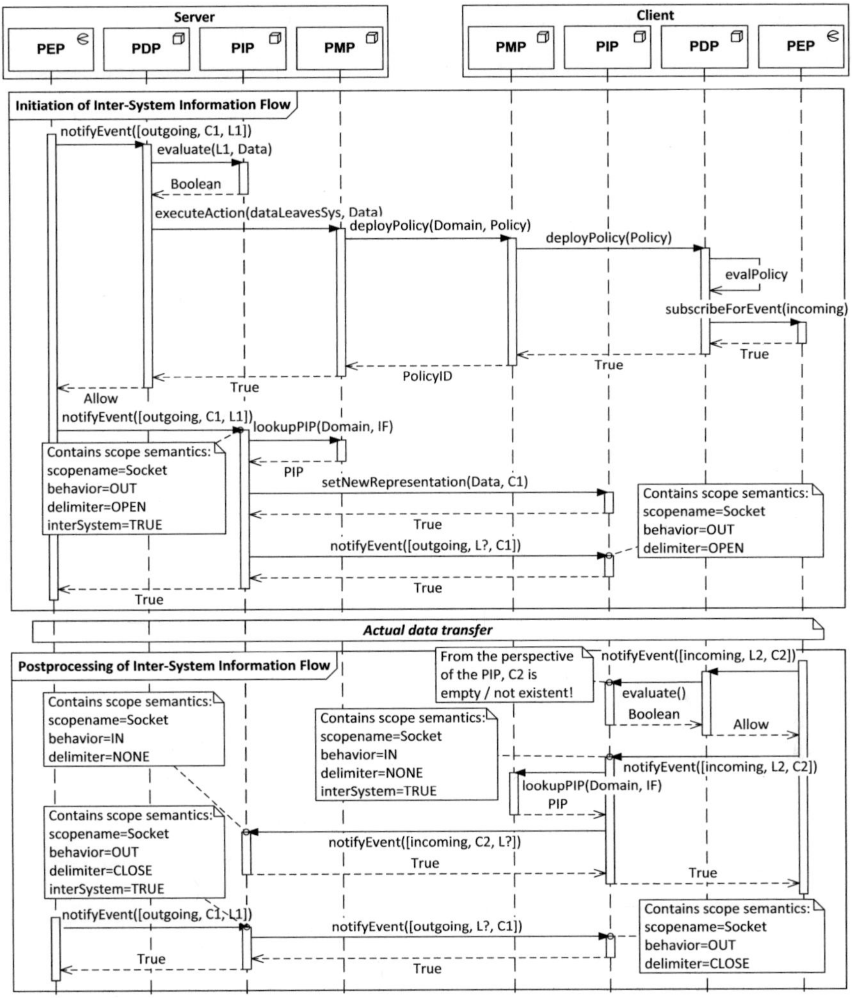


**Figure 6.2:** The procedure of inter-system information flow tracking

### 6.5.1 Inter-System Information Flow Tracking

Video streaming is triggered by a request from the client, which is intercepted on the server side. The according *outgoing* event triggers the steps 1 to 6 (cf. listing 6.1). It indicates an outgoing flow from the local container *L1*, i.e., the actual server process providing the video stream, to a container *C1* representing the network connection to the client from the perspective of the server.

```
<event action="outgoing" timestamp="2015-05-30T09:30:10">
  <parameter name="network" value="192.168.0.2:80;192.168.0.1:49152"><!--C1-->
  <parameter name="process" value="2a26af9d-f565-4775-87b5-8eb1fb987ad5"><!--L1-->
  <parameter name="currentscope" value="192.168.0.2:80;192.168.0.1:49152">
</event>
```

**Listing 6.1:** Outgoing event at the server side

In step 2, a policy deployed at the server side PDP grants access to the video stream under the condition that a policy for protecting the requested video data is deployed at the client side (step 3). The server side policy is shown in listing 6.2, the client side policy is explained in the subsequent section 6.5.2.

Both policies refer to the video data by means of a unique dataID *data*, which represents the video data within PIPs. Thus, when evaluating the *outgoing* event concerning the local container *L1* against the local policy, the server side PDP queries the local PIP whether *L1* contains *data* (cf. *evaluate*-call to the server side PIP in figure 6.2). As the PIP returns *true*, the policy matches the outgoing event and evaluates to *allow* under the condition that a policy protecting the video data is deployed at the client side. This policy demands that the screen must not be captured while an application in the foreground has access to the protected video data. It is shown later in listing 6.7 and explained in section 6.5.2.

```xml
<policy description="Process video requests from clients" name="processVideoRequests">
  <preventiveMechanism name="deployRemotePolicy">
    <description>Deploy remote policy for video data</description>
    <trigger action="videoRequest" isTry="true">
      <paramMatch name="CommunicationContainer" type="xpath" value="contains(//event
            /parameter[@name='CommunicationContainer']/@value,'socket')"/>
    </trigger>
    <condition>
      <true />
    </condition>
    <authorizationAction name="allow">
      <allow>
        <executeAction name="deployPolicy">
          <parameter name="policyName" value="remoteVideoStreamPolicy"/>
          <parameter name="dataId"
            value="string(//event/parameter[@name='dataId']/@value)" type="xpath"/>
          <parameter name="host"
            value="string(//event/parameter[@name='host']/@value)" type="xpath"/>
        </executeAction>
      </allow>
    </authorizationAction>
  </preventiveMechanism>
</policy>
```

**Listing 6.2:** Policy for processing client requests for video data and for deploying another policy at the client side

In step 4 the outgoing event is handled by the server side PIP. The PIP holds a *local semantics* and a *remote semantics* for this type of event. Remote semantics are provided to remote machines that need to process the event as well. The local semantics for the outgoing event is shown in listing 6.3.

The scope attribute $\mathit{interSystem} = \textsc{true}$ in the *outgoing* action description is equivalent to $\mathit{inter} = \textsc{xsystem}$ in the formal model and induces the activation of an *inter-system scope*. The action description also indicates a flow from the local container *L1* into the network container *C1*. According to $\mathit{behavior} = \textsc{out}$ of the scope, *C1* is substituted by the scope's dedicated *intermediate container* within the server side PIP, i.e., as the PIP is aware that *L1* contains *data*, it models this flow by mapping *data* to the *intermediate container*.

```
<ifsemantics>
  <params>
    <param name="network" type="CONTAINER"/>
    <param name="process" type="CONTAINER"/>
  </params>
  <actions>
    <action name="outgoing">
      <scope behavior="OUT" delimiter="OPEN" interSystem="TRUE">
          currentscope</scope>
      <operation name="SF_FLOW">
        <left><operand>network</operand></left><!--C1-->
        <right><operand>process</operand></right><!--L1-->
      </operation>
    </action>
    <action name="close">
      <scope behavior="OUT" delimiter="CLOSE" interSystem="TRUE">
          currentscope</scope>
      <operation name="SF_CLEAR">
        <left><operand>network</operand></left><!--C1-->
        <right></right>
      </operation>
    </action>
  </actions>
</ifsemantics>
```

**Listing 6.3:** Local semantics of the outgoing and close events

The scope specification in the semantics also triggers the server side PIP to signal the upcoming data transfer to the client side PIP. So far, the client side PIP neither knows that this data exists nor that the client requested it from the server. Step 5 takes care of the first part: The server side PIP creates a new representation of the data item to be transferred at the client side PIP, i.e., an initial mapping between the dataID *data* of the video data and the remote network container *C1* is added to the client side information flow model. The server side PIP then forwards the event to the client side PIP. In case the remote semantics for this event has not yet been deployed at the client side PIP, it is attached to this notification (cf. listing 6.4).

In step 6, the client side PIP processes the outgoing event from the server side given the remote semantics (cf. section 6.4.2). According to *delimiter* = OPEN the client side PIP creates a new scope. The semantics further indicates a flow from the network container *C1* into the container *L?*, which is a placeholder for an unknown container that receives the flow at the client side (the local container at the server side included in the event is ignored at the client side). According to *behavior* = OUT of the scope, the client PIP replaces *L?* with the scope's dedicated *intermediate container* (cf. section 6.4.3). The PIP puts this together with the fact that *C1* contains *data* and obtains a flow of *data* from *C1* into the scope's dedicated *intermediate container* at the client side. After this step, the server starts sending video data to the client.

```
<ifsemantics>
  <params>
    <param name="network" type="CONTAINER"/>
    <param name="process" type="CONTAINER"/>
  </params>
  <actions>
    <action name="outgoing">
      <scope behavior="OUT" delimiter="OPEN">currentscope</scope>
      <operation name="SF_FLOW">
        <left><operand>process</operand></left><!--L?-->
        <right><operand>network</operand></right><!--C1-->
      </operation>
    </action>
    <action name="close">
      <scope behavior="OUT" delimiter="CLOSE">currentscope</scope>
      <operation name="SF_CLEAR">
        <left><operand>network</operand></left><!--C1-->
        <right></right>
      </operation>
    </action>
  </actions>
</ifsemantics>
```

**Listing 6.4:** Remote semantics of the outgoing and close events

Steps 7 to 9 of information flow processing are triggered by an *incoming* event, which is intercepted by the client side PEP when receiving data over the network connection with the server (cf. listing 6.5).

```
<event action="incoming" timestamp="2015-05-30T09:30:11">
  <parameter name="process" value="16820cec-18c7-49a2-a443-cd94f0fec3e0"><!--L2-->
  <parameter name="network" value="192.168.0.1:49152;192.168.0.2:80"/><!--C2-->
  <parameter name="currentscope" value="192.168.0.2:80;192.168.0.1:49152">
</event>
```

**Listing 6.5:** Incoming event at the client side

The *incoming* event refers to the same *scope* as the *outgoing* event. It indicates a flow from a network container *C2* representing the network connection from the perspective of the client side PEP into a local container *L2* of the client, i.e., the process accessing the video stream. The client side PDP evaluates this event against the policy that has been deployed in step 3. This requires that the PDP queries the PIP whether this information flow involves a representation of the protected video data identified via the dataID *data* (step 8, cf. *evaluate*-call to the client side PIP in figure 6.2). As the container *C2* is either empty, i.e., it has been created during a prior connection to the server, or does not yet exist, the PIP answers the query with *false*, and the PDP *allows* the incoming event to take place.

In step 9, the *incoming* event is processed at the client side PIP, which holds a local semantics for this type of event. The semantics is shown in listing 6.6. It contains a scope specification with *behavior* = IN and *delimiter* = NONE. It further signals a flow from the network container *C2* into the local container *L2*. The *delimiter* = NONE indicates that the event belongs to an already activated inter-system scope. Due to *behavior* = IN, *C2* is replaced with the scope's *intermediate container* within the PIP at the client side. Putting this together with the state after steps 5 and 6, the client side PIP observes a flow of *data* from the remote container *C1* via the *intermediate container* into the target container *L2*, i.e., as of now, the PIP knows that *L2* contains the video data *data*, which is protected by the policy deployed in step 3. Furthermore, a naming is added to the state of the naming function in order to make *L2* accessible via the process identifier (PID) of the process receiving the video data.

```
<ifsemantics>
  <params>
    <param name="process" type="CONTAINER"/>
    <param name="network" type="CONTAINER"/>
    <param name="process_id" type="CONTAINER_NAME"/>
  </params>
  <actions>
    <action name="incoming">
      <scope behavior="IN" delimiter="NONE">currentscope</scope>
      <operation name="SF_FLOW">
        <left><operand>process</operand></left><!--L2-->
        <right><operand>network</operand></right><!--C2-->
      </operation>
      <operation name="NF_ADD_NAMING">
        <left><operand>process_id</operand></left>
        <right><operand>process</operand></right><!--L2-->
      </operation>
    </action>
  </actions>
</ifsemantics>
```

**Listing 6.6:** Local semantics of the incoming event

As soon as the client disconnects from the video stream, the established inter-system state is no longer needed, i.e., the scopes are deactivated and the intermediate containers at the server side PIP as well as at the client side PIP are deleted. In the example, the termination of the network connection is first observed by the server side PEP (step 10). The according event is processed at the server side PIP (step 11) and forwarded to the client side PIP. In line with algorithm 1, this server side event is processed with scope delimiter CLOSE at server side and at the client side according to the scope specification of the local semantics (cf. Listing 6.3) and the remote semantics deployed in step 5 (cf. listing 6.4). As *C1* has been replaced by the *intermediate container* at the server side in step 4, the event has no effect except for closing the scope locally.

Tracking this inter-system information flow terminates after the close event has been interpreted at the client side (step 12).

### 6.5.2 Client Side Policy Enforcement

```xml
<policy description="Handle screen captures on clients" name="remoteVideoStreamPolicy">
  <preventiveMechanism name="inhibitScreenCaptures">
    <description>Inhibit screen captures of protected video data</description>
    <trigger action="intent:startService" isTry="true">
      <paramMatch name="component" value="com.android.systemui/com.android.systemui.screenshot.TakeScreenshotService"/>
      <paramMatch name="dataId" value="[data]" type="dataUsage"/>
    </trigger>
    <condition>
      <true/>
    </condition>
    <authorizationAction name="Inhibit">
      <inhibit/>
    </authorizationAction>
    <executeAction name="notify">
      <parameter name="msg" value="Capturing the screen is not allowed while visualizing protected video data!"/>
    </executeAction>
  </preventiveMechanism>
</policy>
```

**Listing 6.7:** Policy for inhibiting screen captures at the client while protected video data is visualized

At the client side, data of the video stream is protected against duplication (iii) by means of the policy depicted in listing 6.7,[2] which has been deployed in step 3. The *dataUsage* type (cf. section 2.5.1) of the parameter *dataId* indicates that the policy applies for all representations of the corresponding data item (the actual dataId referring to the video stream is set when instantiating the policy at the client side PDP in step 3). Accordingly, the PIP's knowledge is inquired

[2] This policy is understood by a usage control implementation for the Android operating system done by Feth [FP12].

every time a user triggers an event indicating an according information flow, e.g., when trying to capture the screen.
The event of taking a screen capture is intercepted by a PEP on the client and is only allowed if no application in the foreground has access to the protected video stream. For this, the PIP can be queried using the PIDs of questionable processes (cf. section 6.5.1, step 9). The PIP will apply the naming function on the PID of the application accessing the video stream and answer that this container is a representation of the data item, for which the policy applies. Accordingly, the event, i.e., the screen shot, is inhibited.

The reliability of this distributed usage control enforcement is based on the assumptions explained in section 2.5.2. In particular, it is assumed that confidential communication channels are used and that the client is trustworthy, i.e., it is ensured that usage control components are up and running and not tampered with. In practice, such clients will most likely be managed devices provided by the corresponding organization with usage control components integrated within their firmware.

## 6.6 Conclusions

This chapter introduced a generic, extensible and application-oriented approach for dynamic information flow modeling and processing of explicit flows, also across the boundaries of systems equipped with usage control technology. By this means usage control requirements can be enforced on representations of protected data items on remote systems after the initial access to the data has been granted.

A set of generic primitives for specifying information flow semantics of events enables engineers to develop information flow monitors (PEPs), which can easily be plugged into existing usage control infrastructures, and thus facilitates the deployment of information flow tracking technology in evolving scenarios. These primitives as well as the protocol for distributed processing of information flow-relevant events cover inter-layer and particularly inter-system flows, which requires the synchronization of remote information flow tracking components (PIPs). Eliminating the interdependency between event capturing and information flow tracking at development time facilitates the practical application of state-based usage control enforcement based on information flow tracking.

With the demonstrated instantiation of usage control and inter-system information flow tracking, video data disseminated from a video surveillance system to mobile clients is protected against illegitimate redistribution so as to confirm research question **TS-4**.

# 7 Anonymization of Video Data

Anonymization functions, which are also referred to as *privacy filters*, aim to obfuscate video data so as to avoid that captured persons can be identified by observers. As explained in the analysis of legal requirements (cf. section 4.1), a smart video surveillance system may only disclose video data to operators in an anonymized fashion until a detected incident has turned out to be a concrete threat situation. The rationale behind this requirement is that abstract threat situations and suspected dangers do not yet justify the collection and processing of personal data. Besides, first-level situation assessment is a matter of *what* people are doing and not of *who* people are. From a technical perspective, disclosing anonymized video data also reduces the risk of unnecessary privacy breaches due to false positive detections of video analysis algorithms (cf. section 4.2.3). Anonymization of video data, i.e., applying privacy filters in order to obfuscate the identities of observed individuals when video data is disclosed to an operator, is thus a key privacy protection mechanism in smart video surveillance. As expressed in the research question **TS-2**, it is equally important to preserve the utility of video data for situation assessment, i.e., the activities of observed individuals must remain recognizable for operators. Privacy filters are particularly important for realizing a privacy-preserving default mode as well as privacy-preserving assessment modes in situation-dependent smart video surveillance workflows as introduced in section 4.4 and section 5.1.1.

In this research, the first large-scale online user study with a response of 103 participants evaluated privacy filters for video data in terms of privacy protection *and* utility based on a formalized methodology. Participants were asked to identify persons and to recognize activities. In the context of this study, identification means that obfuscated persons shown in a video clip are recognized in a larger set of unmodified still images of persons. Based on the *privacy evaluation video data set (PEViD)* [KE13] this study is also the first one to consider utility with respect to activities that are specific for common purposes of (smart) video surveillance. This data set includes video clips of the activities *fighting*, *stealing*, and *abandoning an object*, in which occurring persons were anonymized using the obfuscating pixel operations *pixelization*, *reduction to silhouette*, *edge detection*, and *Gaussian blurring* (gray scale and color resolution).

Regarding the activities taking place in these video clips, the results of the study indicate that recognizing activities on obfuscated video data may indeed be possible for operators, which contradicts with the common hypothesis that privacy and utility of video data are necessarily trade-off. In particular, the user study covers the following aspects related to utility, privacy, as well as perceived image quality:

**Privacy Protection and Utility.** Privacy protection is considered in terms of identity leakage, i.e., whether participants are able to correctly identify anonymized persons in a candidate set. Utility is investigated in terms of whether participants are able to correctly recognize an activity, which is taking place in an anonymized video clip.

**Effects of Anonymization Functions on Evidences and Identification.** In terms of protecting privacy in video data, an *evidence* is an information of visual appearance, which reveals or contributes to revealing the identity of an occurring individual. It is also common to distinguish between *explicit* and *implicit* evidences:

- Explicit evidence := An evidence, which is directly visible in a video clip, e.g., a person's hair color, features of the face, body shape and body size, or gait.
- Implicit evidence := An evidence, which is not directly visible in a video clip, but deduced from explicit evidences, e.g., a person's age, gender, or ethnicity.

Evidences reveal an individual's identity with different certainty [Sai+10]. One can directly identify a known person when getting to see her or his face. By means of a person's clothes identification is not necessarily possible. In order to understand how humans identify other people, this work studies the influences of explicit and implicit evidences on identification. For this, the prominence of evidences for identifying persons is compared.

**Subjective Evaluation of Privacy Protection and Video Quality.** A certain level of perceptual quality of disclosed video data is not only essential in order to enable situation assessment, but also to not strain operators unnecessarily. At the same time, people's confidence into anonymization functions as privacy protection mechanisms also depends on their subjective perception of effectiveness. This study thus covers perceived video quality and perceived privacy protection by inquiring subjective ratings from the participants.

## 7.1 Related Work

While a great variety of works has considered privacy aspects of images and video data, i.e., in terms of obfuscating persons, hiding faces, masking out license plates, etc., only few of them consider the utility of such data with respect to certain purposes. Considering collaboration systems for distributed work groups, Hudson and Smith [HS96] claim that the trade-off between awareness and privacy is fundamental and unavoidable, but that privacy filters and also abstraction techniques are promising approaches towards realizing appropriate trade-offs in terms of providing awareness and preserving privacy at the same time. In [ZS98], Zhao and Stasko present a small scale user study on how image filtering techniques convey or suppress activity, identification, and presence information in media space applications. Again with focus on media space applications and common workplace activities Boyle et al. [BEG00] investigate how blurring and pixelization with different levels of fidelity affect awareness and privacy of video data. Although they only inquire subjective feedback concerning perceived privacy protection from their participants, their results already show that privacy filters can be parametrized in a way such that people can still recognize the availability of each other (in terms of looking busy, serious, or approachable) while being confident with the level of privacy protection. Babaguchi et al. [Bab+09] analyze factors of disclosable privacy in a user study with obfuscated still images. Saini et al. [Sai+10] investigate privacy issues regarding video data, define visually accessible information as *evidences*, and propose a model to calculate the privacy loss of video data. In [Sai+14], Saini et al. distinguish the concepts of privacy loss and identity leakage. They estimate the utility of video data that has been obfuscated with different filters in terms of distortion in [Sai+12]. In recent work by Nawaz et al. [NF15] the privacy level of obfuscated video data is calculated as an appearance similarity metric in relation to the original images, whereas the utility level is calculated as a structural similarity metric.

## 7.2 Formal Model

The procedure of anonymizing video data, the experimental design of the online user study, as well as the metrics for privacy protection and utility are described using a formal anonymization model, which is introduced in the following.

### 7.2.1 Definitions

**Definition 7.1 (Video Data)** *A unit of video data $\mathbb{V}$ (i.e., a video clip) is a time sequence of images $I$. $\mathbb{V} = (I^t)^{t \in \mathbb{N}}$. An image $I$ is a matrix of pixels with size $w \times h \times c$. Each pixel $p \in I$ has a value in $\{0, 1, \ldots, 255\}^3$ for red-green-blue (RGB) images (three channels), or in $\{0, 1, \ldots, 255\}$ for gray-scale images (one channel).*

**Definition 7.2 (Image Segmentation)** *An image segmentation is a function $F : I \rightarrow I_{RoI}$ partitioning an image into segments, so-called* Regions of Interest *(RoIs). $I_{RoI}$ and $I$ have the same size, i.e., $I_{RoI}$ is a binary mask of the image differentiating between RoIs to be obfuscated and regions not to be obfuscated.*

$I_{RoI}$ can be the result of face detection, pedestrian detection, background subtraction, etc. Furthermore, video segmentation $F_v : \mathbb{V} \times F \rightarrow \mathbb{V}_{RoI}$ performs image segmentation $F$ on each image $I \in \mathbb{V}$ with output $I_{RoI} \in \mathbb{V}_{RoI}$.

**Definition 7.3 (Personal Information)** *The personal information of an individual $\mathcal{P}$ embedded in $\mathbb{V}$ is a vector of attributes (id, activity, age, gender, hair color, ethnicity, ...), where*

- *id $\in \mathbb{N}$ is a unique identifier of a person (such as a social security number or a unique index in a personnel database). Within the scope of this study it is a person's index in a set of candidates.*
- *activity $\in \mathbb{A}$ indicates a person's activity in the given video clip $\mathbb{V}$. The set $\mathbb{A}$ of activities contains all activities, which are relevant to operators in terms of surveillance tasks being performed, such as $\{fighting, stealing, abandoning\ an\ object, \ldots\}$.*
- *age $\in \mathbb{N}$ is a person's age. Likewise gender $\in \{male, female\}$, hair color $\in \{blonde, black, \ldots\}$ and ethnicity $\in \{African, Asian, European, \ldots\}$ are corresponding attributes of a personal information vector.*

Note that attributes have to be differentiated from evidences. Attributes describe a person in the real world. Evidences are a map of attributes that appear in a video clip. Evidences can be changed through conditions of illumination and also by means of image filters (such as used for anonymization), while attributes are immutable to any operation on video data. A RoI in $I_{RoI}$ can be considered as map of a person's explicit evidences $\mathcal{P}$ embedded in a given video clip.

**Definition 7.4 (Anonymization Function)** *An image anonymization function $A : I_{RoI} \rightarrow I_{anon}$ is an image processing function on RoIs.*[1] *$I_{RoI}$ and $I_{anon}$ have the same size. Analogously, a video anonymization function $A_v : \mathbb{V}_{RoI} \rightarrow \mathbb{V}_{anon}$ is applied on all RoIs in a video clip $\mathbb{V}_{RoI}$.*

Anonymization functions aim to protect a person's *id* either by obfuscating its entire visual appearance or particular features. An anonymization function can be a pixel operation or a combination of pixel operations. In practice, image filters such as blurring and pixelization are commonly used.

### 7.2.2 Assumptions

The anonymization model introduced in the subsequent paragraphs is based on the following assumptions:

> **Assumption 1.** Operators have no background knowledge concerning the persons appearing in the video clips. They identify persons only based on information embedded in the video clips, whereby identification means that obfuscated persons are recognized in a larger set of unmodified still images of persons.
>
> **Assumption 2.** All operators have the same working capabilities including identifying persons and recognizing persons' activities.
>
> **Assumption 3.** All operators work independently.

### 7.2.3 Anonymization Model

An anonymization model is a tuple $(\mathbb{V}, F_v, A_v, \mathbb{A}, \mathbb{T}, \mathbb{C}, operator)$, where

- $\mathbb{V}$ is the original video clip or stream from a camera.
- $F_v$ is a segmentation function applied on $\mathbb{V}$.

[1] Note that this implies a conscious decision against applying anonymization functions on entire images. By means of only obfuscating glsplRoI, persons or other foreground objects stand out from the background, which has been considered as an improvement in terms of image quality.

- $A_v$ is an anonymization function applied on $F_v(\mathbb{V})$.
- $\mathbb{A}$ is a set of attributes concerning a person's identity.
- $\mathbb{T}$ is a set of activities relevant to ongoing video surveillance tasks.
- $\mathbb{C}$ is a set of persons. Every person $\mathcal{P} \in \mathbb{C}$ is called a candidate.
- The *operator* is a person working with the given surveillance system. In the scope of this study, an *operator* (i.e., a participant) is asked to determine the activities of individuals in video clips and to identify each occurring person in a candidate set $\mathbb{C}$.

The evaluation system for anonymization functions works as follows:

1. $\mathbb{V}_{anon} \leftarrow A_v(F_v(\mathbb{V}))$ : Perform a segmentation function $F_v$ and an anonymization function $A_v$ on a video clip $\mathbb{V}$ to obtain an anonymized video clip $\mathbb{V}_{anon}$.
2. $\mathbb{V}_{anon}$, $F_v$, $A_v$, $\mathbb{A}$, $\mathbb{T}$ are given to the *operator*.
   a) The *operator* is asked to choose evidences of each individual in $\mathbb{V}_{anon}$ from $\mathbb{A}$.
   b) The *operator* is asked to choose an activity $\mathcal{T}$ of the individual(s) in $\mathbb{V}_{anon}$ from $\mathbb{T}$.
3. $\mathbb{C}$ is given to the *operator*.
4. $C \xleftarrow{choose} operator(\mathbb{V}_{anon}, \mathbb{C})$ : The *operator* is asked to choose a candidate $C \in \mathbb{C}$ for each person $\mathcal{P} \in \mathbb{V}_{anon}$, where the *operator* thinks that $C$ is anonymized $\mathcal{P}$.

The *utility* of an obfuscated video clip is defined as the probability that the *operator* correctly determines the activities of the occurring persons.

$$utility := Prob[\mathcal{T} = \mathcal{P}.activity] \quad (7.1)$$

The *identity leakage* due to a video clip obfuscated by a given anonymization function is the probability that the *operator* correctly determines the person(s) occurring in the anonymized video clip in the candidate set.

$$identity\ leakage := Prob[C.id = \mathcal{P}.id | C \xleftarrow{choose} operator(\mathbb{V}_{anon}, \mathbb{C})] \quad (7.2)$$

## 7.3 Detecting and Obfuscating Regions of Interest

In practice, perfectly robust segmentation functions for detecting RoIs do not exist. As explained in section 4.2.3, there is an inherent trade-off, which can either be shifted towards reducing false positive detections or towards reducing false negative detections. In other words, there is no useful segmentation function, for which false negative detections can be excluded completely. In this case, a false negative detection means that a RoI, i.e., a person, is missed in one or more frames and thus would appear in the output in an unanonymized fashion. The following procedure has been developed in order to avoid such privacy breaches due to missed RoIs and to obtain robust anonymization. For the segmentation function $F_v(\mathbb{V})$ a background estimator introduced by Monari [MP07] is used. By this means, foreground objects are detected, i.e., the RoI to be anonymized, and a long-term background model of the scene is learned:

1. $(I_{fg}, I_{bg}) \leftarrow BGSubtractor(I)$ : Generate foreground $I_{fg}$ and long-term background image $I_{bg}$ by running the background estimator on $I \in \mathbb{V}$. Each pixel $p \in I_{fg}$ has a value in $\{0,1\}$. Each $p \in I_{bg}$ has a value in $\{0, 1, \ldots, 255\}$. $I_{fg}$, $I_{bg}$ and $I$ have the same size.

2. $I_{RoI} \leftarrow I_{fg} \wedge I$ : Obtain the RoI image $I_{RoI}$ by calculating a mask from $I$ and the foreground image $I_{fg}$.

RoIs are extracted from each frame and obfuscated using an anonymization function $A_v : F_v(\mathbb{V}) \rightarrow \mathbb{V}_{anon}$. Eventually anonymized RoIs are put back onto the long-term background model of the scene.[2] Missed RoIs thus do not appear in the output images at all, which has hardly been recognizable in the obtained video clips. Hence, using this procedure the risk of privacy breaches due to missing RoIs is eliminated.[3]

In this study the image filters *silhouette, pixelization, Gaussian blurring* and *edge detection* are used as anonymization functions $A_v$:

- Reduction to silhouette $A_v^{sil}(F_v(\mathbb{V}))$:
  1. Perform a segmentation on the input images: $(I_{fg}, I_{bg}, I_{RoI}) \leftarrow F_v(\mathbb{V})$
  2. Perform bit-wise inversion on the RoI image: $I'_{fg} \leftarrow \neg I_{fg}$
  3. Obtain the silhouette by removing pixels of the RoI: $I_{anon} \leftarrow I'_{fg} \wedge I_{bg}$
- Pixelization $A_v^{pix}(F_v(\mathbb{V}))$:
  1. Perform a segmentation on the input images: $(I_{fg}, I_{bg}) \leftarrow F_v(\mathbb{V})$
  2. Find contours and bounding rectangles of the RoIs. Each $p \in I_{rec}$ has a value in [0,1]: $I_{rec} \xleftarrow{rectangle} I_{fg}$
  3. Generate rectangle-shaped RoIs: $I_{RoI} \leftarrow I_{rec} \wedge I$
  4. Divide RoIs into blocks and calculate the average pixel value of each block. Assign the average value to all pixels in the corresponding block: $I_{block} \xleftarrow{pixelization} I_{RoI}$
  5. Embed $I_{block}$ into the long-term background image: $I_{anon} \leftarrow \neg I_{rec} \wedge I_{bg} + I_{block}$

[2] Note that depending on the scenario, one could also think about removing the background of the scene from disclosed video data in order to avoid *when* and *where* evidences [Sai+14], which otherwise could also increase the risk of stolen video data to be misused, e.g., for blackmailing.

[3] Note that a similar procedure can be used if RoIs are obtained via face detection, pedestrian detection, etc. Background estimation is then only used for learning the long-term background model of the scene.

- Blurring $A_v^{blr}(F_v(\mathbb{V}))$:
  1. Perform a segmentation on the input images:
     $(I_{fg}, I_{bg}, I_{RoI}) \leftarrow F_v(\mathbb{V})$
  2. Blur the RoI by applying a Gaussian filter: $I_{blur} \xleftarrow{Gaussian} I_{RoI}$
  3. Embed $I_{blur}$ into the long-term background image:
     $I_{anon} \leftarrow \neg I_{fg} \wedge I_{bg} + I_{blur}$
- Edge detection $A_v^{edg}(F_v(\mathbb{V}))$:
  1. Perform a segmentation on the input images:
     $(I_{fg}, I_{bg}, I_{RoI}) \leftarrow F_v(\mathbb{V})$
  2. Obtain edges of the RoIs by applying a Sobel filter on $I_{RoI}$:
     $I_{edge} \xleftarrow{Sobel} I_{RoI}$
  3. Embed $I_{edge}$ into the long-term background image:
     $I_{anon} \leftarrow \neg I_{fg} \wedge I_{bg} + I_{edge}$

A gray-scale version $A_v^{gblr}$ of $A_v^{blr}$ has also been employed, i.e., RoIs are reduced to gray-scale before applying the Gaussian filter. Figure 7.1 shows example images of the particular anonymization functions employed for this user study. It also seems natural to combine such operations, e.g., by applying the silhouette function first and then employ Gaussian blurring afterwards in order to erase smaller structures at the borders of silhouettes, which otherwise may reveal visual information about clothes and/or body shapes of persons. This user study, however, aims to investigate the effects of each anonymization function separately so as to lay the foundations for more sophisticated privacy filters to be developed in the future.

**Figure 7.1:** Anonymization functions: original, silhouette, pixelization, gray-scale blurring, blurring, edge detection

## 7.4 Scenarios

The PEViD data set [KE13] employed for this user study is to date the only public data set for visual privacy tasks. It includes the activities *dropping a bag*, *fighting*, *stealing*, and *walking*. The scenarios for this study, i.e., tuples of $(video\,clip, anonymization\,function)$ as well as the parameters of the particular anonymization functions, were obtained in a small pre-study.

To obtain a representative sample for the parameter space of $anonymization\ functions \times activities \times video\,clips$ one either needs a large number of video clips so as to be able to show $|anonymization\ functions| \cdot |activities|$ to every participant (which would also occupy participants for a long time), or a large number of participants so as to be able to only show $|anonymization\,functions|$ video clips to each participant. As the scale of responses to this user study was unclear, a moderate number of eight scenarios has been used (cf. figures 7.2 to 7.9), which were given to each participant: Three video clips of dropping a bag were obfuscated with the silhouette, gray-scale blurring, and color blurring functions. Three video clips of fighting were obfuscated with the pixelization, edge detection, and color blurring functions. Two video clips of stealing were obfuscated with the edge detection and color blurring functions. The actual meta data concerning each scenario are given in tables 7.1 to 7.8. The video clips $\mathbb{V}_4$ and $\mathbb{V}_6$ were used twice, i.e., using pixelization and color blurring respectively edge detection and and color blurring functions.[4] The fact that the blurring function is overrepresented in these scenarios is due to the prior expectation that it would deliver the most promising trade-off between privacy protection and utility. The activity set $\mathbb{T}$ contains *dropping a bag*, *fighting*, and *stealing* (*walking* video clips were not used). For the candidate set $\mathbb{C}$, the person(s) appearing in the given video clip is/are complemented with randomly chosen persons from the data set so as to obtain ten candidates in total. All candidates are presented as whole-body images.

[4] Participants were shown the video clips obfuscated with the stronger privacy filter first (pixelization/edge detection), whereby identity leakage was expected to be very low according to the pre-study. Gaussian blurring was then used a few rounds later.

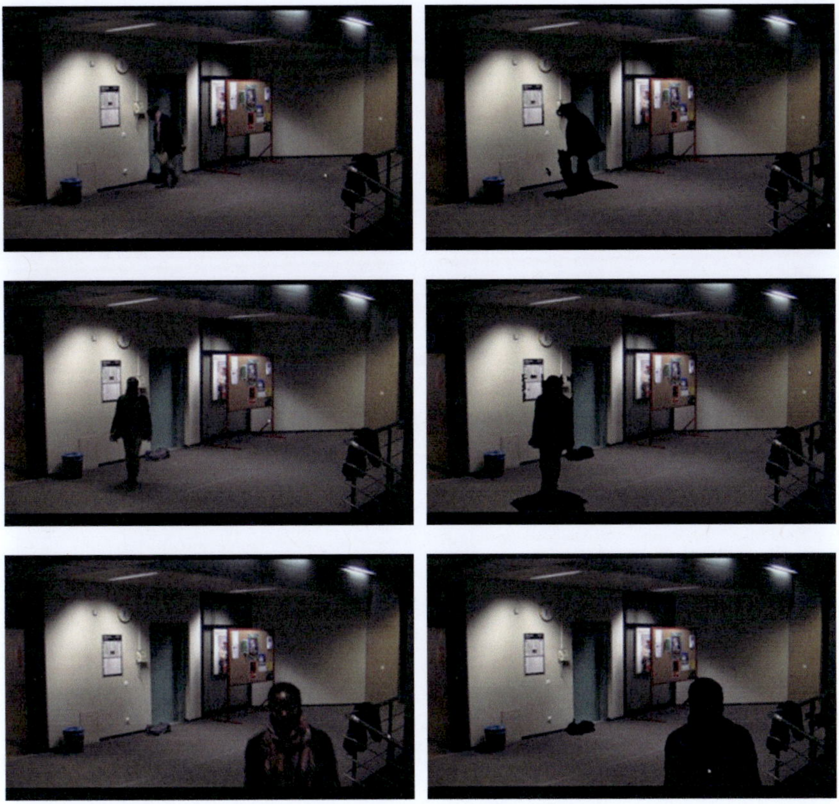

**Figure 7.2:** Original and anonymized video clip of scenario 1

| Vid. | Anon. | Activity | $\mathcal{P}.id$ | Gen. | Hair | Ethnicity | Age |
|---|---|---|---|---|---|---|---|
| $\mathbb{V}_1$ | $A_v^{sil}$ | dropping a bag | 3 | f | black | African | 20–40 |

**Table 7.1:** Setting of scenario 1

**Figure 7.3:** Original and anonymized video clip of scenario 2

| **Vid.** | **Anon.** | **Activity** | $\mathcal{P}.id$ | **Gen.** | **Hair** | **Ethnicity** | **Age** |
|---|---|---|---|---|---|---|---|
| $\mathbb{V}_4$ | $A_v^{pix}$ | fighting | 4 | m | black | European | 20–40 |
| | | | 7 | f | black | Asian | 20–40 |

**Table 7.2:** Setting of scenario 2

**Figure 7.4:** Original and anonymized video clip of scenario 3

| Vid. | Anon. | Activity | $\mathcal{P}.id$ | Gen. | Hair | Ethnicity | Age |
|---|---|---|---|---|---|---|---|
| $\mathbb{V}_6$ | $A_v^{edg}$ | stealing | 8 | f | brown | European | 20–40 |
| | | | 9 | m | black | European | 20–40 |

**Table 7.3:** Setting of scenario 3

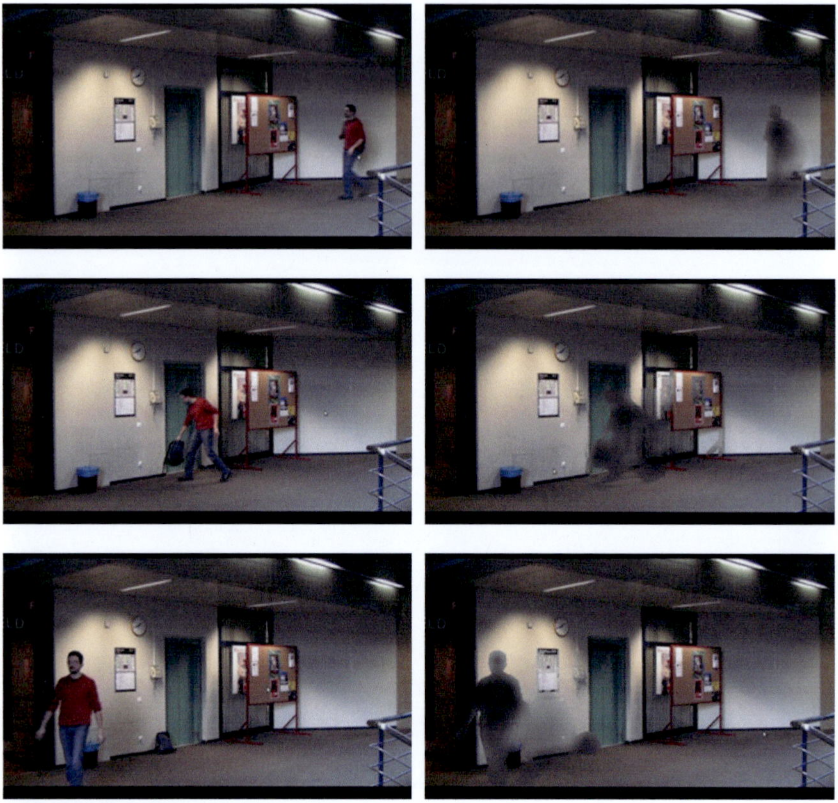

**Figure 7.5:** Original and anonymized video clip of scenario 4

| Vid. | Anon. | Activity | $\mathcal{P}.id$ | Gen. | Hair | Ethnicity | Age |
|---|---|---|---|---|---|---|---|
| $\mathbb{V}_2$ | $A_v^{gblr}$ | dropping a bag | 1 | m | brown | European | 20–40 |

**Table 7.4:** Setting of scenario 4

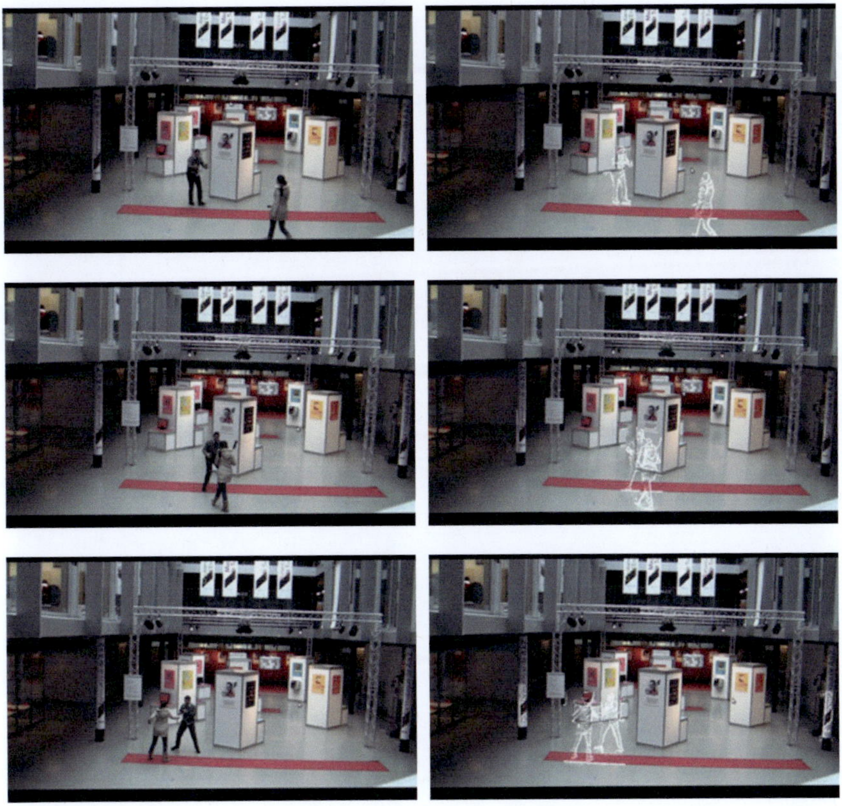

**Figure 7.6:** Original and anonymized video clip of scenario 5

| Vid. | Anon. | Activity | $\mathcal{P}.id$ | Gen. | Hair | Ethnicity | Age |
|---|---|---|---|---|---|---|---|
| $\mathbb{V}_5$ | $A_v^{edg}$ | fighting | 5 | m | black | European | 40–60 |
| | | | 6 | f | brown | European | 20–40 |

**Table 7.5:** Setting of scenario 5

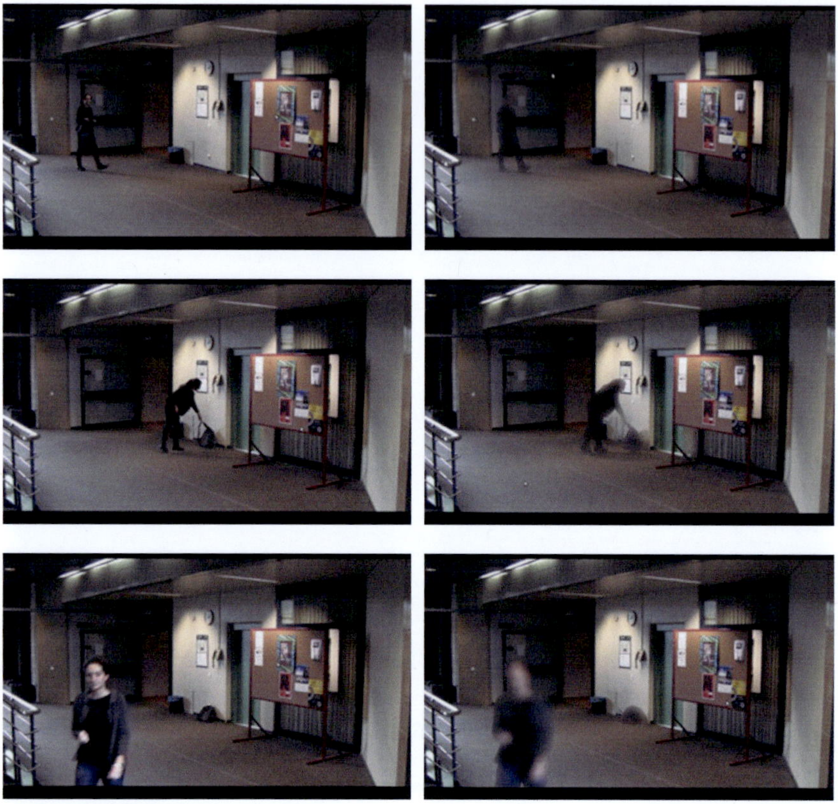

**Figure 7.7:** Original and anonymized video clip of scenario 6

| Vid. | Anon. | Activity | $\mathcal{P}.id$ | Gen. | Hair | Ethnicity | Age |
|---|---|---|---|---|---|---|---|
| $\mathbb{V}_3$ | $A_v^{blr}$ | dropping a bag | 2 | f | brown | European | 20–40 |

**Table 7.6:** Setting of scenario 6

**Figure 7.8:** Original and anonymized video clip of scenario 7

| Vid. | Anon. | Activity | $\mathcal{P}.id$ | Gen. | Hair | Ethnicity | Age |
|---|---|---|---|---|---|---|---|
| $\mathbb{V}_6$ | $A_v^{blr}$ | stealing | 8 | f | blond | European | 20–40 |
| | | | 9 | m | black | European | 20–40 |

**Table 7.7:** Setting of scenario 7

**Figure 7.9:** Original and anonymized video clip of scenario 8

| Vid. | Anon. | Activity | $\mathcal{P}.id$ | Gen. | Hair | Ethnicity | Age |
|---|---|---|---|---|---|---|---|
| $\mathbb{V}_4$ | $A_v^{blr}$ | fighting | 4 | m | black | European | 20–40 |
| | | | 7 | f | black | Asian | 20–40 |

**Table 7.8:** Setting of scenario 8

## 7.5 Questionnaire

For this user study a questionnaire Q has been developed and published as an online survey based on the platform LimeSurvey.[5] The participants had to answer the following questions for each anonymized video clip:

1. *What do you think the person(s) in the video clip is/are doing?* [stealing, walking, dropping something, fighting, falling down, I don't know]
   This single choice question targets the activity taking place in the anonymized video clip. Giving predefined options may seem counter-intuitive, however, a smart video surveillance system will also tell the operator *why* a certain scene demands attention. The utility of an anonymized video clip is calculated from the answers to this question.

2. *What is the gender of the person(s) appearing in the video clip?* [male, female, I don't know]

3. *What is the hair color of the person(s) appearing in the video clip?* [blond, brown, red, black, white, bright, dark, I don't know]

4. *What is the ethnicity of the person(s) appearing in the video clip?* [African, Asian, European, I don't know]

5. *What is the age of the person(s) appearing in the video clip?* [<20, 20-40, 40-60, >60]
   These four single choice questions ask about features of the person(s) in the video clip.

6. *Which candidate(s) is/are the person(s) appearing in the video clip?* [single selection from the candidate set, I don't know]
   The participants had to choose the person shown in the anonymized video clip from a candidate set. Identity leakage for a scenario is (partially) calculated based on the answers to this question (cf. section 7.6).

[5] https://www.limesurvey.org

7. *Why are you sure about this/these candidate(s)?* [multiple selections from face, gender, body shape, hair color, age, gait, body size, clothes, or rough guess]
   This multiple choice question aims to explore which features the participants used for identifying a person under a given anonymization function. This questions is only asked if the participant did *not* select *I don't know* when asked to choose a candidate/candidates.

8. *Which candidates are NOT the person(s) appearing in the video clip?* [multiple selections from the candidate set, I don't know]
   If question 6 was answered with *I don't know*, participants were asked to exclude candidates, if possible. After excluding some candidates a participant can identify the person in the video clip with higher probability in the remaining candidate set. This fact is also considered when calculating identity leakage for a scenario (cf. section 7.6).

9. *Why are you sure these candidates are not the person(s) appearing in the video clip?* [multiple selections from face, gender, body shape, hair color, age, gait, body size, clothes, or rough guess]
   This question is similar to question 7, but is only asked if the participant excluded at least one candidate.

10. *Do you think this anonymization function is suitable for protecting the privacy of the person(s) shown in the video clip?* [1 (absolutely not suitable), ..., 5 (absolutely suitable)]
    These subjective ratings indicate the acceptance of an anonymization function from the perspective of observed people.

11. *How straining is working with the anonymization function used on this video clip?* [1 (totally straining), ..., 5 (not straining at all)]
    Participants rate the perceived video quality for the given anonymization function, which is crucial for the acceptance among operators of video surveillance systems.

Participants had to answer 88 questions in total, which took them between 30 and 45 minutes.

## 7.6 Measuring Utility and Privacy

Referring to the model introduced in section 7.2, the *utility* of an anonymized video clip is defined as the probability of an operator to recognize the activity of the person(s) in the video clip, i.e., to answer question 1 correctly. When calculating the *utility* for a scenario the answers of all participants are aggregated, i.e., all participants together are treated as one operator whose working capability is the arithmetic average of the working capabilities of all participants. The utility for one participant $u_P$ in a scenario is defined as:

$$u_P = \begin{cases} 1 & \text{if P answers question 1 correctly} \\ 0 & \text{otherwise} \end{cases} \tag{7.3}$$

The utility $u$ of an anonymized video clip is accordingly defined as:

$$u = \frac{1}{N} \sum_{i=1}^{N} u_{P_i} \quad \text{where } N \text{ is the number of participants} \tag{7.4}$$

Privacy is measured in terms of identity leakage of an anonymized video clip. When defining identity leakage for one participant $l_P$ in a scenario, the answers to questions 6 and 8 are considered. If the participant was able to reduce the candidate set without excluding the correct candidate, the identity leakage of the anonymized video clip is defined as the probability of a random guess from the reduced candidate set $\mathbb{C}_{reduced}$:

$$l_P = \begin{cases} 1 & \text{if P answers question 6 correctly} \\ \frac{1}{\|\mathbb{C}_{reduced}\|} & \text{if P does not exclude the right candidate in question 8} \\ 0 & \text{otherwise} \end{cases} \tag{7.5}$$

The identity leakage for an anonymized video $l$ is again defined as the arithmetic average of identity leakage over all participants:

$$l = \frac{1}{N}\sum_{i=1}^{N} l_{P_i} \quad \text{where } N \text{ is the number of participants} \tag{7.6}$$

## 7.7 Results

The following paragraphs introduce the results that were obtained from 103 full responses to the online survey. Around the same number of participants did not complete the questionnaire.

### 7.7.1 Evidences and Features

The effects of anonymization functions on the evidences *gender, hair color, ethnicity,* and *age* have been clustered into the categories *erasure (ERS), strong reduction (RED+), reduction (RED), preservation (PRS),* and *change (CHG)* according to the relative frequency of these evidences to be recognized correctly by the participants:

$$\mathcal{E}_{anon} = \begin{cases} ERS & P_{\text{TRUE}} < 0.2 \\ RED+ & 0.2 \leq P_{\text{TRUE}} < 0.5 \\ RED & 0.5 \leq P_{\text{TRUE}} < 0.8 \\ PRS & P_{\text{TRUE}} \geq 0.8 \\ CHG & P_{\text{TRUE}} \leq P_{\text{FALSE}} \end{cases} \tag{7.7}$$

Table 7.9 summarizes the effects of anonymization functions on evidences of individuals' appearance. The *silhouette* and *pixelization* functions obfuscate most evidences. The *edge detection* and *gray blurring* functions erase color information and strongly obfuscate *ethnicity.* In comparison with other anonymization functions, *color blurring* preserves more information of individuals' appearance.

| | $\mathcal{E}_{sil}$ | $\mathcal{E}_{pix}$ | $\mathcal{E}_{edg}$ | $\mathcal{E}_{gblr}$ | $\mathcal{E}_{blr}$ |
|---|---|---|---|---|---|
| *Gender* | RED | RED+/CHG | PRS | PRS | PRS |
| *Hair color* | ERS | RED+ | ERS | ERS | RED |
| *Ethnicity* | ERS | ERS | RED+ | RED+ | RED |
| *Age* | RED | RED | PRS | PRS | PRS |

**Table 7.9:** Effects of anonymization functions on evidences

**Gender.** Figure 7.10 shows the probabilities for recognizing obfuscated persons' gender. The silhouette function reduced the *gender* evidence in scenario 1. In scenario 2 the pixelization function slightly reduced the gender evidence of one person and strongly changed the gender evidence of the other. In all other scenarios the gender evidences are preserved.

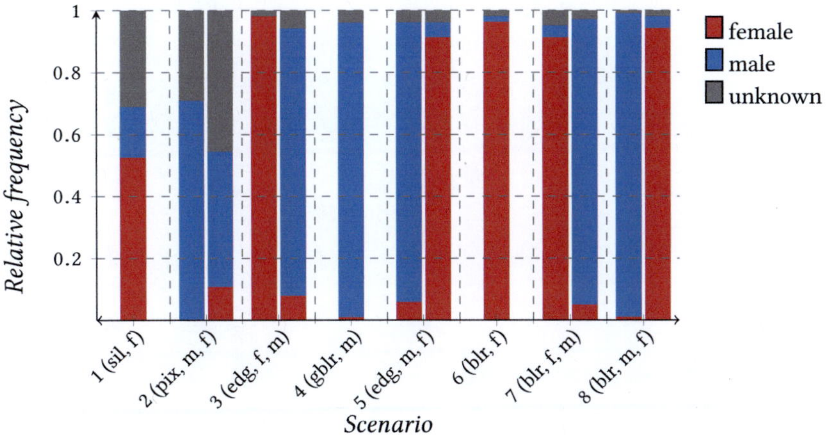


**Figure 7.10:** Evidences on the gender of anonymized persons

**Hair Color.** The probabilities for recognizing anonymized persons' hair color are depicted in figure 7.11. In scenarios 1, 4, and 5 hair color evidences are clearly erased. In scenario 2 most of the participants were not able to recognize hair color, while about 20% of the participants could see that the persons in the video clip have dark hair. Therefore the evidences are not completely erased but strongly reduced. In scenario 3 the edge detection function does not reveal color information of the RoI. However, about 40% of participants selected a hair color for the persons shown in the video clip. In the remaining three scenarios persons were anonymized with the blurring filter on colored RoIs. In scenario 6 more than 40% of the participants accurately recognized the hair color, i.e., *brown*, and about 20% of the participants roughly recognized the hair color as *dark* (both recognitions are correct). The evidence is only slightly reduced. In scenarios 7 and 8 the evidence is also reduced, since about 40% – 50% of the participants recognized the hair color of the persons in the video correctly.

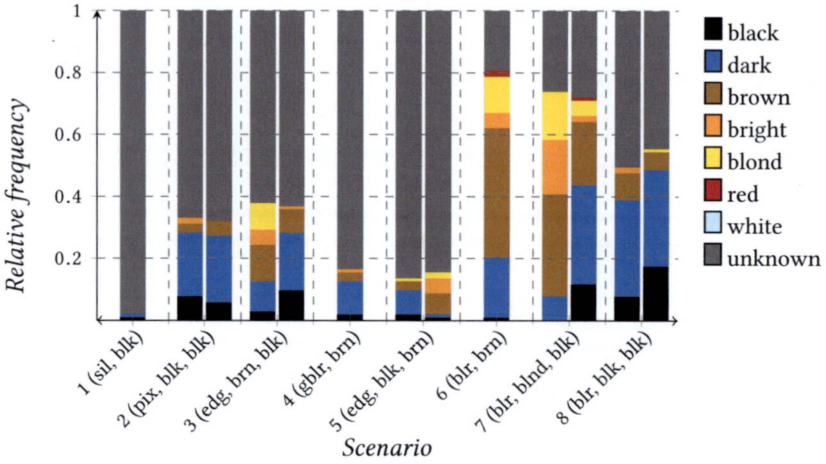


**Figure 7.11:** Evidences on the hair color of anonymized persons

**Ethnicity.** Figure 7.12 shows the probabilities to recognize anonymized persons' ethnicities. In scenarios 1 and 2 the ethnicity evidences are erased, in all other scenarios they are reduced.

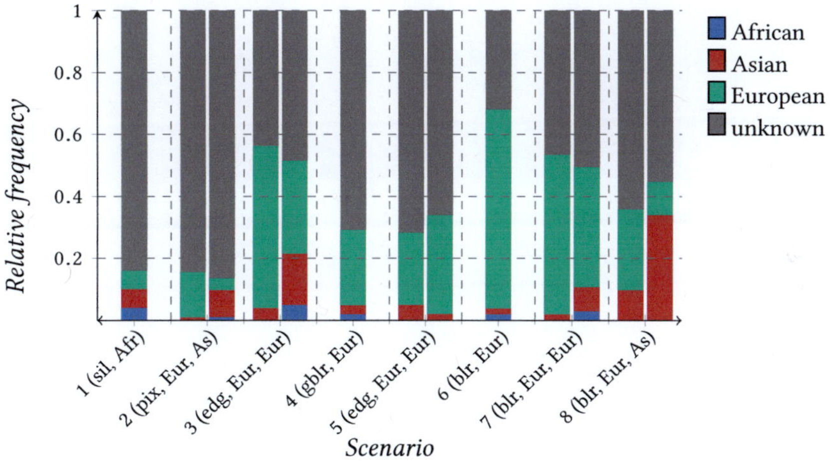


**Figure 7.12:** Evidences on the ethnicity of anonymized persons

**Age.** The probabilities to recognize anonymized persons' age are depicted in figure 7.13. In all scenarios persons are mostly thought to be between 20 and 40 years old, which is correct in almost all cases. Only in scenarios 1 and 2 about 30% to 40% of participants were not able to recognize the age of persons. Like gender and ethnicity, age is an implicit evidence which is deduced from explicit evidences such as face, gait or body shape. The probabilities $P_{\text{unknown}}$ for these three evidences in scenario 1 and 2 are considerably higher than in other scenarios. This indicates that the silhouette and pixelization functions erase more explicit evidences than other functions.

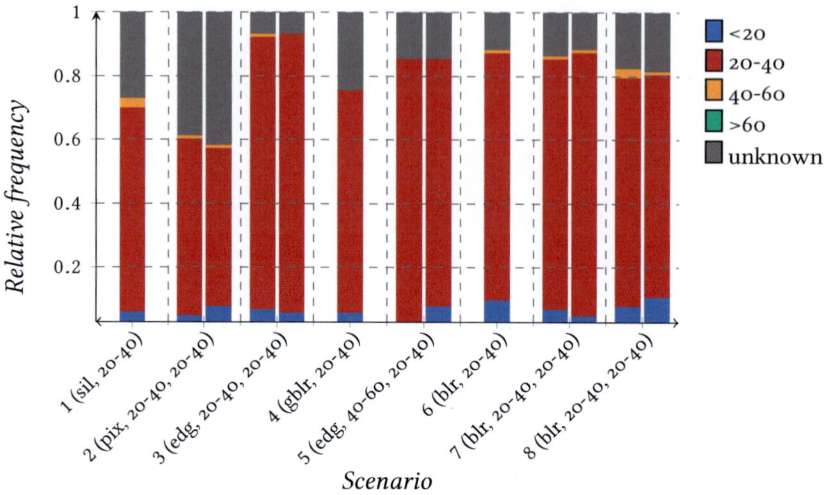


**Figure 7.13:** Evidences on the age of anonymized persons

### 7.7.2 Utility and Identity Leakage

Results for utility and identity leakage (cf. Eq. (7.4) and (7.6)) for each scenario are shown in table 7.10 and in figure 7.14. Two values for identity leakage given for a scenario refer to the first and the second person appearing in the scene. It can be observed that the utility is higher than 90% for all scenarios, while identity leakage differs considerably. Participants could easily distinguish the activities. In scenarios 2 and 8 the same video [6] clip has been anonymized with pixelization and with blurring of colored RoIs. For scenario 8, utility is about 5% higher, however, on the cost of considerably higher identity leakage compared to scenario 2. In scenarios 3 and 7 the same video clip [6] has been anonymized with edge detection and with blurring of colored RoIs. While the utility is almost the same for both anonymization functions, identity leakage is again considerably higher in the blurring scenario.

[6] Participants were shown the video clips obfuscated with the stronger privacy filter first (pixelization/edge detection), whereby identity leakage was expected to be very low according to the pre-study. Gaussian blurring was then used a few rounds later.

| Scenario | Video | Anon. | Utility | Person | Id. Leakage |
|---|---|---|---|---|---|
| 1 | $\mathbb{V}_1$ | $A_v^{sil}$ | 0.9902 | $P_1$ | 0.31 |
| 2 | $\mathbb{V}_4$ | $A_v^{pix}$ | 0.9029 | $P_1$ | 0.30 |
| | | | | $P_2$ | 0.17 |
| 3 | $\mathbb{V}_6$ | $A_v^{edg}$ | 0.9902 | $P_1$ | 0.05 |
| | | | | $P_2$ | 0.06 |
| 4 | $\mathbb{V}_2$ | $A_v^{gblr}$ | 0.9902 | $P_1$ | 0.33 |
| 5 | $\mathbb{V}_5$ | $A_v^{edg}$ | 0.9320 | $P_1$ | 0.35 |
| | | | | $P_2$ | 0.57 |
| 6 | $\mathbb{V}_3$ | $A_v^{blr}$ | 1.0000 | $P_1$ | 0.74 |
| 7 | $\mathbb{V}_6$ | $A_v^{blr}$ | 0.9902 | $P_1$ | 0.37 |
| | | | | $P_2$ | 0.17 |
| 8 | $\mathbb{V}_4$ | $A_v^{blr}$ | 0.9514 | $P_1$ | 0.51 |
| | | | | $P_2$ | 0.71 |

**Table 7.10:** Utility and identity leakage

Edge detection erases all color evidences, while preserving the outline of face, body shape, and clothes. Color blurring only reduces evidences about color, which mainly works for smaller structures of clothes, whereas it preserves the body shape evidence. In comparison, pixelization leads to the strongest reduction of the body shape evidence. Therefore it can be assumed that the body shape was the most helpful evidence for recognizing activities, since the body shape over time reveals a person's movements. This is supported in particular by the high utility obtained in scenario 1, where the silhouette function erased all explicit evidences but body shape. Regarding identity leakage, persons anonymized with the blurring function on colored RoIs were easier to recognize than persons anonymized with silhouette, pixelization, and blurring on gray-scale RoIs. As already discussed, blurring on colored RoIs preserves more evidences than the other anonymization functions that were used.

Generally speaking, these results do not support the hypothesis of a trade-off relationship between privacy in terms of identity leakage and utility in terms of recognizing activities. A likely reason for this observation is that the activities in this data set are rather easy to recognize. Future works need to study whether these findings can be generalized to realistic video surveillance scenarios where operators have to assess more complex situations.

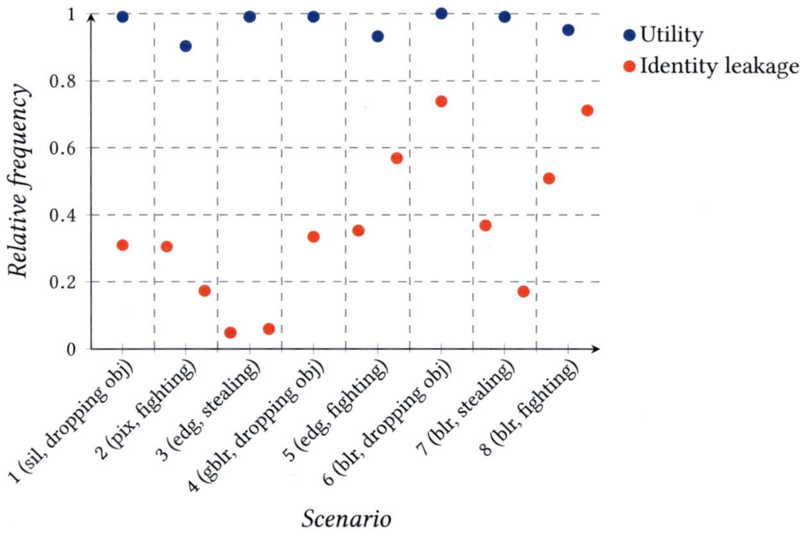


**Figure 7.14:** Utility and identity leakage

### 7.7.3 Subjective Evaluation

In questions 10 and 11 participants were asked to give subjective ratings of the anonymized video clips regarding perceived privacy protection as well as perceived image quality. Figure 7.15 compares the subjective ratings to the experimental results (dots) that were obtained for utility and for identity leakage. The subjective ratings indeed suggest a trade-off relationship between privacy protection and video quality. The silhouette and the pixelization function (scenarios 1 and 2) are perceived better at protecting privacy while being more straining to work with. Conversely, edge detection and color blurring (scenarios 3, 5, 6, 7, and 8) seem to result in better image quality, but are considered less suitable for protecting privacy by the participants.

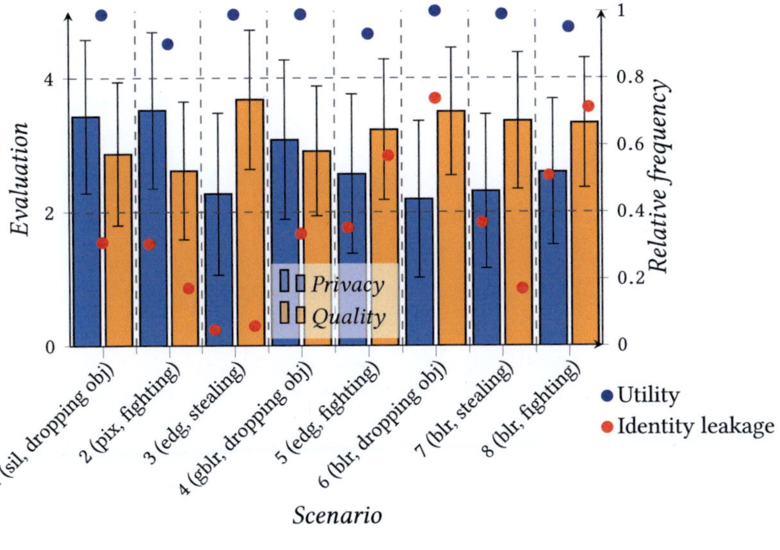


**Figure 7.15:** Subjective evaluation of privacy protection and perceptual video quality

When comparing these observations with the experimental results, the ratings for perceived image quality do not correspond to the statistics for utility: Subjectively lower image quality does not necessarily result in a lower utility of the anonymized video clips, i.e., operators might be able to get used to working with any of the anonymization functions. Perceived privacy protection also does not align too well with the experimental results for identity leakage: The edge detection scenarios 3 and 5 exhibit very low values for identity leakage even though the participants do not consider edge detection to perform very well in terms of privacy protection.

### 7.7.4 Insights on Identification

In order to understand the effects of different anonymization functions and to learn how participants identified the persons in the videos, the relationships between evidences and identity leakage have to be analyzed. For this, the answers to question 7 about evidences that have been used for identification are grouped according to whether or not participants selected the correct candidate in question 6. The positive x-axis of figure 7.16 shows the evidences employed by participants who identified the person(s) in the video clip correctly, the negative x-axis shows the evidences on which false identifications were based. The y-axis indicates the frequencies of the evidences to be used. It can be observed that *clothes*, *body shape*, and *gender* are said to be the most helpful evidences for identification. Yet these are also the most important evidences for false identifications. From the distribution across the scenarios it can be observed that these evidences led to false identifications in scenarios 1, 2, 3, and 7 and to correct identifications in scenarios 5, 6, and 8.

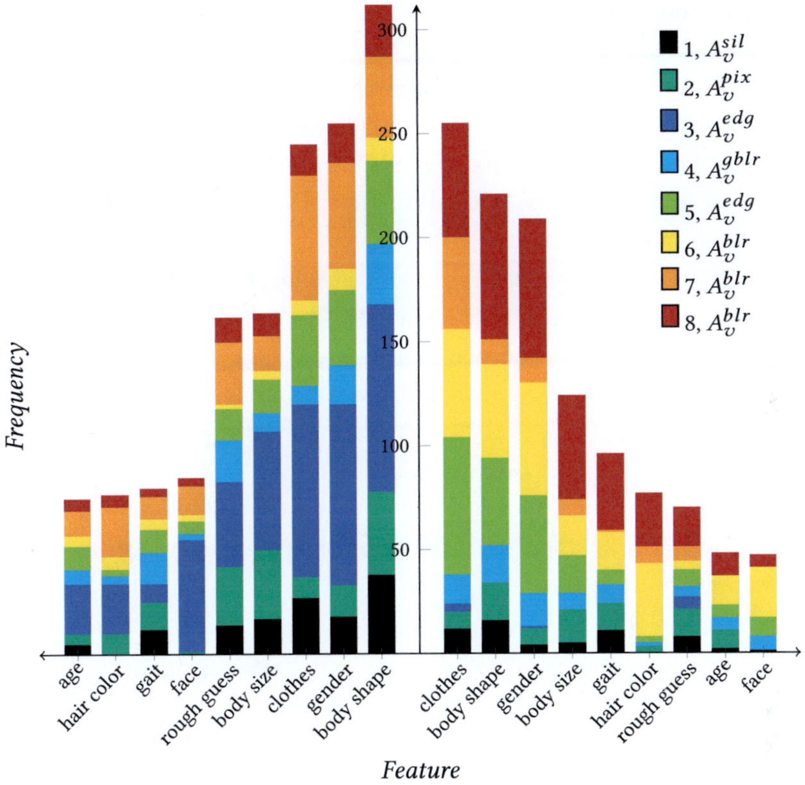


**Figure 7.16:** This plot shows the features used for identification. Answers of participants who were not able to identify the anonymized person(s) in the candidate set are shown on the negative x-axis, answers of participants who correctly identified the anonymized person(s) are depicted on the positive x-axis.

**Implicit Evidences and Identification.** Since gender is an implicit evidence, which is deduced from explicit evidences like face, body shape, or gait, and does not reveal any distinctive information of appearance, the observation that gender was said to be an important factor for identifying persons was not necessarily expected. As the participants have also been asked directly about the gender of the person(s) in the anonymized video clips in question 2, this observation can be double-checked.

If the gender evidence is helpful for identification, then participants recognizing gender correctly should be able to identify the anonymized person correctly with higher probability in question 6. $P(Id.\ leak.\mid gender)$, i.e., identity leakage under the condition of recognizing gender correctly is calculated as:

$$P(Id.\ leak.\mid gender) := \frac{P(Q2 \cap Q6)}{P(Q2)} \tag{7.8}$$

Figure 7.17 compares the results for $P(Id.\ leak.\mid gender)$ with the general results for identity leakage.

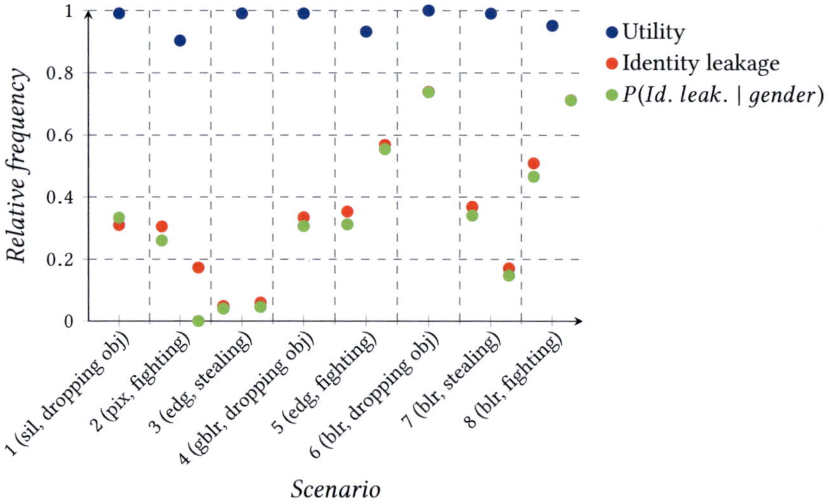


**Figure 7.17:** Probability of identification under gender recognition

It shows that $P(Id.\ leak.\mid gender)$ is not higher than identity leakage. Participants who recognized the gender correctly were not better at identifying the anonymized person than general participants. They do not seem to recognize the anonymized person's gender at first, and then select a candidate based on the gender evidence. Even though recognizing gender obviously helps to reduce the candidate set, it does not necessarily help with the final decision for particular candidates.

**Explicit Evidences and Identification.** Hair color is the only explicit evidence about which the participants have been asked directly (cf. question 3), and which can be compared to the findings about the gender evidence in order to explain the role of explicit evidences. Even though hair color was not among the most helpful evidences for identification named by the participants (cf. figure 7.16), it is interesting to look into $P(Id.\ leak.\mid hair\ cl.)$, i.e., identity leakage under the condition of recognizing hair color correctly:

$$P(Id.\ leak.\mid hair\ cl.) := \frac{P(Q3 \cap Q6)}{P(Q3)} \tag{7.9}$$

As color information is erased by all other anonymization functions, $P(Id.\ leak.\mid hair\ cl.)$ is only calculated for scenarios anonymized with blurring on colored and gray-scale RoIs. Figure 7.18 compares the results for $P(Id.\ leak.\mid hair\ cl.)$ with general identity leakage for these scenarios. It can be observed that $P(Id.\ leak.\mid hair\ cl.)$ is slightly higher than identity leakage in scenarios 6 and 7 and clearly higher in scenarios 4 and 8. Participants who correctly recognized the hair color were a little bit better at identifying the anonymized persons than the participants of the study in general.

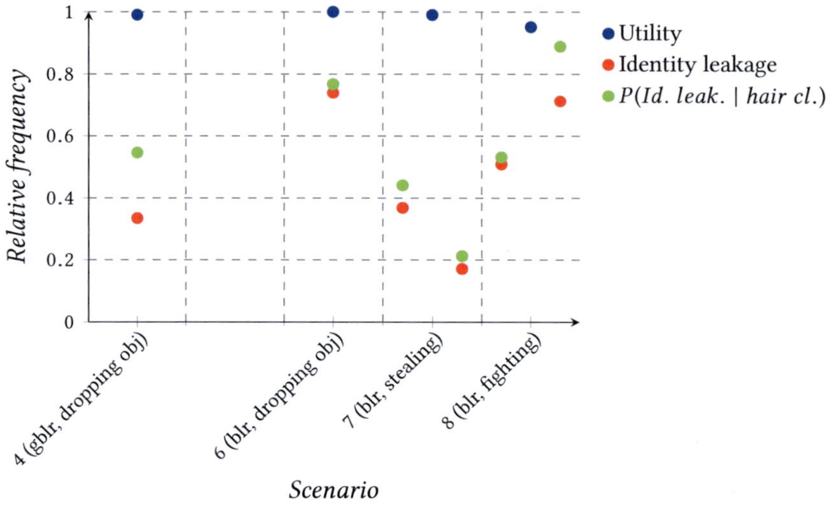


**Figure 7.18:** Probability of identification under hair color recognition

## 7.8 Conclusions and Outlook

Acceptable privacy protection can be achieved with most of the anonymization functions that have been evaluated. The stronger privacy filters such as the silhouette function and the pixelization function are also capable to erase evidence concerning observed individuals' ethnicity and thus protect against racial discrimination by operators. Combinations of the anonymization functions may further improve privacy protection without reducing the utility of video data for activity or situation recognition, e.g., by applying the silhouette function first and then employ Gaussian blurring afterwards in order to erase smaller structures at the borders of silhouettes, which otherwise may reveal visual information about clothes and/or body shapes of persons. Disclosing evidences concerning color and outline of a person as with color blurring leads to higher identity leakage. For the small set of activities provided in the PEViD data set the obtained results do not support the common hypothesis of a trade-off relationship between utility and privacy of video data, which indicates that

**TS-2** can indeed be accomplished, i.e., that activity recognition on obfuscated video data may indeed be possible for operators. Even in scenarios with a low rating of perceived image quality, a high utility has been observed, while at the same time the identities of observed individuals were protected with high probability. Thus, operators may be able to adapt to working with stronger anonymization functions such as the pixelization function. Empirically, explicit evidences play the key role for identification, namely body shape and clothes, even though the participants of the study considered gender as the second most important factor.

The aforementioned observations have been made under the assumption that operators, i.e., the participants of the user study, do not have context knowledge about the persons appearing in the obfuscated video clips (cf. section 7.2.2 and also section 5.7.1). In daily practice of video surveillance measures this assumption does not hold in any case. If, for instance, video surveillance is employed on premises and in buildings of a company, it must be assumed that operators of such systems indeed know at least a certain fraction of the people captured by the cameras. With regard to video surveillance measures in publicly accessible spaces, identity leakage due to operators' context knowledge is less likely. However, while it seems negligible on urban squares, it is not when considering shops or boutiques and their regular customers.

The presented user study experienced an encouragingly large response of volunteer participants. Further studies in this subject could thus count on this broad support and give different combinations of video clips and privacy filters to each participant so as to obtain a better data basis for comparing anonymization functions. In this regard the presented user study was large, but not large enough. Another issue to be stressed is that further data sets are required for investigations of this kind. More persons appearing in longer video clips and being involved in more complex activities or situations may allow to obtain a more profound understanding of the effects of anonymization functions on the utility of video data, particularly in the application domain of video surveillance. To sum up, further investigation is needed in order to study whether the findings of this work can be generalized to realistic video surveillance scenarios where operators have to assess more complex situations. Future work may also want to compare results of user studies with recent approaches towards objectively measuring the privacy level of obfuscated video data in terms of appearance similarity and the utility level in terms of structural similarity with the original images [NF15].

# 8 Evaluation of Utility

As the study on anonymization functions presented in the previous chapter already indicated, it is hardly possible to validate the utility of video surveillance technology under laboratory conditions. A fair number of datasets is available for evaluating the accuracy and the robustness of tracking algorithms and also for benchmarking activity recognition, but even these are mainly self-made video clips with amateur actors. When aiming at a proof of concept of an entire system design as introduced in this research, these datasets are only suitable to a limited extent. To get an indication on whether or not a system operating according to the concept of situation-dependent smart video surveillance workflows (cf. section 4.4) may be usable in practice, an experiment has been set up based on three clips from the Soft-Biometric in Surveillance (SoBiS) dataset [Sch14]. The SoBiS dataset has been recorded in the premises of Fraunhofer IOSB and contains video data for evaluating video analysis algorithms for person detection, person tracking, person re-identification, as well as soft-biometric attribute recognition. It includes scenes of persons leaving behind and picking up/stealing luggage objects, which serve as "incidents" to be handled by the participants of an application study.

This study was conducted with 31 employees from Fraunhofer IOSB without prior working experience with video surveillance. For comparison, participants were asked to handle such incidents using a conventional video surveillance system, the smart video surveillance system NEST [MVK08; Bau+08; MRV10] without any privacy-preserving mechanisms in place, and the extended NEST system operating according to the situation-dependent smart video surveillance workflow introduced in section 5.2. In the following, the latter system is denoted as *Usage Control for Network Enabled Surveillance and Tracking (UC4NEST)*. The main goal of the experiments was to find out to what extent the different operating modes of a situation-dependent smart video surveillance workflow actually detain users when handling incidents.

## 8.1 Scenario: Handling Incidents Concerning Abandoned Objects

As mentioned above, the experiments conducted in this evaluation were based on video clips of people leaving behind and picking up luggage. The scene was shown to the participants from the perspectives of two cameras, which overlap to some extent (cf. figure 8.1).

**Figure 8.1:** Scene of the incidents to be handled by the participants

| | **Video clip 1** | **Video clip 2** | **Video clip 3** |
|---|---|---|---|
| *Activity* | object dropped & stolen | object dropped & picked up | object dropped & picked up |
| *Incident duration* | 21s | 15s | 24s |

**Table 8.1:** Video clips used in the experiments

Three video clips were chosen for the experiments. They last 2–3 minutes and involve at least six people moving around in the area, one of whom leaves behind a luggage object. In two video clips, the luggage object is picked up by its owner after a short time; in the third one, it is stolen, i.e., picked up by someone who flees with the object. The people appearing in the video clips were essentially the same throughout all video clips.

Participants were asked to handle such incidents in terms of deciding whether or not a luggage object has been abandoned by its owner (assessment), and in terms of determining the owner of the luggage object and also the person picking it up/stealing it later on (investigation), i.e., by this means each incident has a well-defined end. For this purpose, a screenshot control has been integrated into the HMI, since timestamps of screenshots are particularly helpful in order to measure *assessment times* and *investigation times* for the incidents given to the participants. The first screenshot indicates that the participants were sure that the luggage object has been left behind. The second screenshot indicates that the investigation of the incident is completed. In terms of utility, assessment times and investigation times give an indication of whether situation assessment and incident handling becomes more difficult or more tedious due to a given system design. In the real practice of smart video surveillance, the procedure of taking screenshots as evidence could also be substituted by means of activating a biometric face recognition algorithm as described in section 5.2. Note that false alerts and actually critical incidents did not require different actions of the participants, since this kind of differentiation could not be expected on the basis of the self-made video clips being used.

Each participant was asked to handle three incidents successively, whereby the sequence of the particular video clips was permuted each time. Due to its easier handling participants began the experiment using the conventional video surveillance system. For the second video clip they had to work with the smart video surveillance system NEST without any privacy-preserving mechanisms in place. Eventually participants used the UC4NEST system operating according to the situation-dependent smart video surveillance workflow introduced in section 5.2. These particular system designs were expected to be used as explained in the following.

**Conventional Video Surveillance.** The HMI shows the live video streams of the two cameras (cf figure 8.2). It is controlled via a touch screen and provides controls for freezing the current images and for taking screenshots. Furthermore, it offers a timeline control for accessing recorded video data and a control for switching back to the live streams. Participants observe the video streams and are asked to pay attention to objects that are left behind. As soon as they think that an object is abandoned, they rewind the video to the time when the luggage object has been left behind and determine its owner (i.e., participants access recorded video data). Then they switch back to the live video streams. If the object is still there, they further observe the scene until the object is picked up by again, either by its owner or by someone else. Participants were instructed to take a screenshot of the person picking up the luggage object in any case. (In practice, an operator would at some point notify mobile security personnel or the police to look after the object.) In case the object is already gone, participants have to rewind the video once more in order to determine the person who picked up the object.

**Figure 8.2:** Conventional surveillance system

**Smart Video Surveillance.** When using the smart video surveillance system NEST, the HMI additionally shows an overview map of the observed area, on which the positions of persons detected by video analysis are visualized using pictographs (cf. figure 8.3). Video analysis also automatically detects abandoned objects, which appear as suitcase pictographs on the overview map so as to notify the operator. Accordingly, it was left to the participants to decide whether to observe the overview map, the video streams, or both. When using the timeline control, they would not only rewind the video, but also the overview map, i.e., they would also access recorded tracking information of the persons detected in the observed area.

**Figure 8.3:** Smart Video Surveillance: NEST

**Situation-dependent Smart Video Surveillance.** Eventually the participants were asked to work with the UC4NEST system operating according to the situation-dependent smart video surveillance workflow introduced in section 5.2. In terms of noticeable constraints, honest users essentially notice that video streams are obfuscated using privacy filters and that recorded data is not accessible at all until an abandoned object has been detected by video analysis (cf. figure 8.4). Once an alert concerning a left behind object appears on the overview map, a certain timeframe of recorded data becomes accessible. Originally, the workflow would explicitly require the users to confirm the incident before being granted access to recorded data. However, pre-testing the workflow showed that this additional intermediate step was too confusing for users that were not familiar with the system. Accordingly, the workflow was modified so as to automatically switch to the investigation mode as soon as the user tries to access recorded data after an abandoned luggage object has been detected. Participants were also told that they implicitly switch the workflow into its investigation mode once they try to access recorded data in the assessment mode, that this constitutes a severe intrusion into observed people's privacy, which should be well-considered, and that this action of switching to the investigation mode is written to the system log. Participants were also instructed to actually switch to investigation mode once they would be sure that an object has been left behind. As explained in section 5.2 this would deactivate privacy filtering and thus allow to take screenshots on which the persons are identifiable.

**Figure 8.4:** Situation-dependent Smart Video Surveillance: UC4NEST

## 8.2 Results

31 participants took part in the study. Thus, for each combination of a particular video surveillance system design and a video clip, 10 – 11 measurements were obtained so as to give a first impression of the effects of situation-dependent smart video surveillance workflows on the procedure of handling incidents. Figures 8.5 to 8.7 show the mean assessment times and investigation times that have been measured as well as the standard deviations for each setting.

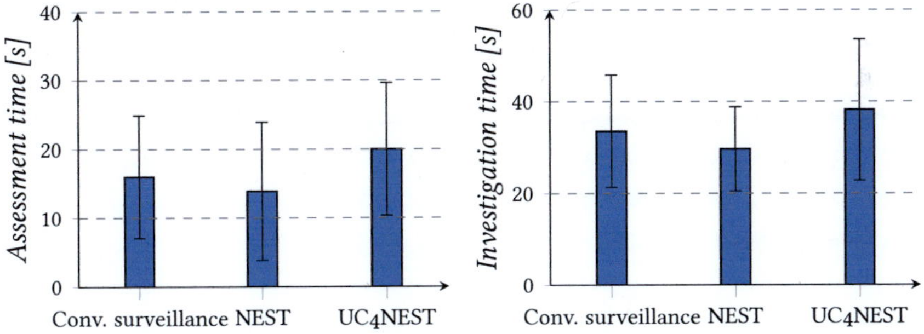


**Figure 8.5:** Assessment and investigation time for video 1, incident duration: 21$s$

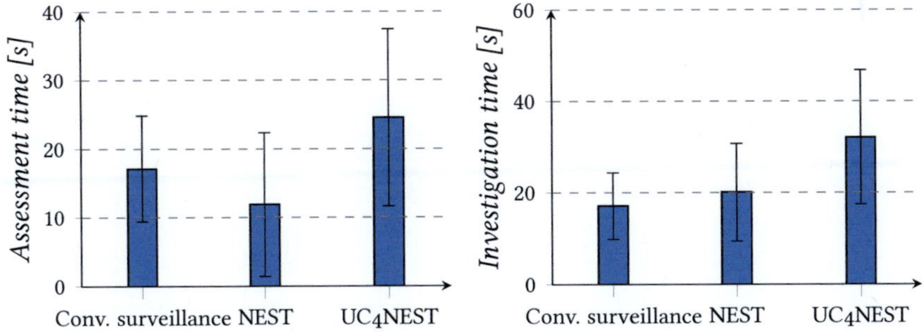


**Figure 8.6:** Assessment and investigation time for video 2, incident duration: 15$s$

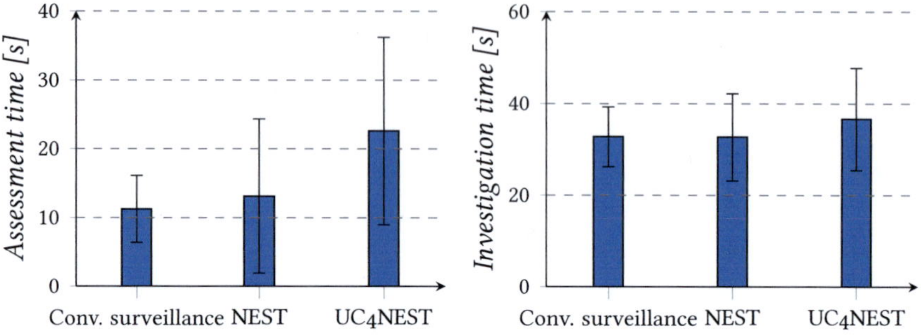


**Figure 8.7:** Assessment and investigation time for video 3, incident duration: 24*s*

Assessment times indicate that it took participants a bit more time to assess situations when they had to work with the anonymized video data of the UC4NEST system. Regarding conventional video surveillance and NEST, assessment times are even closer. When observing the participants working with the particular systems, it became apparent that the NEST system's notification about a detection of an abandoned object in some cases accelerated the decision that a given incident required further investigations. On the other hand, participants seemed to consider situations more carefully when using the UC4NEST system, since it required interaction with the timeline control to switch to the investigation mode, which also led to noticeable changes to the system's behavior, in particular to the deactivation of the privacy filters.

As was expected, investigation times are in most cases close to the durations of the incidents. However, as the incidents to be handled by the participants have rather short durations of $15 - 24s$, longer assessment times also increase the risk of missing the second action, i.e., while searching the person who abandoned the luggage object, participants were more likely to initially miss that the object has already been picked up or stolen. As a consequence, when they eventually noticed that the considered object was gone, they again had to retrieve the person who picked it up by means of accessing buffered video data. This may explain why investigation times also tend to be longer when using the UC4NEST system.

## 8.3 Discussion and Feedback of Participants

The incidents to be handled by the participants in this application study were clearly easy ones. The results show that the enforcement of operating modes to be passed through by the users do only induce a small delay to investigations and thus indicate that acceptable efficiency as demanded in **TS-5** might also be achievable in practice. As conventional video surveillance does not scale with the number of cameras, its advantage over the situation-dependent approach as observed in this experiment cannot be expected for larger video surveillance deployments. Furthermore, when used without any privacy-preserving mechanisms in place as in this user study, the smart video surveillance system NEST is not likely to be considered proportionate in most scenarios.

However, the evaluation of smart video surveillance systems still remains a largely unsolved problem, particularly in terms of utility for realistic scenarios. For specific video analysis tasks or for privacy filters, methodologies have been proposed (cf. chapter 7), but public video data sets do not seem to be anywhere close to realistic video surveillance scenarios. As a minimum requirement, data sets for evaluating the utility of video surveillance systems should include longer video clips with more persons (even crowded scenes would be helpful in fact). A larger number of persons or more complex activities would render situation recognition and assessment more challenging and closer to reality, and would also allow to obtain a more profound understanding of the effects of privacy filters on the utility of the systems.

It is also obvious that the utility of such system is strongly influenced by their usability. Non of the employed prototype systems was optimized in this respect – also due to the fact that operating workflows and usability of smart video surveillance have not yet been thoroughly investigated in the research community. This observation can also be confirmed based on the informal feedback for which participants were asked. Several participants found it strenuous to work with dual HMIs as with the NEST system as well as the UC4NEST system. This effect is reinforced by the fact that from spending roughly 30 minutes with the systems during the experiments, the participants were not able to profoundly assess the reliability of the video analysis algorithm for abandoned object detection. At least a few of the participants said that they felt the need to constantly view the video streams, as they did not want to miss a potentially critical incident. Regarding the UC4NEST system some participants appreciated the application of privacy filters while others felt hindered from fulfilling the assigned task properly. Eventually, the three systems had to be controlled via touch screens, which was also criticized by a smaller fraction of the participants. They would have preferred to use a mouse for interacting with the surveillance systems.

# 9 Conclusions and Outlook

An inherent problem of video surveillance is that a good balance must be found between confidence in and control over operators' actions. On the one hand we put the responsibility for assessing situations and coordinating interventions to operators, but then, next to privacy intrusions due to the general presence of the cameras, they are considered as the most likely attackers who deliberately misuse the systems to commit privacy intrusions. In the face of the continuing expansion of video surveillance, there are no real doubts regarding whether the number of *smart* video surveillance systems in use will also increase in the near future. As these system are more powerful yet even more privacy-intrusive, legal scholars do not consider them permissible without a responsible technology design, i.e., effective mechanisms have to be in place for restricting intrusions into observed individuals' privacy. By means of the conceptual framework for privacy-respecting smart video surveillance introduced in this research, privacy intrusions to be permitted can be dosed in proportion to the substantiation of threat situations and criminal offenses.

Based on ideas introduced by legal scholars among Roßnagel [RDH11] the concept of situation-dependent smart video surveillance workflows separates the systems' capabilities into operating modes with different levels of functionality and different levels of privacy protection (cf. section 4.4). Operating modes encapsulate function usage constraints, data access constraints, as well as privacy filters and accountability requirements to be enforced according to the substantiation of a threat situation and depending on the type of incident that is detected by the system. Sensing for potentially critical incidents has to be performed continuously and necessarily takes place in an unselective manner. Due to this groundless and unjustified observation the default mode of a smart video surveillance system must be optimized so as to protect observed individuals' privacy, i.e., disclosed data is reduced to a minimum and must not exhibit personal connections. Disclosing video data should either be avoided, or, if not possible, privacy filters must be applied in order to protect the identities of individuals in the monitored area.

Once the system detects a potentially critical incident, assessment modes create privacy-preserving views of the scene, which enable operators to distinguish actual threats from false alarms while still not disclosing captured individual's identities. The research on privacy filters conducted in this thesis indicates that it is actually possible to disclose video data in a form, which allows activity recognition and protects identities at the same time (cf. chapter 7). Assessment modes may also unlock functions for keeping track of the persons associated to the incident or for tracking back where these persons came from. They are executed until the operator either recognizes and confirms a concrete threat situation or discards the incident.

Once an investigation mode is entered, the physical integrity of people is at risk, property is damaged, or a criminal act has been observed. This justifies further investigations involving the collection and processing of personal data for initiating countermeasures as well as for identifying offenders. In other words, the functionality of the system is increased to a level, which is appropriate for handling a given incident. At the same time the selectivity of the surveillance process is further increased, i.e., investigations are restricted to persons that are associated to the incident. Usages of privacy-intrusive functions are also logged in order to be able to reveal misuse in hindsight. As has been shown in chapter 5, usage control monitoring capabilities enable the enforcement of constraints that are required to implement such situation-dependent smart video surveillance workflows.

Combined with the enforcement of privacy privileges and selective processing of detections from video analysis during information fusion at the world model, system designs are enabled, which balance low selectivity with a low privacy impact, whereas deeper privacy intrusions are compensated with a high selectivity and accountability. Countermeasures in the face of a concrete threat situation require that interventions are coordinated with the police or emergency personnel on site. Chapter 6 has shown that distributed usage control extended with inter-system information flow tracking even allows to protect data after it has been transmitted from control rooms to devices carried by mobile personnel.

The concept of situation-dependent smart video surveillance workflows is based on the assumption that false positive detections of critical activities by video analysis do only occur occasionally. Otherwise the low privacy impact of the default mode cannot serve as an argument in favor of situation-dependent smart video surveillance over conventional video surveillance. Moreover, assessment modes should not be activated without cause, since they provide means for specific observation of individuals even though the application of privacy filters is usually enforced. Reliable enforcement of situation-dependent smart video surveillance workflows as well as the enforcement of policies on data transferred to mobile devices is based on all assumptions that are commonly made by instantiations of usage control (cf. section 5.1). In particular, the assumption that components are not tampered with and do not leak any data via implementation errors must also be made for all components of the smart video surveillance system.

Even though realistic video surveillance scenarios are doubtlessly difficult to be reproduced under laboratory conditions, this research has tried to obtain an indication on whether the constraints of situation-dependent smart video surveillance workflows may still allow operators to fulfill their duties with acceptable overhead. While the incidents to be handled by non-experienced participants in the conducted application experiments were clearly easy ones, i.e., people abandoning luggage objects, they still show that the enforced operating modes to be passed through only induce a small delay to investigations.

## 9.1 Conclusion

The thesis confirmed the first part of the initial hypothesis and showed that usage control mechanisms and privacy filters for video data can actually fulfill the (partly predicted) requirements of lawful smart video surveillance and is capable of protecting the identities of observed individuals against malicious operators. For the second part, which claimed that the utility of smart video surveillance is preserved in terms of allowing situation assessment and collection of evidence with acceptable efficiency, at least some indications could be obtained. While it can be argued that anonymization functions for video data can be evaluated on non-realistic data sets, for workflows of an entire (smart) video surveillance system this seems rather questionable. In terms of the research questions introduced in section 1.3 the following insights have been obtained:

- Usage control monitoring capabilities as described in chapter 5 enable the enforcement of all the constraints that are required to implement situation-dependent smart video surveillance workflows, which confirms **TS-1**. By this means it might be possible to develop and operate smart video surveillance systems which are not only privacy-respecting, but indeed lawful.

- The results obtained in an evaluation of privacy filters (cf. chapter 7) do not support the common hypothesis of a trade-off relationship between utility and privacy of video data, which indicates that **TS-2** can indeed be accomplished, i.e., operators may actually be able to recognize activities based on obfuscated video data. The stronger privacy filters are also capable to erase evidence concerning observed individuals' ethnicity and thus protect against racial discrimination by operators.

- The enforcement of privacy privileges as well as selective processing of detections from video analysis during information fusion at the world model balances privacy impact with selectivity and accountability in terms of making misuse traceable (cf chapter 5). This confirms **TS-3**.

- With a generalization from inter-layer information flow tracking of explicit flows to inter-system settings and its instantiation with distributed usage control enforcement it has been shown that (video) data disseminated from a video surveillance system to mobile clients can be protected against illegitimate redistribution so as to confirm **TS-4** (cf. chapter 6).

- When participants assessed and investigated incidents in experiments of an application study as described in chapter 8, the restrictions and privacy filters in place did not induce a considerable operating overhead measured in terms of delay. As stated before, these experiments cannot claim to be close to reality. However, the results indicate that **TS-5** might also be achievable in practice. The situation-dependent approach proposed in this research should eventually be conceived as a toolkit for tailoring proportionate and privacy-respecting smart video surveillance systems for all kinds of scenarios.

## 9.2 Outlook

This research does not cover the issue of privacy breaches due to context knowledge that an operator may have. If operators must be expected to have such additional knowledge about people concerned by a given video surveillance measure, identities of these people may even leak via a site map view, which only visualizes the positions of otherwise anonymous person objects detected by video analysis. As the purposes and applications for which abstracted data is disclosed to operators or further analyzed by algorithms are still at an early stage of development, criteria for the utility of abstracted data can hardly be identified. It is thus not clear to what extent this issue can be mitigated by means of applying privacy filters on abstracted data, i.e., anonymization functions from the field of database privacy. Future work therefore needs to keep an eye on the developments in the area of situation recognition.

With a view to the future, linking data obtained from smart surveillance systems to data from other information sources such as the Internet and other telecommunications networks is considered as a severe threat to privacy and civil rights [Nor03; Cam05; Kam05]. This research assumed that video surveillance systems are operated within an infrastructure, which excludes data extraction as far as possible (cf. appendix A), and developed mechanisms to restrict the purposes for which data is used. However, there is already a trend in video analysis research to address the safety of public events such as music festivals, fairs, large-scale demonstrations, and sports events [Joh+08; Mah+10; MFA15]. In such scenarios other information sources such as data from mobile phone networks and social media are already exploited and may in the future indeed get fused with data obtained from smart video video surveillance. Therefore emerging privacy risks have to be analyzed and according mechanisms for monitoring information fusion have to be developed.

Smart video surveillance systems based on the conceptual framework introduced in this research are controlled via policies. This raises the question of who is in charge of specifying the policies for the situation-dependent smart video surveillance workflows to be enforced during the operation of a given system. Generally speaking, this must be done by a data protection expert, who may not necessarily be a technical expert. Some initial work on graphical model-based policy authoring for smart video surveillance has been published in [BBB15], but has not been evaluated in terms of usability for technical laymen.

The introduced approach on inter-system information flow tracking does not cover recent results for improving the precision of information flow models [LK14; LOP14; Lov+15]. However, since Lovat demonstrated their applicability for tracking inter-layer information flows in [Lov15], they are likely to be applicable to inter-system information flows as well.

A largely unsolved problem is the evaluation of smart video surveillance systems, particularly in terms of utility. For specific video analysis algorithms or privacy filters for video data, methodologies have been proposed, but public video data sets do not seem to be anywhere close to realistic video surveillance scenarios. Criteria for appropriate data sets regarding the evaluation of privacy filters for video data have been identified. More persons appearing in longer video clips and being involved in more complex activities or situations would allow to obtain a more profound understanding of the effects of anonymization functions on the utility of video data. Accordingly, further investigation is needed to study whether the findings of this work can be generalized to realistic video surveillance scenarios where operators have to assess more complex situations. Future work may also want to compare results of user studies with recent approaches towards objectively quantifying the privacy and utility levels of obfuscated video data [NF15].

When trying to evaluate the utility of an entire smart video surveillance system design, there is not only a lack of realistic video data sets, but also a lack of criteria for utility. It is obvious that factors such as usability play an equally important role as that enforced constraints are not too restrictive. However, smart video surveillance systems are still at an early stage of development and not yet used in practice. Future works will thus have to study *how* smart video surveillance system are actually used by operators, e.g., in terms of which functions are needed in which situations and how these functions are actually controlled in the HMIs.

According to Microsoft's identity architect Cameron [Cam05], one must ask the question whether technical approaches to oppose surveillance, such as privacy-enhancing technologies (PETs), will not only further increase society's dependency on technology in a non-desirable fashion. In view of the spread and further expansion of video surveillance, there does not seem to be a real choice. Moreover, assuming that there has been a careful consideration of interests prior to the installation, video surveillance measures are actually lawful. As has been shown, technical mechanisms can ensure to a certain extent that video surveillance system are not deliberately misused by operators and organizations. From the perspective of people concerned, the presence of such mechanisms may thus also be able to mitigate the panoptical effect/chilling effect caused by an omnipresence of video surveillance cameras, the capabilities of which are widely unknown and mostly overestimated by the public.

# A Appendix: Secure Infrastructure for Smart Video Surveillance

With a focus on the operation of a privacy-enabled smart video surveillance system as proposed in this research (cf. chapter 5), two supervised student projects have been following up on the assumptions under which usage control enforcement unfolds its effectiveness (cf. section 2.5.2, section 5.7.1) as well as on how to set up a secure network architecture so as to eliminate threats on the level of the infrastructure (cf. section 4.2.1). The subsequent sections briefly summarize the results of these student projects.

## A.1 Protecting the Usage Control Components Against Manipulation and Deactivation

Components of the usage control infrastructure must be protected against deactivation and manipulation. This particularly applies for the components that are also required on the machine, which executes the frontend of the smart video surveillance system. If these components are installed as services,[1] which are executed in the context of another user and launched automatically at start-up, the operator is unable to kill the respective processes. As long as they do not require write permissions, even components to be executed in the operator's user context, such as the HMI of the smart video surveillance system, and also their configuration files can be protected against manipulation by not granting the user write access to the respective files.

Given physical access to the machine which runs the frontend, an attacker can easily obtain local administrator rights, either by removing the hard disk

[1] e.g., via service managers such as NSSM (`http://nssm.cc`)

or by using tools such as *Offline NT Password & Registry Editor* [2] or *Kon-Boot.* [3] Suchlike offline attack methods can be avoided by means of hard disk encryption or by locating the frontend machine in a secure data center outside the control room of the smart video surveillance system (preferably both measures should be taken). The frontend can then either be accessed via remote desktop solutions, which can be protected against illegitimate data extraction and infiltration with malware by means of deactivating the client clipboard as well as the forwarding of client resources, e.g., via Windows Group Policies. Another option for excluding physical access to the machine that executes the frontend could be realized by only providing monitors and possibly input devices for the frontend in the control room. Using solutions for tunneling High Definition Multimedia Interface (HDMI) over IP as well as Universal Serial Bus (USB) device servers, a small number of Ethernet lines is required to connect the input and output devices to the remotely located frontend machine.

## A.2 Secure Network Infrastructure for Smart Video Surveillance

As explained in section 4.2.1, protective mechanisms against external attackers can be implemented on the level of the network infrastructure. Such mechanisms are also effective for reducing the threats posed by malicious administrators and malicious operators as will be explained in the following.

Any attack to be performed by an external attacker first of all requires access to the network infrastructure of a (smart) video surveillance system. In particular, the network ports used by the cameras are physically exposed to such attackers. Several mechanisms can be employed on the link layer as well as on the network layer in order to eliminate the threat of external attackers obtaining access to the network infrastructure.

[2] `http://pogostick.net/~pnh/ntpasswd`
[3] `http://thelead82.com`

On the link layer, devices can be enforced to authenticate with the switches via *network access control.*[4] The *port security feature* of Ethernet switches also allows to use sticky MAC addresses, i.e., an according switch port only accepts links from the specified MAC address of a certain camera. Either of these options should be combined with monitoring the cameras' availability at frequent intervals. In case a camera becomes unreachable, the according port must be shut down and an administrator should by notified. By this means external attackers only have very limited chances to gain unnoticed access to the network infrastructure.

On the network layer and transport layer the level of security can be further increased by means of *network separation.* Using a zone firewall separate networks can be configured for the components of the back-end, for the components of the front-end, for the cameras, as well as a transfer network for maintenance access (cf. figure A.1). By this means the following access restrictions can be enforced:

- No connections can be initiated from within the camera network;
- A minimal set of necessary connections can be initiated from within the front-end network into the back-end network, i.e., connections for controlling the system, for pulling data, and updating the HMI;
- Unrestricted access from within the back-end network into the camera network and the front-end network;
- Temporary access from within the transfer network into other networks for maintenance purposes.

By this means also neither a malicious administrator nor a malicious operator can obtain illegitimate access to the camera network or to the back-end network. Under the assumption that any communication between components takes place via encrypted and authenticated channels, the risk of illegitimate data

[4] e.g., IEEE 802.1X (Extensible Authentication Protocol (EAP) over IEEE 802) as specified in RFC 3748 (`https://tools.ietf.org/html/rfc3748`)

access as well as an attacker gaining illegitimate control over (parts of) the smart video surveillance system through tapping attacks or signal manipulation is thus minimized (cf. section 4.2.1).

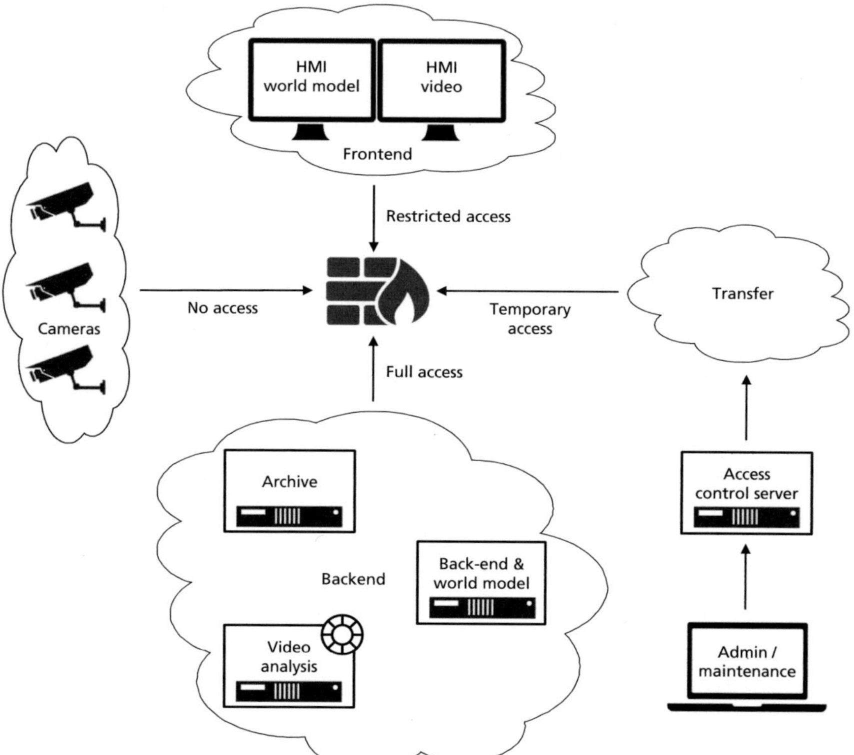


**Figure A.1:** Required network zones for separating the components of smart video surveillance systems

**Granting Temporary Access for Maintenance Purposes.** Administrators are responsible for maintenance tasks. Therefore they must be granted extensive permissions on the machines executing the components of the smart video surveillance system. As this poses a high risk for misuse and sabotage, administrator should only be granted access to the machines on an on-demand and temporary basis. This can be achieved by means of providing a separate transfer network and an *access control server*, which is able to log in to the firewall (e.g., via `ssh`) in order to create or remove access control lists (ACLs).[5] The access control server furthermore hosts a service, which allows operators to file support requests in case of technical problems with the system. Access to a protected network is then only granted depending on the existence of a support request to a particular operator for a predefined period of time. For this, support requests are handled as follows:

- An operator must file a support request on the access control server.
- The access control server creates a short-lived invitation link, which can be employed exactly once and which requires an authentication of an authorized administrator.
- An administrator follows the invitation link and is asked to authenticate with a directory service (such as `ldap`).
- The access control server temporarily adds the client IP address of the administrator's machine to the access list for the front-end, back-end, or camera network, writes a log entry (e.g., via `rsyslog`) and notifies the department head or works council (if applicable).

This procedure enables a particular administrator to establish connections into the protected networks for remote maintenance. After a predefined period of time the access list is reset and connections from the client machine are dropped by the firewall. Durations of such support connections should also

[5] In principle, the firewall and the access control server could also be operated on the same physical/virtual host system. However, one may not want to deploy additional services on a specifically hardened firewall.

be logged. By this means, the access control server can grant on-demand and temporary access to protected networks so as to minimize the potential of misuse or sabotage by a malicious administrator.

# B Appendix: Graphical Model-based Policy Editor

Poor usability and, as a consequence, human errors can render security and privacy mechanisms useless. This observation also applies for the specification of UC policies such as those shown in chapter 5, which describe the constraint profiles of situation-dependent smart video surveillance workflows. Editing the machine-readable XML syntax using text editors is effortful, error-prone, and requires deep knowledge of technical details of the system.

This issue has been addressed in [BBB15], where a graphical policy editor for smart video surveillance was proposed. This tool borrows from the concept of visual programming and enables users to assemble policies from readily understandable graphical blocks, which can be exported as machine-readable UC policies. A meta model of a generalized smart video surveillance architecture equipped with UC provides the editor with semantics so that users can be relieved from knowing syntax rules and details of the system's technical implementation. The details of this meta model can be found in [Bur14] and [BBB15]. These works also instantiate the editor for a scenario in which smart video surveillance is deployed for fall detection in medical facilities. Figure B.1 shows an exemplary assessment mode policy for this scenario. Upon observing an event indicating a potential fall an anonymized view is created using a privacy filter, which reduces observed individuals to blurred silhouettes, so as to hide their identities. The responsible nurse can then proceed by either confirming the incident, discarding it as a false detection, or by requesting a $2^{nd}$ level assessment mode in case the provided view does not provide enough evidence for situation assessment.

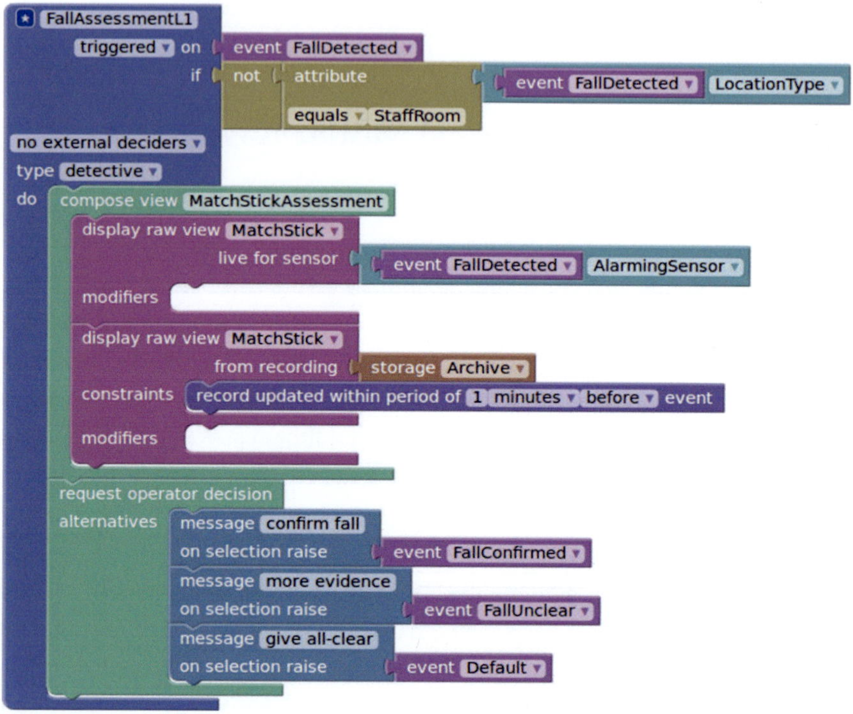


**Figure B.1:** Assessment mode for privacy-respecting fall detection

# C Appendix: Usage Control Policy Syntax

## C.1 XML-Scheme of the Enforcement Language

The following XML scheme shows the complete specification of the usage control policy syntax, which was introduced in section 2.5.1 and used in the instantiations of chapters 5 and 6.

```
<?xml version="1.0" encoding="UTF-8"?>
<schema
  xmlns = "http://www.w3.org/2001/XMLSchema"
  targetNamespace = "http://www.iese.fhg.de/ind2uce/1.0/enforcementLanguage"
  xmlns:tns = "http://www.iese.fhg.de/ind2uce/1.0/enforcementLanguage"
  elementFormDefault = "qualified">

  <attributeGroup name="TimeAmountAttributeGroup">
    <attribute name="amount" type="long" use="required"/>
    <attribute name="unit" type="tns:TimeUnitType" use="optional" default="TIMESTEPS"/>
  </attributeGroup>

  <complexType name="TimeAmountType">
    <annotation>
      <documentation>
        A time amount is a sum of elapsed time, which need not be of any specific intervals.
      </documentation>
    </annotation>
    <attributeGroup ref="tns:TimeAmountAttributeGroup"/>
  </complexType>

  <simpleType name="TimeUnitType">
    <annotation>
      <documentation>
        Possible time units to quantify a time amount. One month is 30 days and a year is 12 months or 360 days.
```

```
      </documentation>
    </annotation>
    <restriction base="string">
      <enumeration value="TIMESTEPS"/>
      <enumeration value="NANOSECONDS"/>
      <enumeration value="MICROSECONDS"/>
      <enumeration value="MILLISECONDS"/>
      <enumeration value="SECONDS"/>
      <enumeration value="MINUTES"/>
      <enumeration value="HOURS"/>
      <enumeration value="DAYS"/>
      <enumeration value="WEEKS"/>
      <enumeration value="MONTHS"/>
      <enumeration value="YEARS"/>
    </restriction>
  </simpleType>

  <simpleType name="EventParameterDataTypes">
    <restriction base="string">
      <enumeration value="string"/>
      <enumeration value="binary"/>
      <enumeration value="int"/>
      <enumeration value="long"/>
      <enumeration value="bool"/>
      <enumeration value="stringArray"/>
    </restriction>
  </simpleType>

  <complexType name="EventParameterType">
    <attribute name="name" type="string" use="required"/>
    <attribute name="value" type="string" use="required"/>
    <attribute name="type" type="tns:EventParameterDataTypes" default="string"/>
  </complexType>

  <complexType name="ComplexEventParameterType">
    <choice maxOccurs="unbounded">
      <element name="complexParameter" type="tns:ComplexEventParameterType"
          minOccurs="0" maxOccurs="unbounded"/>
      <element name="parameter" type="tns:EventParameterType" minOccurs="0"
          maxOccurs="unbounded"/>
```

```
    </choice>
    <attribute name="name" type="string"/>
  </complexType>

  <complexType name="EventType">
    <annotation>
      <documentation>
        Events have a name as well parameters.
        Classes of events are: usage, signaling, and other.
        A try event represents an attempted usage event by a user.
      </documentation>
    </annotation>
    <choice maxOccurs="unbounded">
      <element name="complexParameter" type="tns:ComplexEventParameterType"
            minOccurs="0" maxOccurs="unbounded"/>
      <element name="parameter" type="tns:EventParameterType" minOccurs="0"
            maxOccurs="unbounded"/>
    </choice>
    <attribute name="action" type="string"/>
    <attribute name="timestamp" type="time:TimestampType"/>
    <attribute name="isTry" type="boolean" default="false"/>

    <!-- Event signaler (PEP) -->
    <attribute name="signallerComponent" type="string"/>
    <attribute name="subject" type="string"/>
    <attribute name="target" type="string"/>
  </complexType>

  <simpleType name="ParamMatchDataTypes">
    <restriction base="string">
      <pattern value="string|dataUsage|xpath|regex|binary|int|long|bool|stringArray"/>
    </restriction>
  </simpleType>

  <complexType name="ParamMatchType">
    <attribute name="name" type="string" use="required"/>
    <attribute name="value" type="string" use="required"/>
    <attribute name="type" type="tns:ParamMatchDataTypes" default="string"/>
    <attribute name="negate" type="boolean" use="optional" default="false"/>
  </complexType>
```

```
<complexType name="EventMatchingOperatorType">
  <sequence>
    <element name="paramMatch" type="tns:ParamMatchType" minOccurs="0"
          maxOccurs="unbounded"/>
  </sequence>
  <attribute name="action" type="string"/>
  <attribute name="class" type="action:ActionClassType"/>
  <attribute name="isTry" type="boolean" default="false"/>
</complexType>

<element name="event" type="tns:EventType"/>

<complexType name="conditionType">
  <group ref="tns:OperatorsGroup"/>
</complexType>

<complexType name="EmptyOperatorType" />

<complexType name="UnaryOperatorType">
  <group ref="tns:OperatorsGroup" minOccurs="1" maxOccurs="1"/>
</complexType>

<complexType name="BinaryOperatorType">
  <group ref="tns:OperatorsGroup" minOccurs="2" maxOccurs="2"/>
</complexType>

<complexType name="TimeBoundedUnaryOperatorType">
  <group ref="tns:OperatorsGroup" minOccurs="1" maxOccurs="1"/>
  <attributeGroup ref="time:TimeAmountAttributeGroup"/>
</complexType>

<group name="OperatorsGroup">
  <annotation>
    <documentation>
      Propositional, temporal logic and cardinality operators
    </documentation>
  </annotation>
  <choice>

```

```
<!-- logical constants -->
<element name="true" type="tns:EmptyOperatorType"/>
<element name="false" type="tns:EmptyOperatorType"/>

 <!-- eventMatch = event matching -->
<element name="eventMatch" type="event:EventMatchingOperatorType"/>

<!-- propositional operators -->
<element name="not" type="tns:UnaryOperatorType"/>
<element name="and" type="tns:BinaryOperatorType"/>
<element name="or" type="tns:BinaryOperatorType"/>
<element name="implies" type="tns:BinaryOperatorType"/>

<!-- xpath operator -->
<element name="xPathEval" type="string"/>

<!-- temporal operators -->

<element name="since" type="tns:BinaryOperatorType">
  <annotation>
    <documentation>
      since(A, B) => B since A
      Since the last occurrence of A, B has to hold all the time.
      Alternatively globally B.
      This is equivalent to the LTL weak since operator.
    </documentation>
  </annotation>
</element>

<element name="always" type="tns:UnaryOperatorType">
  <annotation>
    <documentation>
      In the past the formula should have held in all timesteps.
      Equivalent to the LTL globally (G) operator.
    </documentation>
  </annotation>
</element>
```

```
<element name="before" type="tns:TimeBoundedUnaryOperatorType">
  <annotation>
    <documentation>
      Formula has to have held immediately before the given time interval in the past.
      The time interval depends on the monitor's view of time; it should be expressed as timesteps or absolute time values.
      This is similar to the LTL previous operator.
    </documentation>
  </annotation>
</element>

<element name="during" type="tns:TimeBoundedUnaryOperatorType">
  <annotation>
    <documentation>
      A formula should have held constantly during the time interval in the past.
      During (3 hours, A)
      Means A has to be always true in the previous 3 hours (depending on the mechanism's notion of timesteps).
    </documentation>
  </annotation>
</element>

<element name="within" type="tns:TimeBoundedUnaryOperatorType">
  <annotation>
    <documentation>
      A formula should have held at least once during the time interval in the past.
      This is similar to during without the requirement for the formula to hold in every time step.
    </documentation>
  </annotation>
</element>

<!-- cardinality operators -->

<element name="repLim">
  <annotation>
    <documentation>
      Specifies a lower and upper bound of occurrences within a fixed time interval in which a formula should hold.
      repLim(lower=0, upper=3, 1 hour, A)
```

```
          In 3 hours min 0 max 3 times A has to hold.
        </documentation>
      </annotation>
      <complexType>
        <complexContent>
          <extension base="tns:TimeBoundedUnaryOperatorType">
            <attribute name="lowerLimit" type="nonNegativeInteger" use="required"/>
            <attribute name="upperLimit" type="positiveInteger" use="required"/>
          </extension>
        </complexContent>
      </complexType>
    </element>

    <element name="repSince">
      <annotation>
        <documentation>
          repSince(3, A, B)
          Limits the maximum number of times (here 3) the subformula (B) may hold
                since subformula (A) has held.
          Alternatively limits the amount, subformula B may hold globally, similar to
                since and LTL weak since operator.
        </documentation>
      </annotation>
      <complexType >
        <complexContent>
          <extension base="tns:BinaryOperatorType">
            <attribute name="limit" type="nonNegativeInteger" use="required"/>
          </extension>
        </complexContent>
      </complexType>
    </element>

    <element name="repMax">
      <annotation>
        <documentation>
          The maximum number of times a formula should occur all the time.
        </documentation>
      </annotation>
      <complexType>
        <complexContent>
```

```
          <extension base="tns:UnaryOperatorType">
            <attribute name="limit" type="nonNegativeInteger" use="required"/>
          </extension>
        </complexContent>
      </complexType>
    </element>

  </choice>
</group>

<complexType name="DelayActionType">
  <attributeGroup ref="time:TimeAmountAttributeGroup" />
</complexType>

<complexType name="ModifyActionType">
  <sequence>
    <element name="parameter" type="action:ParameterInstance" minOccurs="0" maxOccurs="unbounded"/>
  </sequence>
</complexType>

<complexType name="AuthorizationInhibitType">
  <sequence>
    <element name="delay" type="tns:DelayActionType" minOccurs="0" maxOccurs="1"/>
  </sequence>
</complexType>

<complexType name="AuthorizationAllowType">
  <annotation>
    <documentation>
      Mechanisms that only contain allow action without modify/delay and no actions do not make sense.
      Allows the trigger event to take place.
      In our concrete semantics this means that the action behind the event should be allowed to take place.
    </documentation>
  </annotation>
  <sequence>
    <element name="delay" type="tns:DelayActionType" minOccurs="0" maxOccurs="1"/>
```

```
      <element name="modify" type="tns:ModifyActionType" minOccurs="0" maxOccurs="1" />
      <element name="executeAction" type="action:ExecuteActionType" minOccurs="0" maxOccurs="unbounded"/>
    </sequence>
  </complexType>

  <complexType name="AuthorizationActionType">
    <choice>
      <element name="allow" type="tns:AuthorizationAllowType"/>
      <element name="inhibit" type="tns:AuthorizationInhibitType"/>
    </choice>
    <attribute name="name" type="string" use="required"/>
    <!-- indicates starting point in authorizationAction hierarchy -->
    <attribute name="start" type="boolean" use="optional" default="false"/>
    <!-- reference to fallback authorizationAction (name), if executeActions/modification could not be performed successfully -->
    <attribute name="fallback" type="string" use="optional" default="inhibit"/>
  </complexType>

  <!-- Preventive mechanisms can only come to decisions on the grounds of their current knowledge, so
    they use past formulas. The mechanism consists of an Event, a Condition, and an Action part (ECA).
    The Event is called trigger Event. When the condition evaluates to true the action part is executed. -->
  <complexType name="MechanismBaseType">
    <sequence>
      <element name="description" type="string" minOccurs="0" maxOccurs="1"/>
      <!-- Timestep size must not use timestep time unit! -->
      <element name="timestep" type="time:TimeAmountType" minOccurs="1" maxOccurs="1"/>
      <element name="trigger" type="event:EventMatchingOperatorType" minOccurs="0" maxOccurs="1"/>
      <element name="condition" type="tns:conditionType" minOccurs="0" maxOccurs="1"/>

    </sequence>
    <attribute name="name" type="string" use="required"/>
  </complexType>

```

```
<complexType name="DetectiveMechanismType">
  <complexContent>
    <extension base="tns:MechanismBaseType">
      <sequence>
        <element name="executeAction" type="action:ExecuteActionType" minOccurs="0" maxOccurs="unbounded"/>
      </sequence>
    </extension>
  </complexContent>
</complexType>

<complexType name="PreventiveMechanismType">
  <annotation>
    <documentation>
      Trigger is always a try action for preventive mechanisms.
    </documentation>
  </annotation>
  <complexContent>
    <extension base="tns:MechanismBaseType">
      <sequence>
        <element name="authorizationAction" type="tns:AuthorizationActionType" minOccurs="1" maxOccurs="unbounded"/>
        <element name="executeAction" type="action:ExecuteActionType" minOccurs="0" maxOccurs="unbounded"/>
      </sequence>
    </extension>
  </complexContent>
</complexType>

<complexType name="PolicySetType">
  <sequence>
    <choice minOccurs="0" maxOccurs="unbounded">
      <element name="detectiveMechanism" type="tns:DetectiveMechanismType"/>
      <element name="preventiveMechanism" type="tns:PreventiveMechanismType"/>
    </choice>
  </sequence>
  <attribute name="name" type="string" use="required"/>
  <attribute name="description" type="string" use="optional"/>
</complexType>

```

```
  <element name="policy" type="tns:PolicySetType">
    <annotation>
      <documentation>
        Actions and parameter names are keys. Action names and parameters are referenced
            by the mechanism trigger, the eventMatch operator and the execution action.
      </documentation>
    </annotation>
  </element>

</schema>
```

## C.2 Extension of Event Declarations

In order to support nested parameters in events as required for the instantiations of usage control described in chapters 5 and 6 the OSL syntax by Hilty et al. [Hil+07] must be extended. The necessary extensions are specified in the syntax form of OSL based on Z. In the standard form, an event consists of the event name and parameters, represented by a partial function ($\nrightarrow$) from parameter names to parameter values. For nested parameters, the partial function *Params* is now defined as follows:

$$
\begin{aligned}
&[EventName, ParamName, ParamValue] \\
&EventClass == \{usage, signalling, other\} \\
&getclass : EventName \rightarrow EventClass \\
&Params : ParamName \nrightarrow (Params \cup ParamValue) \\
&Event == EventName \times Params
\end{aligned}
\tag{C.1}
$$

An event declaration specifies the events that can be observed in a concrete system. Event declarations are defined as follows:

$$
\begin{aligned}
&EventDecl == EventName \times EventClass \times ParamDecl \\
&ParamDecl : (ParamName \nrightarrow \mathbb{P}\,(ParamDecl \cup ParamValue)
\end{aligned}
\tag{C.2}
$$

# D Appendix: Syntax for Information Flow Semantics Specification

The following XML scheme shows the syntax specification for information flow semantics descriptions as used in the instantiation of chapter 6.

```
<?xml version="1.0" encoding="UTF-8"?>
<xs:schema xmlns:xs="http://www.w3.org/2001/XMLSchema"
        elementFormDefault="qualified">
  <xs:element name="ifsemantics">
    <xs:complexType>
      <xs:sequence>
        <xs:element ref="params"/>
        <xs:element ref="actions"/>
      </xs:sequence>
    </xs:complexType>
  </xs:element>
  <xs:element name="params">
    <xs:complexType>
      <xs:sequence>
        <xs:element maxOccurs="unbounded" ref="param"/>
      </xs:sequence>
    </xs:complexType>
  </xs:element>
  <xs:element name="param">
    <xs:complexType>
      <xs:attribute ref="name" use="required"/>
      <xs:attribute ref="type" use="required"/>
    </xs:complexType>
  </xs:element>
  <xs:element name="actions">
    <xs:complexType>
      <xs:sequence>
        <xs:element maxOccurs="unbounded" ref="action"/>
```

```
      </xs:sequence>
    </xs:complexType>
  </xs:element>
  <xs:element name="action">
    <xs:complexType>
      <xs:sequence>
        <xs:element minOccurs="0" maxOccurs="unbounded" ref="scope"/>
        <xs:element maxOccurs="unbounded" ref="operation"/>
      </xs:sequence>
      <xs:attribute ref="name" use="required"/>
    </xs:complexType>
  </xs:element>
  <xs:element name="scope">
    <xs:complexType>
      <xs:simpleContent>
        <xs:extension base="xs:string">
          <xs:attribute ref="behavior" default="INTRA"/>
          <xs:attribute ref="delimiter" default="NONE"/>
          <xs:attribute ref="interSystem" default="FALSE"/>
        </xs:extension>
      </xs:simpleContent>
    </xs:complexType>
  </xs:element>
  <xs:element name="operation">
    <xs:complexType>
      <xs:sequence>
        <xs:element ref="left"/>
        <xs:element ref="right"/>
      </xs:sequence>
      <xs:attribute ref="name" use="required"/>
    </xs:complexType>
  </xs:element>
  <xs:element name="left">
    <xs:complexType>
      <xs:sequence>
        <xs:element minOccurs="1" maxOccurs="1" ref="operand"/>
      </xs:sequence>
    </xs:complexType>
  </xs:element>
  <xs:element name="right">
```

```
      <xs:complexType>
        <xs:sequence>
          <xs:element minOccurs="0" maxOccurs="unbounded" ref="operand"/>
        </xs:sequence>
      </xs:complexType>
    </xs:element>
    <xs:element name="operand" type="xs:NCName"/>
    <xs:attribute name="type" type="xs:NCName"/>
    <xs:attribute name="name" type="xs:NCName"/>
    <xs:attribute name="behavior" type="behaviors"/>
    <xs:attribute name="delimiter" type="delimiters"/>
    <xs:attribute name="interSystem" type="boolean"/>
    <xs:simpleType name="behaviors">
      <xs:restriction base="xs:string">
        <xs:enumeration value="IN"/>
        <xs:enumeration value="OUT"/>
        <xs:enumeration value="INTRA"/>
      </xs:restriction>
    </xs:simpleType>
    <xs:simpleType name="delimiters">
      <xs:restriction base="xs:string">
        <xs:enumeration value="OPEN"/>
        <xs:enumeration value="CLOSE"/>
        <xs:enumeration value="NONE"/>
      </xs:restriction>
    </xs:simpleType>
    <xs:simpleType name="boolean">
      <xs:restriction base="xs:string">
        <xs:enumeration value="TRUE"/>
        <xs:enumeration value="FALSE"/>
      </xs:restriction>
    </xs:simpleType>
</xs:schema>
```

# Own Publications


[BBB15] P. Birnstill, C. Burkert, and J. Beyerer. “Graphical Model-based Privacy Policy Editing for Smart Video Surveillance.” In: *10th Future Security. Security Research Conference. Proceedings.* Berlin, Sept. 2015, pp. 81–88. URL: http://publica.fraunhofer.de/dokumente/N-362488.html.

[BDF10] P. Birnstill, P. Di, and T. Fuhrmann. “Using asymmetric links to improve SSR’s routing performance.” In: *9th IFIP Annual Mediterranean Ad Hoc Networking Workshop, Med-Hoc-Net.* June 2010, pp. 1–6. URL: http://dx.doi.org/10.1109/MEDHOCNET.2010.5546852.

[BF10] P. Birnstill and T. Fuhrmann. “Getting things straight - comparing ISPRP to linearization.” In: *Wireless On-demand Network Systems and Services (WONS), 7th International Conference on.* Feb. 2010, pp. 74–81. URL: http://dx.doi.org/10.1109/WONS.2010.543712.

[Bie+12] C. Bier et al. “Enhancing Privacy by Design from a Developer’s Perspective.” In: *Privacy Technologies and Policy - First Annual Privacy Forum, APF.* Oct. 2012, pp. 73–85. URL: http://dx.doi.org/10.1007/978-3-642-54069-1_5.

[Bir+15] P. Birnstill et al. “Privacy-preserving surveillance: an interdisciplinary approach.” In: *International Data Privacy Law* (2015). eprint: http://idpl.oxfordjournals.org/content/early/2015/09/25/idpl.ipv021.full.pdf+html. URL: http://idpl.oxfordjournals.org/content/early/2015/09/25/idpl.ipv021.abstract.

[Bir13] P. Birnstill. "Usage Controlled Video Surveillance–Revealing its Potentials for Privacy." In: *8th Future Security. Security Research Conference. Proceedings.* Berlin, Sept. 2013, pp. 502–503. URL: http://publica.fraunhofer.de/dokumente/N-276001.html.

[BKB15] S. Bretthauer, E. Krempel, and P. Birnstill. "Intelligente Videoüberwa-chung in Kranken- und Pflegeeinrichtungen von morgen: eine Analyse der Bedingungen nach den Entwürfen der EU-Kommission und des EU-Parlaments für eine DS-GVO." In: *Computer und Recht: CR; Zeitschrift für die Praxis des Rechts der Informationstechnologien* 31.31 (2015), pp. 239–245.

[BP13] P. Birnstill and A. Pretschner. "Enforcing privacy through usage-controlled video surveillance." In: *Advanced Video and Signal Based Surveillance (AVSS), 2013 10th IEEE International Conference on.* Aug. 2013, pp. 318–323. URL: http://dx.doi.org/10.1109/AVSS.2013.6636659.

[BRB15] P. Birnstill, D. Ren, and J. Beyerer. "A user study on anonymization techniques for smart video surveillance." In: *Advanced Video and Signal Based Surveillance (AVSS), 2015 12th IEEE International Conference on.* Aug. 2015. URL: http://dx.doi.org/10.1109/AVSS.2015.7301805.

[Fis+14] Y. Fischer et al. "Privacy-Aware Smart Video Surveillance Revisited." In: *9th Future Security. Security Research Conference. Proceedings.* Berlin, Sept. 2014, pp. 91–99. URL: http://publica.fraunhofer.de/dokumente/N-311337.html.

[Gre+13] S. Greiner et al. "Privacy Preserving Surveillance and the Tracking-Paradox." In: *8th Future Security. Security Research Conference. Proceedings.* Berlin, Sept. 2013, pp. 296–302. URL: http://publica.fraunhofer.de/dokumente/N-275999.html.

[KBB16] E. Krempel, P. Birnstill, and J. Beyerer. “A Privacy-aware Fall Detection System for Hospitals and Nursing Facilities.” In: *CPDP Computers, Privacy & Data Protection (to appear)*. 2016.

# Supervised Student Theses


[Bur14] Christian Burkert. "Model-Driven Generation of Privacy Policies for Smart Video Surveillance Systems." Diploma Thesis. Karlsruhe Institut für Technology (KIT), 2014.

[Kop15a] Christian Kopetschny. "Netzwerkarchitektur für ein intelligentes VÜ-System im produktiven Einsatz." Project Thesis. Duale Hochschule Baden-Württemberg Karlsruhe (DHBW), 2015.

[Kop15b] Christian Kopetschny. "Sicherheitsanalyse der Demonstratorplattform des intelligenten VÜ-Systems NEST." Project Thesis. Duale Hochschule Baden-Württem-berg Karlsruhe (DHBW), 2015.

[Ren15] Daoyuan Ren. "A User Study on Anonymization Techniques for Smart Video Surveillance." Master Thesis. Karlsruhe Institut für Technology (KIT), 2015.

# Literature

[Ain98] Rosa Ainley. "Watching the detectors: control and the Panopticon." In: *New Frontiers of Space, Bodies and Gender. London: Routledge* (1998), pp. 88–100.

[Bab+09] Noboru Babaguchi et al. "Psychological Study for Designing Privacy Protected Video Surveillance System: PriSurv." English. In: *Protecting Privacy in Video Surveillance.* Ed. by Andrew Senior. Springer London, 2009, pp. 147–164. URL: http://dx.doi.org/10.1007/978-1-84882-301-3_9.

[Bas+13] David A. Basin et al. "Monitoring Data Usage in Distributed Systems." In: *IEEE Trans. Software Eng.* 39.10 (2013), pp. 1403–1426. URL: http://doi.ieeecomputersociety.org/10.1109/TSE.2013.18.

[Bau+08] A. Bauer et al. "N.E.S.T. - Network Enabled Surveillance and Tracking." In: *3rd Future Security. Security Research Conference. Proceedings.* Karlsruhe, Sept. 2008, pp. 349–353.

[Bau+09] A. Bauer et al. "Object Oriented World Model for Surveillance Systems." In: *4th Future Security. Security Research Conference. Proceedings.* Karlsruhe, Sept. 2009, pp. 339–345.

[BEG00] Michael Boyle, Christopher Edwards, and Saul Greenberg. "The Effects of Filtered Video on Awareness and Privacy." In: *Proceedings of the 2000 ACM Conference on Computer Supported Cooperative Work.* CSCW '00. Philadelphia, Pennsylvania, USA: ACM, 2000, pp. 1–10. URL: http://doi.acm.org/10.1145/358916.358935.

[BG15] J. Beyerer and J. Geisler. “A quantitative risk model for a uniform description of safety and security.” In: *10th Future Security. Security Research Conference. Proceedings.* Berlin, Sept. 2015, pp. 317–324.

[BK14] S. Bretthauer and E. Krempel. “Videomonitoring zur Sturzdetektion und Alarmierung – Eine technische und rechtliche Analyse.” In: *17. Internationales Rechtsinformatik Symposion (IRIS) 2014 – Transparenz.* zugleich online in: Jusletter IT 20. Februar 2014, http://jusletter-it.weblaw.ch/]. 2014, pp. 525–534.

[BS07] Manfred Bornewasser and Franziska Schulz. “Systematische Videoüberwachung am Beispiel einer Maßnahme in Brandenburg.” In: *Poli-zeiliche Videoüberwachung öffentlicher Räume. Duncker & Humblot. Berlin. S* 75 (2007).

[BS12] Christoph Bier and Indra Spiecker gen. Döhmann. “Intelligente Video-überwachungstechnik: Schreckensszenario oder Gewinn für den Datenschutz?” In: *Computer Und Recht: Forum für die Praxis des Rechts der Datenverarbeitung, Information und Automation.* Vol. 28. 9. Otto Schmidt. 2012, pp. 610–618.

[Cam05] Kim Cameron. “The laws of identity.” In: *Microsoft Corp* (2005).

[CWF13] Lulu Chen, Hong Wei, and James Ferryman. “A survey of human motion analysis using depth imagery.” In: *Pattern Recognition Letters* 34.15 (2013), pp. 1995–2006.

[Dav01] Garland David. *The culture of control: Crime and social order in contemporary society.* 2001.

[Dem11] Brian Demsky. “Cross-application Data Provenance and Policy Enforcement.” In: *ACM Trans. Inf. Syst. Secur.* 14.1 (June 2011), 6:1–6:22. URL: `http://doi.acm.org/10.1145/1952982.1952988`.

[Dit00] Jason Ditton. “Crime and the City.” In: *British journal of criminology* 40.4 (2000), pp. 692–709.

[DLM03] John Dixon, Mark Levine, and Rob McAuley. "Street drinking legislation, CCTV and public space: Exploring attitudes towards public order measures." In: *Online Report for Home Office* (2003).

[Dom98] Mona Domosh. "Those "gorgeous incongruities": Polite politics and public space on the streets of nineteenth-century New York City." In: *Annals of the Association of American Geographers* 88.2 (1998), pp. 209–226.

[Enc+14] William Enck et al. "TaintDroid: An Information-Flow Tracking System for Realtime Privacy Monitoring on Smartphones." In: *ACM Trans. Comput. Syst.* 32.2 (June 2014), 5:1–5:29. URL: http://doi.acm.org/10.1145/2619091.

[Esp14] S. Degli Esposti. "A Roadmap for developing acceptable surveillance-based security measures." In: *Future Security. 9th Security Research Conference. Proceedings.* Berlin, Sept. 2014, pp. 71–80.

[FB12a] Yvonne Fischer and Jürgen Beyerer. "A Top-Down-View on Intelligent Surveillance Systems." In: *Proceedings of the Seventh International Conference on Systems.* Saint Gilles, Reunion, Feb. 2012, pp. 43–48.

[FB12b] Yvonne Fischer and Jürgen Beyerer. "Defining Dynamic Bayesian Networks for Probabilistic Situation Assessment." In: *Proceedings of the 15th International Conference on Information Fusion.* Singapore, July 2012.

[FGR06] Silvia Ferrando, Gianluca Gera, and Carlo Regazzoni. "Classification of unattended and stolen objects in video-surveillance system." In: *Video and Signal Based Surveillance, 2006. AVSS'06. IEEE International Conference on.* IEEE. 2006, pp. 21–21.

[FHW08] DI Martin Forster, Mag. Edith Huber, and Andreas Wüster. "Subjektives Sicherheitsgefühl und Überwachung." In: (2008), pp. 44–51.

[Fis01] John Fiske. "Die Überwachung der Stadt: Weißsein, der schwarze Mann und demokratischer Totalitarismus." In: *Die Fabrikation des Populären. Der John-Fiske Reader. Bielefeld* (2001), pp. 309–338.

[FNT04] Douglas A Fidaleo, Hoang-Anh Nguyen, and Mohan Trivedi. "The networked sensor tapestry (NeST): a privacy enhanced software architecture for interactive analysis of data in video-sensor networks." In: *Proceedings of the ACM 2nd International Workshop on Video Surveillance & Sensor Networks.* ACM. 2004, pp. 46–53.

[Fou77] Michel Foucault. *Discipline and punish: The birth of the prison.* Vintage, 1977.

[Fou84] Michel Foucault. "What is Enlightenment?" In: *Berlinische Monatsschrift* (1984).

[FP12] Denis Feth and Alexander Pretschner. "Flexible data-driven security for android." In: *Software Security and Reliability (SERE), 2012 IEEE Sixth International Conference on.* IEEE. 2012, pp. 41–50.

[GBA07] Martin Gill, Jane Bryan, and Jenna Allen. "Public Perceptions of CCTV in Residential Areas "It Is Not As Good As We Thought It Would Be."" In: *International Criminal Justice Review* 17.4 (2007), pp. 304–324.

[GH04] Martin Gill and Martin Hemming. "Evaluation of CCTV in the London borough of Lewisham." In: *PRCI Ltd: Leicester* (2004).

[Gil05] ML Gill. *Control room operation: findings from control room observations.* Home Office, 2005.

[Goo03] Benjamin J Goold. "Public area surveillance and police work: the impact of CCTV on police behaviour and autonomy." In: *Journal of Surveillance and Society* 1.2 (2003), pp. 191–203.

[Goo04] Benjamin Jervis Goold. *CCTV and policing: Public area surveillance and police practices in Britain.* Oxford University Press, 2004.

[Gra86] Jennifer Mulhern Granholm. "Video surveillance on public streets: The constitutionality of invisible citizen searches." In: *U. Det. L. Rev.* 64 (1986).

[GS05] Martin Gill and Angela Spriggs. *Assessing the impact of CCTV.* Home Office Research, Development and Statistics Directorate London, 2005.

[Gup+09] Arpan Gupta et al. "Understanding videos, constructing plots learning a visually grounded storyline model from annotated videos." In: *Computer Vision and Pattern Recognition, 2009. CVPR 2009. IEEE Conference on.* IEEE. 2009, pp. 2012–2019.

[H+92] Terry Honess, Elizabeth Charman, Crime Prevention Unit, et al. *Closed circuit television in public places: Its acceptability and perceived effectiveness.* Home Office London, 1992.

[Ham+05] A. Hampapur et al. "Smart video surveillance: exploring the concept of multiscale spatiotemporal tracking." In: *IEEE Signal Processing Magazine* 22.2 (Mar. 2005), pp. 38–51.

[HB07] Leon Hempel and Peter Bittner. "Zur Evaluation von Videoüberwachung." In: *Surveillance Studies. Perspektiven eines Forschungsfeldes* (2007), pp. 117–147.

[HD11] Gerrit Hornung and Monika Desoi. "'Smart Cameras' und automatische Verhaltensanalyse – Verfassungs- und datenschutzrechtliche Probleme der nächsten Generation der Videoüberwachung." In: *Kommunikation & Recht* 3 (2011), pp. 153–158.

[Hil+07] Manuel Hilty et al. "A Policy Language for Distributed Usage Control." In: *ESORICS.* Ed. by Joachim Biskup and Javier Lopez. Vol. 4734. Lecture Notes in Computer Science. Springer, 2007, pp. 531–546. URL: http://dblp.uni-trier.de/db/conf/esorics/esorics2007.html#HiltyPBSW07.

[HP09] Matús Harvan and Alexander Pretschner. "State-Based Usage Control Enforcement with Data Flow Tracking using System Call Interposition." In: *Third International Conference on Network and System Security, NSS 2009, Gold Coast, Queensland, Australia, October 19-21, 2009.* 2009, pp. 373–380. URL: http://dx.doi.org/10.1109/NSS.2009.51.

[HS96] Scott E Hudson and Ian Smith. "Techniques for addressing fundamental privacy and disruption tradeoffs in awareness support systems." In: *Proceedings of the 1996 ACM Conference on Computer Supported Cooperative Work.* ACM. 1996, pp. 248–257.

[Hue10] Laura Huey. "False security or greater social inclusion? Exploring perceptions of CCTV use in public and private spaces accessed by the homeless." In: *The British journal of sociology* 61.1 (2010), pp. 63–82.

[Joh+08] Anders Johansson et al. "From crowd dynamics to crowd safety: a video-based analysis." In: *Advances in Complex Systems* 11.04 (2008), pp. 497–527.

[Kam05] Dietmar Kammerer. *"Are you dressed for it?": der Mythos der Videoüber-wachung in der visuellen Kultur.* suhrkamp taschenbuch wissenschaft, 2005.

[Kam08] Dietmar Kammerer. *Bilder der Überwachung*. Suhrkamp, 2008.

[KE13] Pavel Korshunov and Touradj Ebrahimi. "PEViD: privacy evaluation video dataset." In: vol. 8856. 2013. URL: http://dx.doi.org/10.1117/12.2030974.

[Kev06] Hina Keval. "CCTV Control Room Collaboration and Communication: Does it Work?" In: *Proceedings of Human Centred Technology Workshop.* 2006.

[Kim+09] Hyung Chan Kim et al. “Capturing Information Flow with Concatenated Dynamic Taint Analysis.” In: *Proceedings of the The Forth International Conference on Availability, Reliability and Security, ARES 2009, March 16-19, 2009, Fukuoka, Japan.* 2009, pp. 355–362. URL: http://dx.doi.org/10.1109/ARES.2009.56.

[Kla06] Francisco Reto Klauser. *Die Videoüberwachung öffentlicher Räume: zur Ambivalenz eines Instruments sozialer Kontrolle.* Vol. 902. Campus Verlag, 2006.

[Kla07] Martin Klamt. *Verortete Normen: öffentliche Räume, Normen, Kontrolle und Verhalten.* Springer-Verlag, 2007.

[Kos00] Hille Koskela. “‘The gaze without eyes’: video-surveillance and the changing nature of urban space.” In: *Progress in Human Geography* 24.2 (2000), pp. 243–265.

[Kos02] Hille Koskela. “Video Surveillance, Gender, and the Safety of Public Urban Space:" Peeping Tom" Goes High Tech?” In: *Urban Geography* 23.3 (2002), pp. 257–278.

[KP13] Florian Kelbert and Alexander Pretschner. “Data Usage Control Enforcement in Distributed Systems.” In: *Proceedings of the Third ACM Conference on Data and Application Security and Privacy.* CODASPY ’13. San Antonio, Texas, USA: ACM, 2013, pp. 71–82. URL: http://doi.acm.org/10.1145/2435349.2435358.

[KP14] Florian Kelbert and Alexander Pretschner. “Decentralized Distributed Data Usage Control.” In: *Cryptology and Network Security - 13th International Conference, CANS 2014, Heraklion, Crete, Greece, October 22-24, 2014. Proceedings.* 2014, pp. 353–369. URL: http://dx.doi.org/10.1007/978-3-319-12280-9_23.

[Kra05] Susanne Krasmann. *Mobilität: Videoüberwachung als Chiffre einer Gouvernmentalität der Gegenwart.* na, 2005.

[Leo05] Nils Leopold. *Rechtskulturbruch: die Ausbreitung der Videoüberwachung und die unzulängliche Reaktion des Rechts.* suhrkamp taschenbuch wissenschaft, 2005.

[LK14] Enrico Lovat and Florian Kelbert. "Structure Matters - A New Approach for Data Flow Tracking." In: *35. IEEE Security and Privacy Workshops, SPW 2014, San Jose, CA, USA, May 17-18, 2014.* 2014, pp. 39–43. URL: http://dx.doi.org/10.1109/SPW.2014.15.

[LOP14] Enrico Lovat, Johan Oudinet, and Alexander Pretschner. "On quantitative dynamic data flow tracking." In: *Fourth ACM Conference on Data and Application Security and Privacy, CODASPY'14, San Antonio, TX, USA - March 03 - 05, 2014.* 2014, pp. 211–222. URL: http://doi.acm.org/10.1145/2557547.2557551.

[Lov+15] Enrico Lovat et al. "SHRIFT System-Wide HybRid Information Flow Tracking." In: *ICT Systems Security and Privacy Protection.* Springer, 2015, pp. 371–385.

[Lov15] Enrico Lovat. "Cross-layer Data-centric Usage Control." Dissertation. München: Technische Universität München, 2015.

[Lyo01] David Lyon. *Surveillance society: Monitoring everyday life.* McGraw-Hill Education (UK), 2001.

[Mah+10] Vijay Mahadevan et al. "Anomaly detection in crowded scenes." In: *Computer Vision and Pattern Recognition (CVPR), 2010 IEEE Conference on.* IEEE. 2010, pp. 1975–1981.

[McC98] Michael McCahill. "Beyond Foucault: towards a contemporary theory of surveillance." In: *Surveillance, closed circuit television and social control. Aldershot: Ashgate* (1998), pp. 41–65.

[MFA15] E. Monari, Y. Fischer, and M. Anneken. "NEST-CrowdControl – Advanced Video-based Crowd Monitoring for Large Public Events." In: *10th Future Security. Security Research Conference. Proceedings.* Berlin, Sept. 2015, pp. 49–45.

[MN02] Michael McCahill and Clive Norris. "CCTV in London." In: *Report deliverable of UrbanEye project* (2002).

[MP07] E. Monari and C. Pasqual. "Fusion of background estimation approaches for motion detection in non-static backgrounds." In: *Advanced Video and Signal Based Surveillance, 2007. AVSS 2007. IEEE Conference on.* Sept. 2007, pp. 347–352.

[MRV10] J. Moßgraber, F. Reinert, and H. Vagts. "An Architecture for a Task-Oriented Surveillance System: A Service- and Event-Based Approach." In: *Systems (ICONS), 2010 Fifth International Conference on.* Apr. 2010, pp. 146–151.

[Mün+11] David Münch et al. "High-level situation recognition using fuzzy metric temporal logic, case studies in surveillance and smart environments." In: *Computer Vision Workshops (ICCV Workshops), 2011 IEEE International Conference on.* IEEE. 2011, pp. 882–889.

[MVK08] E. Monari, S. Voth, and K. Kroschel. "An Object- and Task-Oriented Architecture for Automated Video Surveillance in Distributed Sensor Networks." In: *Advanced Video and Signal Based Surveillance, 2008. AVSS '08. IEEE Fifth International Conference on.* Sept. 2008, pp. 339–346.

[NA99] Clive Norris and Gary Armstrong. *The maximum surveillance society: The rise of CCTV.* Berg Publishers, 1999.

[NF15] Tahir Nawaz and James Ferryman. "An annotation-free method for evaluating privacy protection techniques in videos." In: *Advanced Video and Signal Based Surveillance (AVSS), 2015 12th IEEE International Conference on.* Aug. 2015.

[NMW02] Clive Norris, Mike McCahill, and David Wood. "The growth of CCTV: a global perspective on the international diffusion of video surveillance in publicly accessible space." In: *Surveillance & Society* 2.2/3 (2002).

[Nog02] Detlef Nogala. "Ordnung durch Beobachtung: Videoüberwachung als urbane Einrichtung." In: *Jahrbuch StadtRegion* (2002), pp. 33–54.

[Nor03] Clive Norris. "From personal to digital: CCTV, the panopticon, and the technological mediation of suspicion and social control." In: *Surveillance as Social Sorting: Privacy, Risk and Digital Discrimination. New York: Routledge* (2003), pp. 249–281.

[PHB06] Alexander Pretschner, Manuel Hilty, and David A. Basin. "Distributed usage control." In: *Commun. ACM* 49.9 (2006), pp. 39–44. URL: http://doi.acm.org/10.1145/1151053.

[PLB11] A. Pretschner, E. Lovat, and M. Büchler. "Representation-Independent Data Usage Control." In: *Data Privacy Management and Autonomous Spontaneus Security - 6th International Workshop, DPM 2011, and 4th International Workshop, SETOP 2011, Leuven, Belgium, September 15-16, 2011, Revised Selected Papers.* 2011, pp. 122–140. URL: http://dx.doi.org/10.1007/978-3-642-28879-1_9.

[RDH11] Alexander Roßnagel, Monika Desoi, and Gerrit Hornung. "Gestufte Kontrolle bei Videoüberwachungsanlagen - Ein Drei-Stufen-Modell als Vorschlag zur grundrechtsschonenden Gestaltung." In: *Datenschutz und Datensicherheit* 35.10 (2011), pp. 694–701. URL: http://dx.doi.org/10.1007/s11623-011-0166-z.

[Reu01] Karl-Heinz Reuband. "Was die Bürger von der Überwachung halten." In: *Neue Kriminalpolitik* (2001).

[Rol07] Manfred Rolfes. "Konstruktion und Konstrukteure sicherer und unsicherer Räume." In: *Surveillance Studies: Perspektiven eines Forschungsfeldes* (2007).

[Roß11] Alexander Roßnagel. "Das Gebot der Datenvermeidung und -sparsam-keit als Ansatz wirksamen technikbasierten Persönlichkeitsschutzes." In: *Innovation, Recht und öffentliche Kommunikation* 1 (2011), pp. 41–66.

[Rot10] Robert Rothmann. "Sicherheitsgefühl durch Videoüberwachung? Argumentative Paradoxien und empirische Widersprüche in der Verbreitung einer sicherheitspolitischen Maßnahme." In: *Neue Kriminalpolitik* 22.3 (2010), pp. 103–107.

[Rou+07] Caroline Rougier et al. "Fall detection from human shape and motion history using video surveillance." In: *Advanced Information Networking and Applications Workshops, 2007, AINAW'07. 21st International Conference on.* Vol. 2. IEEE. 2007, pp. 875–880.

[RR06] Neil Robertson and Ian Reid. "A general method for human activity recognition in video." In: *Computer Vision and Image Understanding* 104.2 (2006), pp. 232–248.

[Sai+10] Mukesh Saini et al. "Privacy modeling for video data publication." In: *Multimedia and Expo (ICME), 2010 IEEE International Conference on.* IEEE. 2010, pp. 60–65.

[Sai+12] Mukesh Saini et al. "Adaptive Transformation for Robust Privacy Protection in Video Surveillance." In: *Adv. MultiMedia* 2012 (Jan. 2012). URL: http://dx.doi.org/10.1155/2012/639649.

[Sai+14] Mukesh Saini et al. "W3-privacy: Understanding What, when, and Where Inference Channels in Multi-camera Surveillance Video." In: *Multimedia Tools Appl.* 68.1 (Jan. 2014), pp. 135–158. URL: http://dx.doi.org/10.1007/s11042-012-1207-9.

[Sch14] Arne Schumann. "Object instance recognition using motion cues and instance specific appearance models." In: *Proc. SPIE.* Vol. 9026. 2014. URL: http://dx.doi.org/10.1117/12.2038541.

[Sen+05] A. Senior et al. "Enabling video privacy through computer vision." In: *Security & Privacy, IEEE* 3.3 (May 2005), pp. 50–57.

[Shu+05] Chiao-Fe Shu et al. "IBM Smart surveillance system (S3): a open and extensible framework for event based surveillance." In: *Advanced Video and Signal Based Surveillance, 2005. AVSS 2005. IEEE Conference on.* IEEE. 2005, pp. 318–323.

[Spr+05] Angela Spriggs et al. *Public attitudes towards CCTV: results from the Pre-intervention Public Attitude Survey carried out in areas implementing CCTV.* Home Office, 2005.

[SS07] Tobias Singelnstein and Peer Stolle. "Von der sozialen Integration zur Sicherheit durch Kontrolle und Ausschluss." In: *Surveillance Studies: Perspektiven eines Forschungsfeldes* (2007).

[TD08] Son D Tran and Larry S Davis. "Event modeling and recognition using markov logic networks." In: *Computer Vision–ECCV 2008.* Springer, 2008, pp. 610–623.

[Thu+06] Bhavani Thuraisingham et al. "Access Control, Confidentiality and Privacy for Video Surveillance Databases." In: *Proceedings of the Eleventh ACM Symposium on Access Control Models and Technologies.* SACMAT '06. Lake Tahoe, California, USA: ACM, 2006, pp. 1–10. URL: http://doi.acm.org/10.1145/1133058.1133061.

[Töp07] Eric Töpfer. "Videoüberwachung–eine Risikotechnologie zwischen Sicherheitsversprechen und Kontrolldystopien." In: *Surveillance Studies. Perspektiven eines Forschungsfeldes. Opladen, Germany: Budrich* (2007).

[VA13] Sarvesh Vishwakarma and Anupam Agrawal. "A survey on activity recognition and behavior understanding in video surveillance." In: *The Visual Computer* 29.10 (2013), pp. 983–1009.

[Vag13] Hauke-Hendrik Vagts. *Privatheit und Datenschutz in der intelligenten Überwachung: ein datenschutzgewährendes System, entworfen nach dem „Privacy by Design" Prinzip.* Karlsruher Schriften zur Anthropomatik ; 14. Karlsruhe: KIT Scientific Publishing, 2013.

URL: http://digbib.ubka.uni-karlsruhe.de/volltexte/1000035198.

[Van07] Gisbert Van Elsbergen. “Kriminologische Implikationen der Videoüber-wachung.” In: *Surveillance Studies, Perspektiven eines Forschungsfeldes. Opladen: Budrich* (2007).

[VB10] H. Vagts and A. Bauer. “Privacy-Aware Object Representation for Surveillance Systems.” In: *Advanced Video and Signal Based Surveillance (AVSS), 2010 Seventh IEEE International Conference on.* Aug. 2010, pp. 601–608.

[VB11] H. Vagts and J. Beyerer. “Enhancing the acceptance of technology for civil security and surveillance by using Privacy Enhancing Technology.” In: *6th Future Security. Security Research Conference. Proceedings.* Berlin, Sept. 2011, pp. 372–379.

[VBB11] H. Vagts, C. Bier, and J. Beyerer. “Anonymization in Intelligent Surveillance Systems.” In: *New Technologies, Mobility and Security (NTMS), 2011 4th IFIP International Conference on.* Feb. 2011, pp. 1–4.

[VJ12] Hauke Vagts and Andreas Jakoby. “Privacy-aware access control for video data in intelligent surveillance systems.” In: *SPIE Defense, Security, and Sensing.* International Society for Optics and Photonics. 2012.

[Wak02] Alison Wakefield. “The public surveillance functions of private security.” In: *Surveillance & Society* 2.4 (2002).

[Weh02] Jan Wehrheim. “Die überwachte Stadt.” In: *Sicherheit, Segregation und Ausgrenzung. Opladen* (2002).

[WF02] Brandon C Welsh and David P Farrington. *Crime prevention effects of closed circuit television: a systematic review.* Vol. 252. Citeseer, 2002.

[Wic+04] Jehan Wickramasuriya et al. “Privacy protecting data collection in media spaces.” In: *Proc. 12th annual ACM intl. conf. on Multimedia.* 2004, pp. 48–55.

[WP12] Tobias Wüchner and Alexander Pretschner. "Data Loss Prevention Based on Data-Driven Usage Control." In: *23rd IEEE International Symposium on Software Reliability Engineering, ISSRE 2012, Dallas, TX, USA, November 27-30, 2012.* 2012, pp. 151–160. URL: http://dx.doi.org/10.1109/ISSRE.2012.10.

[WR14] Thomas Winkler and Bernhard Rinner. "Security and Privacy Protection in Visual Sensor Networks: A Survey." In: *ACM Comput. Surv.* 47.1 (May 2014), 2:1–2:42. URL: http://doi.acm.org/10.1145/2545883.

[Yin+07] Heng Yin et al. "Panorama: capturing system-wide information flow for malware detection and analysis." In: *Proceedings of the 2007 ACM Conference on Computer and Communications Security, CCS 2007, Alexandria, Virginia, USA, October 28-31, 2007.* 2007, pp. 116–127. URL: http://doi.acm.org/10.1145/1315245.1315261.

[Zha+10] Qing Zhang et al. "Neon: system support for derived data management." In: *Proceedings of the 6th International Conference on Virtual Execution Environments, VEE 2010, Pittsburgh, Pennsylvania, USA, March 17-19, 2010.* 2010, pp. 63–74. URL: http://doi.acm.org/10.1145/1735997.1736008.

[ZS98] Qiang Alex Zhao and John T. Stasko. "Evaluating Image Filtering Based Techniques in Media Space Applications." In: *Proceedings of the 1998 ACM Conference on Computer Supported Cooperative Work.* CSCW '98. Seattle, Washington, USA: ACM, 1998, pp. 11–18. URL: http://doi.acm.org/10.1145/289444.289450.

[Zur07] Nils Zurawski. "Video Surveillance and Everyday Life Assessments of Closed-Circuit Television and the Cartography of Socio-Spatial Imaginations." In: *International Criminal Justice Review* 17.4 (2007), pp. 269–288.

# Glossary

*ACL*

access control list. 183

*BDSG*

Bundesdatenschutzgesetz. 23–25

*BVerfGE*

Federal Constitutional Court of Germany (Bundesverfassungsgericht). 21, 22

*CCTV*

Closed Circuit Television. 2, 15

*CMS*

C++ Messaging Service. 95

*ECA rule*

event-condition-action rule. 30

*ECtHR*

European Court of Human Rights. 4

*GDPR*

General Data Protection Regulation of the European Union. 25–27

*HDMI*

High Definition Multimedia Interface. 180

*HMI*

human machine interface. 37, 38, 59, 64–66, 69–72, 74, 78, 82, 86, 88, 99, 163, 164, 169, 176, 179, 181

*IP*

Internet Protocol. 104, 180

*JMS*

Java Messaging Service. 95

*KASTEL*

Competence Center for Applied IT Security Technology at Karlsruhe Institute of Technology. 42

*MVC*

model-view-controller pattern. 71

*NEST*

Network Enabled Surveillance and Tracking. 12, 38, 57, 66, 69, 71–73, 94, 95, 161, 163–166, 168, 169

*OSL*

Obligation Specification Language for usage control policies. 28, 31, 195

*OVG*

Higher Administrative Court (Oberverwaltungsgericht). 25

*PAP*

Policy Administration Point. 30

*PDP*

Policy Decision Point. 28, 30, 31, 64, 70, 72, 95, 102, 104, 105, 115, 116, 121, 123

*PEP*

Policy Enforcement Point. 28, 30, 57, 64, 67, 69, 70, 72, 88, 94, 102, 103, 105, 107, 111, 112, 115, 121–123

*PET*

privacy-enhancing technology. 17

*PID*

process identifier. 122, 123

*PIP*

Policy Information Point. 30, 31, 102–105, 107, 110, 111, 113, 115, 116, 119–124

*PMP*

Policy Management Point. 30, 92, 116

*PRP*

Policy Retrieval Point. 30

*PTZ camera*

pan-tilt-zoom camera. 2, 15, 38, 44, 71

*PXP*

Policy Execution Point. 28, 30, 57, 64–68, 70, 72, 73, 95

*RFID*

radio-frequency identification. 97

*RGB*

red-green-blue. 128

*RMI*

Remote Method Invocation. 95

*RoI*

Region of Interest. 128, 129, 131–133, 148, 152, 157

*TCP*

Transmission Control Protocol. 95, 104

*UC*

Usage Control. 15, 28, 71, 201

*UC4NEST*

Usage Control for Network Enabled Surveillance and Tracking. 161, 163–169

*UDHR*

Universal Declaration of Human Rights of the United Nations. 3, 4, 21

*USB*

Universal Serial Bus. 180

## Karlsruher Schriftenreihe zur Anthropomatik (ISSN 1863-6489)

Herausgeber: Prof. Dr.-Ing. Jürgen Beyerer

Die Bände sind unter www.ksp.kit.edu als PDF frei verfügbar oder als Druckausgabe bestellbar.

**Band 1** Jürgen Geisler
**Leistung des Menschen am Bildschirmarbeitsplatz.** 2006
ISBN 3-86644-070-7

**Band 2** Elisabeth Peinsipp-Byma
**Leistungserhöhung durch Assistenz in interaktiven Systemen zur Szenenanalyse.** 2007
ISBN 978-3-86644-149-1

**Band 3** Jürgen Geisler, Jürgen Beyerer (Hrsg.)
**Mensch-Maschine-Systeme.** 2010
ISBN 978-3-86644-457-7

**Band 4** Jürgen Beyerer, Marco Huber (Hrsg.)
**Proceedings of the 2009 Joint Workshop of Fraunhofer IOSB and Institute for Anthropomatics, Vision and Fusion Laboratory.** 2010
ISBN 978-3-86644-469-0

**Band 5** Thomas Usländer
**Service-oriented design of environmental information systems.** 2010
ISBN 978-3-86644-499-7

**Band 6** Giulio Milighetti
**Multisensorielle diskret-kontinuierliche Überwachung und Regelung humanoider Roboter.** 2010
ISBN 978-3-86644-568-0

**Band 7** Jürgen Beyerer, Marco Huber (Hrsg.)
**Proceedings of the 2010 Joint Workshop of Fraunhofer IOSB and Institute for Anthropomatics, Vision and Fusion Laboratory.** 2011
ISBN 978-3-86644-609-0

**Band 8** Eduardo Monari
**Dynamische Sensorselektion zur auftragsorientierten Objektverfolgung in Kameranetzwerken.** 2011
ISBN 978-3-86644-729-5

| | | |
|---|---|
| **Band 9** | Thomas Bader<br>**Multimodale Interaktion in Multi-Display-Umgebungen.** 2011<br>ISBN 3-86644-760-8 |
| **Band 10** | Christian Frese<br>**Planung kooperativer Fahrmanöver für kognitive Automobile.** 2012<br>ISBN 978-3-86644-798-1 |
| **Band 11** | Jürgen Beyerer, Alexey Pak (Hrsg.)<br>**Proceedings of the 2011 Joint Workshop of Fraunhofer IOSB and Institute for Anthropomatics, Vision and Fusion Laboratory.** 2012<br>ISBN 978-3-86644-855-1 |
| **Band 12** | Miriam Schleipen<br>**Adaptivität und Interoperabilität von Manufacturing Execution Systemen (MES).** 2013<br>ISBN 978-3-86644-955-8 |
| **Band 13** | Jürgen Beyerer, Alexey Pak (Hrsg.)<br>**Proceedings of the 2012 Joint Workshop of Fraunhofer IOSB and Institute for Anthropomatics, Vision and Fusion Laboratory.** 2013<br>ISBN 978-3-86644-988-6 |
| **Band 14** | Hauke-Hendrik Vagts<br>**Privatheit und Datenschutz in der intelligenten Überwachung: Ein datenschutzgewährendes System, entworfen nach dem „Privacy by Design" Prinzip.** 2013<br>ISBN 978-3-7315-0041-4 |
| **Band 15** | Christian Kühnert<br>**Data-driven Methods for Fault Localization in Process Technology.** 2013<br>ISBN 978-3-7315-0098-8 |
| **Band 16** | Alexander Bauer<br>**Probabilistische Szenenmodelle für die Luftbildauswertung.** 2014<br>ISBN 978-3-7315-0167-1 |
| **Band 17** | Jürgen Beyerer, Alexey Pak (Hrsg.)<br>**Proceedings of the 2013 Joint Workshop of Fraunhofer IOSB and Institute for Anthropomatics, Vision and Fusion Laboratory.** 2014<br>ISBN 978-3-7315-0212-8 |
| **Band 18** | Michael Teutsch<br>**Moving Object Detection and Segmentation for Remote Aerial Video Surveillance.** 2015<br>ISBN 978-3-7315-0320-0 |

**Band 19** Marco Huber
**Nonlinear Gaussian Filtering: Theory, Algorithms, and Applications.** 2015
ISBN 978-3-7315-0338-5

**Band 20** Jürgen Beyerer, Alexey Pak (Hrsg.)
**Proceedings of the 2014 Joint Workshop of Fraunhofer IOSB and Institute for Anthropomatics, Vision and Fusion Laboratory.** 2014
ISBN 978-3-7315-0401-6

**Band 21** Todor Dimitrov
**Permanente Optimierung dynamischer Probleme der Fertigungssteuerung unter Einbeziehung von Benutzerinteraktionen.** 2015
ISBN 978-3-7315-0426-9

**Band 22** Benjamin Kühn
**Interessengetriebene audiovisuelle Szenenexploration.** 2016
ISBN 978-3-7315-0457-3

**Band 23** Yvonne Fischer
**Wissensbasierte probabilistische Modellierung für die Situationsanalyse am Beispiel der maritimen Überwachung.** 2016
ISBN 978-3-7315-0460-3

**Band 24** Jürgen Beyerer, Alexey Pak (Hrsg.)
**Proceedings of the 2015 Joint Workshop of Fraunhofer IOSB and Institute for Anthropomatics, Vision and Fusion Laboratory.** 2016
ISBN 978-3-7315-0519-8

**Band 25** Pascal Birnstill
**Privacy-Respecting Smart Video Surveillance Based on Usage Control Enforcement.** 2016
ISBN 978-3-7315-0538-9